The
Counseling
Dictionary

The Counseling Dictionary

CONCISE DEFINITIONS OF FREQUENTLY USED TERMS

SAMUEL T. GLADDING

Wake Forest University

Upper Saddle River, New Jersey
Columbus, Ohio

Library of Congress Cataloging in Publication Data
Gladding, Samuel T.
    The counseling dictionary : concise definitions of frequently used terms / Samuel T. Gladding.
      p. cm.
    ISBN 0-13-085292-9
    1. Counseling—Dictionaries. 2. Psychotherapy—Dictionaries.   I. Title.
    BF637.C6 G5332   2001
    361′.06′03—dc21   00-028401

Vice President and Publisher: Jeffery W. Johnston
Executive Editor: Kevin M. Davis
Editorial Assistant: Christina M. Kalisch
Production Editor: Linda Hillis Bayma
Copy Editor: Marie Maes
Design Coordinator: Diane C. Lorenzo
Cover Designer: Linda Fares
Text Designer: Sara Arrand
Production Manager: Laura Messerly
Electronic Text Management: Marilyn Wilson Phelps, Karen L. Bretz, Melanie N. Ortega
Director of Marketing: Kevin Flanagan
Marketing Manager: Amy June
Marketing Services Manager: Krista Groshong

This book was set in Garamond by Prentice Hall. It was printed and bound by R.R. Donnelley & Sons Company. The cover was printed by Phoenix Color Corp.

Illustrations on pp. 22, 128 (mid page), and 129 adapted from "Some Effects of Certain Communication Problems on Group Performance" by H. J. Leavitt, 1951, *Journal of Abnormal and Social Psychology, 46*, pp. 38–50. Copyright 1951 by the APA. Reprinted with permission of the American Psychological Association.

Illustrations on pp. 24, 30, 49, 54, 58 (bottom right), 71 (bottom left), and 128 from *Family Therapy: History and Practice*, Second Edition, by Samuel T., Gladding, © 1994; pp. 34 and 44 from *Counseling: A Comprehensive Profession*, Fourth Edition, by Gladding, © 2000; and pp. 55, 63, 89, 98, and 113 from *Group Work: A Counseling Specialty*, by Gladding, © 1991. All are reprinted by permission of Prentice-Hall, Inc., Upper Saddle River, NJ.

10 9 8 7 6 5 4 3 2 1
ISBN: 0-13-085292-9

To my graduate students in counseling
at Fairfield University,
    the University of Alabama at Birmingham, and
        Wake Forest University
Who have taught me to be precise and concise
    with my words
And inspired me to be a better counselor.

Preface

Behind every book there is a story. This dictionary is no exception. The story is simple. A few years ago, one of my students asked me if I could give her a concise definition of a word often used in counseling. I thought I could provide a definition, but I told her I would consult the glossary of a leading book in the field to make sure the definition was concise. To my surprise, that book did not have a glossary. "No problem," I thought. "I'll go to another leading book in the field." However, that book had a glossary but did not include the word I was looking for. "Well, surely another major book in the field will have what I want," I thought. However, I was wrong again!

Not known to give up easily, I decided I would find a dictionary of counseling terms. Surely, going to an authoritative source would solve my problem and save me time. Well, I was incorrect once more. I found a lot of dictionaries for a number of professions, but when it came to counseling, I could locate only three. One had been published in the 1960s, one in the early 1980s, and one more recently—but it contained less than three hundred terms and not the one I wanted. Wow! The task that I expected would be simple had turned out to be anything but that.

Thus the idea to write a concise dictionary of counseling terms was born. The purpose of this book is threefold. First, it is aimed at students who are entering or have entered the profession and wish to better learn the language of counseling. Second, it is intended to serve professors and practicing counselors as a quick reference source to commonly used counseling terms. Finally, this dictionary is meant to be a resource for the public in discerning what counselors and other helping professionals mean when they use specific words.

The Counseling Dictionary will give you basic information on over 2,100 words and abbreviations often used in the profession of counseling. I have italicized words that are defined in this dictionary that are a part of another counseling definition or that are particularly germane to a definition. This dictionary also contains websites that can enrich your understanding in select areas of counseling. It is my hope that you will both enjoy as well as benefit from this reference. If so, your frustration may be lowered and, more importantly, your understanding enhanced.

In writing this dictionary, I am indebted to my teachers, colleagues, students, and clients, both past and present. They are too numerous to name. However, there are some who have been especially helpful in recent years. Anita Hughes, my administrative assistant, read my initial drafts and offered invaluable input and suggestions. Also providing me with excellent feedback were my colleagues Donna Henderson, Pamela Karr, and Debbie Newsome at Wake Forest University; Mike Ryan, my graduate assistant, also at Wake Forest; Mary Guindon at Johns Hopkins University; and these outside reviewers: Bob Barret, University of North Carolina, Charlotte; Carole A. Campbell, California State University, Long Beach; Joseph C. Ciechalski, East Carolina University; Chris Maglio, Truman State University; Lynda K. Mitchell, California State University, Los Angeles; Julia Orza, Western Maryland College; Simeon Schlossberg, Western Maryland College; Michael J. Stevens, Illinois State University; and Claire Cole Vaught, Virginia Polytechnic Institute and State University. I am also grateful to my wife, Claire, and our children, Ben, Nate, and Tim, for their understanding of what I have been doing and for their allowing me use of our home computer. Finally, I appreciate the fine professionals at Merrill/Prentice Hall with whom I have been working since the mid-1980s. Kevin Davis in particular has been most encouraging and supportive. Who could ask for more?

SAMUEL T. GLADDING

Discover the Companion Website Accompanying This Book

The Prentice Hall Companion Website: A Virtual Learning Environment

Technology is a constantly growing and changing aspect of our field that is creating a need for content and resources. To address this emerging need, Prentice Hall has developed an online learning environment for students and professors alike—Companion Websites—to support our textbooks.

In creating a Companion Website, our goal is to build on and enhance what the textbook already offers. For this reason, the content for each user-friendly website is organized by topic and provides the professor and student with a variety of meaningful resources. Common features of a Companion Website include:

For the Professor—

Every Companion Website integrates **Syllabus Manager**™, an online syllabus creation and management utility.

- **Syllabus Manager**™ provides you, the instructor, with an easy, step-by-step process to create and revise syllabi, with direct links into Companion Website and other online content without having to learn HTML.
- Students may logon to your syllabus during any study session. All they need to know is the web address for the Companion Website and the password you've assigned to your syllabus.
- After you have created a syllabus using **Syllabus Manager**™, students may enter the syllabus for their course section from any point in the Companion Website.
- Clicking on a date, the student is shown the list of activities for the assignment. The activities for each assignment are linked directly to actual content, saving time for students.
- Adding assignments consists of clicking on the desired due date, then filling in the details of the assignment—name of the assignment, instructions, and whether or not it is a one-time or repeating assignment.
- In addition, links to other activities can be created easily. If the activity is online, a URL can be entered in the space provided, and it will be linked automatically in the final syllabus.

- Your completed syllabus is hosted on our servers, allowing convenient updates from any computer on the Internet. Changes you make to your syllabus are immediately available to your students at their next logon.

For the Student—

- **Topic Overviews**—outline key concepts in topic areas
- **Electronic Bluebook**—send homework or essays directly to your instructor's email with this paperless form
- **Message Board**—serves as a virtual bulletin board to post—or respond to—questions or comments to/from a national audience
- **Chat**—real-time chat with anyone who is using the text anywhere in the country—ideal for discussion and study groups, class projects, etc.
- **Web Destinations**—links to www sites that relate to each topic area
- **Professional Organizations**—links to organizations that relate to topic areas
- **Additional Resources**—access to topic-specific content that enhances material found in the text

To take advantage of these and other resources, please visit *The Counseling Dictionary: Concise Definitions of Frequently Used Terms* Companion Website at

www.prenhall.com/gladding

The
Counseling
Dictionary

a

AA   See *Alcoholics Anonymous.*

AABT   See *Association for Advancement of Behavior Therapy.*

AAC   See *Association for Assessment in Counseling.*

AACC   See *American Association of Christian Counselors.*

AACD   See *American Association for Counseling and Development.*

AADA   See *Association for Adult Development and Aging.*

AAMFT   See *American Association for Marriage and Family Therapy.*

AAPC   See *American Association of Pastoral Counselors.*

AARP   See *American Association of Retired Persons.*

AASCB   See *American Association of State Counseling Boards.*

AASECT   See *American Association of Sex Educators, Counselors, and Therapists.*

AATA   See *American Art Therapy Association.*

AB research design   A simple time series *experimental design* method in which a *baseline* (A) is established before an intervention strategy (B) is introduced.

ABAB research design   A more complex and involved *experimental design* than an AB simple time series experiment. In this method, a *baseline* (A) is established, followed by an *intervention* (B), which is then discontinued after a time, followed by a second baseline (A) and intervention (B). The ABAB design is used to confirm that the treatment intervention (B) really had an effect on the baseline behavior.

A-B-C theory of personality   Albert Ellis's *rational emotive behavior therapy (REBT)* method of conceptualizing the origin of human feelings and their resulting behaviors. In this model, "A" stands for an objective event or experience, "B" stands for a person's

thought(s) or belief(s) about "A," and "C" represents feeling(s) or emotion(s) resulting from the thought(s) in "B." In this model, the thinking/belief aspect around an event is crucial in regard to the effective outcome.

ABCs of REBT

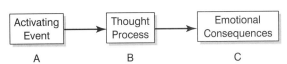

A   B   C

A-B-C-D-E-F paradigm   Albert Ellis's *rational emotive behavior therapy (REBT)* method of correcting illogical or *irrational thinking* and promoting and maintaining change. In this model, the "A," "B," and "C" are the same as in the *A-B-C theory of personality.* "D" is the counselor disputing any irrational thoughts or beliefs of the client. "E" refers to the presumed consequences of the counselor's interventions, that is, the client gaining a different *perception* of an event. "F" represents new feelings the client has in regard to the event or situation in "A." To change a negative or nonproductive feeling, individuals need to think differently, for example, in either a neutral or positive way. See also *rational emotive behavioral therapy (REBT).*

ability test   A test that measures the extent to which a person is presently functioning in a particular area, such as math, and provides an estimate of what the person is capable of performing in regard to a certain task.

abnormal   Functioning that is divergent or maladaptive from what is considered normal among a population, especially if the behavior is persistent. Abnormal is a culturally sensitive concept because what is considered appropriate in one society may not be seen as such in another.

a

abreaction A *psychoanalysis* term for the therapeutic relieving of painful or distressing emotion by a client through calling into awareness experiences or material that has been repressed.

absolutism A term in Jean Piaget's stages of *moral development* for the concern that children, beginning at about age 5, have about right and wrong and the *rules* of life. At this stage, children have absolute faith in the rules their parents have given them.

abstract A brief formal summary at the beginning of a *research* study or theoretical paper.

abstract reasoning The ability to manipulate thoughts that include dealing with situations that have not yet occurred, to use logical thought processes, and to develop symbolic meaning.

absurdity A statement that is half truthful and even silly if followed out to conclusion. For example, "I'll simply fall apart if my son acts that way again." Counselors sometimes work with families by using absurdities and exaggerating client statements in order to help them recognize realities.

abuse All forms of maltreatment or improper behavior of one person or group by another, whether physical, sexual, behavioral, cognitive, economic, or emotional.

ACA See *American Counseling Association*.

ACAF See *American Counseling Association Foundation*.

ACCA See *American College Counseling Association*.

accent Highlighting the last few words of a client's statement. For example, if a client says, "The situation I'm in now is driving me crazy," the counselor might reply, "Driving you crazy?"

acceptance **1.** Also known as *unconditional positive regard;* a deep and genuine caring for the client as a person; a prizing of the person just for being. As outlined by Carl Rogers, acceptance is one of the three necessary and sufficient conditions of counseling, the other two being *congruence (genuineness)* and *empathy*. **2.** A simple acknowledgment by the counselor of the client's previous statement with a response such as "Yes" or "Uh-huh" that encourages the client to continue. See also *minimal encouragers*. **3.** Acknowledging what is happening as opposed to evaluating it.

accommodation **1.** The ability of a person or group to modify cultural ways in order to fit in better with a new *environment* or another group. **2.** The *process* in which a counselor *joins* with a client to achieve a therapeutic alliance based on the nature of the client. In order to accommodate, counselors make personal adjustments, such as modifying their speech patterns or behaviors. **3.** Jean Piaget's term for the way children alter their thinking when new experiences cannot be incorporated through assimilation into their intellectual framework. The opposite of *assimilation*.

accountability Documenting effectiveness through the use of measured means such as *outcome research* or *feedback*. To be responsible to their clients and the profession, counselors must be able to document that the procedures and methods they use are effective.

accreditation An approval process, usually involving an academic program of study, in which members of an outside agency authorized by a profession, such as counseling, inspect and certify that program training standards and practicum/internship site requirements are being met at or above a minimum level. In counseling, approved programs of study are accredited by the *Council for Accreditation of Counseling and Related Educational Programs (CACREP)*.

acculturation **1.** The ways people learn the customs, beliefs, behaviors, and traditions of a *culture*. **2.** The degree to which individuals from minority cultures identify with or conform to the attitudes, lifestyles, and values of the majority culture.

ACEG See *Association for Counselors and Educators in Government*.

ACES   See *Association for Counselor Education and Supervision.*

ACGPA   See *American Council of Guidance and Personnel Associations.*

achievement   The degree of success, accomplishment, attainment, or competence of a person in a particular area.

achievement test   An instrument that measures an individual's degree of competence or learning in regard to a given subject or skill (e.g., the *National Counselor Examination*).

ACoAs   See *Adult Children of Alcoholics.*

ACPA   See *American College Personnel Association.*

acquired culture   Learned habits picked up from others outside one's own culture.

Acquired immune deficiency syndrome (AIDS)   The most advanced phase of the *human immune deficiency virus (HIV)*. AIDS breaks down the body's immunization system and is fatal. Both HIV infection and AIDS are considered to be *chronic* illnesses and are managed with both pharmaceutical therapies (pharmacy drugs) and complementary (alternative) therapies. See also *human immune deficiency virus (HIV)*.

acrophobia   An exaggerated fear of being in high places or being up in the air.

ACT   See *American College Testing, Inc.*

acting "as if"   An *Adlerian counseling* technique in which clients are instructed to act "as if" they were the person they wanted to be, the ideal person they envision.

acting out   **1.** A psychoanalytic term for the direct or indirect enactment of *unconscious* tensions or wishes by a client in the form of disruptive or irrational behaviors.   **2.** A term for the disruptive and inappropriate behavior(s) of children.

action   When a client translates insights gained in counseling into changed behaviors (e.g., a client realizes s/he can obtain more of what s/he desires in life by using the assertiveness skills learned in counseling).

action exercises   Sensory awareness methods or guided imagery used in the warm-up phase

of a group session or a *psychodrama* to help members discover common themes within the group as well as focus more on individual concerns.

action phase   **1.** When clients in counseling put insights into action.   **2.** The second part of a *psychodrama* process that involves the enactment of a protagonist's concerns.

action research   Research that is *"experience-near"* and that focuses on resolving practical relevant problems that counselors routinely encounter, such as evaluating the effects of a *psychoeducational* program or treatment on clients. This type of research may not be as tightly controlled or as easily generalized as other types of research.

action stage   The working stage in a counseling session in which clients focus on changing their behaviors.

action therapy   A term for the treatment procedures that are based on direct alterations of behavior, such as *behavior modification*.

active listening   Attending to verbal and nonverbal aspects of a client's communication without judging or evaluating in order to encourage *trust*, client *self-disclosure*, and *exploration* within the counseling *relationship*. Hearing what is being implied as well as what is explicitly stated.

activity   **1.** Movement or *behavior,* including mental processes, on the part of a person.   **2.** In *transactional analysis*, an activity is a way of structuring time that deals with external reality (e.g., work).

activity group guidance (AGG)   Group guidance that involves activities that are *developmental* in nature (e.g., learning proper dating behaviors). AGG typically includes coordinated guidance topics.

actors   Individuals (also known as *auxiliaries*) who play the parts of important people or objects in a *psychodrama* play. With prompting from the protagonist, actors play the protagonist's double, an antagonist, or even a piece of furniture. In the same psychodrama,

a

an auxiliary can play more than one part, such as being the protagonist's best friend and worst enemy.

actualizing tendency An innate tendency or motivation in human beings toward growth and the fulfilling of their potential—an important concept in the *person-centered counseling* theory of Carl Rogers and in the *humanistic approach* to counseling. See also *self-actualization.*

acute The relatively rapid onset of a condition.

ADA See *Americans with Disabilities Act.*

adaptation See *adaptive behavior.*

adaptive behavior Also known as *adaptation* and *adjustment;* a response intended to deal positively with changes in one's environment (e.g., working harder instead of complaining at certain times of the day when the workload picks up).

adaptive child A term in *transactional analysis* theory for the part of the *child ego state* that learns to adapt to the expectations of others in order to gain acceptance and approval.

ADD See *Attention deficit disorder.*

addiction Psychological or physiological dependence on a *substance* (e.g., alcohol, tobacco, cocaine) or *activity* (e.g., gambling, sex) in order to function. Addiction is characterized by increased tolerance of the drug or behavior and *withdrawal* symptoms when the substance or activity is unavailable.

addiction counseling Counseling that focuses on working with clients who have *addictions.*

adding cognitive constructions The verbal component of *structural family therapy* consisting of *advice*, information, pragmatic fictions, and *paradox.*

additive responses Empathetic verbal responses counselors give that add to a client's understanding of a situation. Additive responses clarify as well as provide a fresh perspective of meaning.

ADHD See *Attention Deficit Hyperactivity Disorder.*

Adjective Checklist A pencil-and-paper *personality test* generally used with adults. The test contains 300 adjectives and measures 37 dimensions of *personality*. It is not timed but usually takes from 15 to 20 minutes.

adjourning The final stage in *group development,* when counseling comes to an end. Adjourning is also referred to as *mourning* and *termination.*

adjustment The degree of harmony between people and their environments. Successful adjustment results in *adaptive behavior;* unsuccessful adjustment results in behavior that is *maladaptive.*

adjustment disorders A *DSM-IV* category of *diagnosis* for people who are responding to either negative (e.g., divorce) or positive (e.g., marriage) *stressors.* Appropriate modifiers, such as "with depressed mood" or "with *anxiety,*" must accompany the diagnosis. Impairment of persons under this category should have occurred within 3 months of the *stressor(s).* The diagnosis itself, which is considered among the mildest in the *DSM-IV* classification, is time limited and must be changed after 6 months. Most individuals appropriately diagnosed with adjustment disorders respond well to counseling.

adjustment test A *personality test* that measures the ability of a person to function well in society and achieve personal needs.

Adlerian counseling An approach to counseling devised by Alfred Adler. It includes an emphasis on the *family constellation* (especially birth order), *fictions* (subjective evaluations about oneself or the environment), and an analysis of a client's *lifestyle.* Treatment involves both the promotion of insight and reeducation with accompanying behavioral changes. See also *Individual Psychology.*

administrative (regulatory) law Specialized regulations passed by authorized government agencies that pertain to certain specialty areas, such as the profession of counseling.

administrative model A model of providing student activities in which professionals in college administration (i.e., admissions, records, food, health, and financial aid) are put in charge of offering services.

adolescence A term originated by G. Stanley Hall at the beginning of the 20th century for the age span between *childhood* and *adulthood* beginning at puberty. Adolescence is characterized as a period of transitions, a time of unevenness and paradoxes marked by physical, emotional, moral, and intellectual change. The basic challenge of adolescence according to Erik Erikson is to develop a *self-identity*. Failure to do so leads to *role confusion* and an *identity crisis*.

ADTA See *American Dance Therapy Association*.

Adult Children of Alcoholics (ACoAs) Adults who, as children, spent part or all of their *childhood* in a stressful family environment in which one or more *caregivers* abused *alcohol*. Many ACoAs have special issues to resolve through counseling, such as establishing *trust* and establishing a clear *identity*. Many ACoAs suffer from similar emotional disorders, including *depression*, *anxiety*, low *self-esteem*, and anger.

Adult ego state A term in *transactional analysis* for the objective part of the *personality* that functions rationally in a planned and organized way. The adult ego state receives and processes materials from the parent and the child ego states as well as the environment and makes decisions based on available information.

adulthood A somewhat nebulous term implying that a person has reached physical, mental, social, and emotional maturity. Adulthood encompasses a wide range of ages, from 18 years and up. It is usually broken down into early, middle, and late periods. According to Erik Erikson, the challenge of young adulthood is to achieve *intimacy* (i.e., a sharing of self) with others. A failure to do so leads to *isola-*

tion. The challenge of middle adulthood is to become generative (i.e., to create and become productive through one's career, family, or leisure time). A failure to achieve *generativity* leads to *stagnation*. Finally, according to Erikson, the task of late adulthood is to achieve a sense of *integrity* (i.e., acceptance of life in all its multiple dimensions). The opposite of such an accomplishment is *despair*.

advanced empathy A process in which the counselor gets at feelings and meanings in the client's life that are hidden or beyond the immediate *awareness* of the client. Advanced empathy goes beyond what has been stated to what is implied. Sometimes advanced empathy is expressed in the identification of and/or linking of themes in the client's life. See also *primary empathy*.

advice A suggestion or recommendation.

advice giving Instructing or providing someone with information or recommendations about what to do in a particular situation. Advice was one of the main techniques of E. G. Williamson and his *directive counseling* approach of the 1930s. Advice giving was challenged as a technique by Carl Rogers because of its tendency to promote client *dependency* and interfere with the client's growth. Advice is sparingly used in most counseling approaches today. It is employed mainly in *crisis* situations in which it either prevents clients from engaging in destructive acts or gives clients something beneficial to do when they are not able to generate constructive plans of action because of being overwhelmed by *trauma*. Advice giving, if not used judiciously, prevents clients from struggling with their own thoughts, feelings, and behaviors.

advocacy Actively working for, supporting, or espousing a cause or person(s) (e.g., lobbying, writing, petitioning, speaking, or politicking). Advocacy occurs on many levels (e.g., local, state, national). Counselors advocate for the welfare of their clients and the profession of counseling.

affect   Pertaining to emotion, feeling, mood, a person's overt emotional state. Affect is a primary emphasis of some counseling approaches.

affect disorder   Also known as *mood disorder;* a disorder associated with inappropriate expression of emotion (e.g., depression).

affective-oriented counseling   Theories in counseling, such as *gestalt therapy*, that focus on making an impact on clients' emotions to bring about *change*. The objective is to arouse, handle, and/or modify emotional responses in clients.

affiliation   A positive emotional relationship with someone (e.g., it might include smiling and talking) but without *attachment.*

affirmation   When a counselor affirms the correctness of information or encourages a client's efforts at self-determination. For example, the counselor might state "That's helpful new information" or "You seem to be gaining more control."

African Americans   People in the United States whose ancestry came from Africa. African Americans constitute approximately 12% of the total population of the United States.

AFTA   See *American Family Therapy Association.*

aftercare   Any *follow-up* or continued care services given to clients after their release from counseling (e.g., individuals released from mental health facilities are often seen in aftercare groups periodically).

age discrimination   The unfair treatment of individuals based on their age.

age norms   Scores or values on tests that represent the typical or average performance of individuals at certain *chronological ages.*

ageism   The untrue assumption that *chronological age* is the primary determinant of human characteristics. People who practice ageism *stereotype* and *discriminate* against older people based on their age.

aging   A biological and psychological phenomenon composed of physiological changes as well as a mental process of considering oneself older. See also *gerontology.*

AGLBIC   See *Association for Gay, Lesbian, and Bisexual Issues in Counseling.*

agoraphobia   An exaggerated and irrational fear of being in an unfamiliar place or of leaving one's home.

AGPA   See *American Group Psychotherapy Association.*

aha reaction   A sudden insight into one's situation or environment; it may be accompanied by the exclamation of the word "aha."

AHEAD   See *Counseling Association for Humanistic Education and Development (C-AHEAD).*

AIDS   See *Acquired immune deficiency syndrome.*

Al-Anon   A voluntary *mutual help group* organization founded in 1951. It is comprised of relatives of alcohol abusers who meet regularly in order to discuss common *problems.*

Albert Ellis Institute   Formerly known as the *Institute for Rational-Emotive Therapy;* a not-for-profit educational organization founded in 1968 to promote *rational emotive behavior therapy (REBT).* The institute is located at 45 E. 65th Street, New York, NY 10021 (800-323-4738; http://www.REBT.org/).

alcohol   Also known as ethyl alcohol (ethanol); a clear liquid with a bitter taste that acts as a *depressant,* to which someone can become physically addictive. Alcohol is the most widely used *drug* in the United States. When abused, it can detrimentally affect almost every organ in the body. Withdrawal symptoms are often severe. See also *alcoholism; delirium tremens.*

Alcoholics Anonymous (AA)   An organization that helps alcohol abusers gain and maintain control of their lives by remaining sober. Established in the late 1930s, there is a dependence within the AA program on a higher power outside oneself. Much of the work of Alcoholics Anonymous is carried out in *self-help groups.* AA's address is P.O. Box 459, Grand Central Station, New York, NY 10163 (212-870-3400;

http://www.alcoholics-anonymous.org/). See also *self-help groups*.

alcoholism The chronic abuse of and compulsive increased use and tolerance of *alcohol*. Alcoholism is considered a progressive disease in which the client becomes physically and psychologically dependent on drinking alcohol.

alienation Feelings of being estranged or cut off from a group; a term often used for the separation of persons from their cultural groups.

alignments The ways family members join together or oppose one another in carrying out a family activity.

allopastic approach An *adjustment* to a culturally different environment through confronting obstacles in the *environment* and changing them. The opposite of the *autoplastic approach*.

all-or-nothing thinking A type of *cognitive distortion* characterized by assuming that things are absolutely perfect or absolutely terrible.

alter ego A *psychodrama* term for another version of oneself, usually the opposite of oneself.

alternate form A different but comparable form of a *standardized test*, such as *achievement* or *aptitude tests*. If a person is tested twice, the second test can consist of the alternate form of the first test.

alternative hypothesis Possible outcome not covered by the *null hypothesis*.

altruism Being concerned for others rather than oneself; sharing experiences and thoughts with others; helping others by giving of one's self unselfishly; working for the common good.

Alzheimer's disease An organic mental disease, occurring mostly in older people, characterized by disorientation, forgetfulness, confusion, and mood swings.

ambivalence When an individual experiences two opposite feelings at the same time (e.g., wanting help and being afraid to ask for it).

AMCD See *Association for Multicultural Counseling and Development*.

American Art Therapy Association (AATA) The primary association for promoting the visual arts therapies in the United States. AATA is located at 1202 Allanson Road, Mundelein, IL 60060 (847-949-6064; http://www.arttherapy.org/). See also *art therapy*.

American Association for Counseling and Development (AACD) The name of the *American Counseling Association (ACA)* from 1984 to 1992.

American Association for Marriage and Family Therapy (AAMFT) The oldest and largest association for couple and family counseling in the United States, established in 1942. AAMFT is located at 1133 NW 15th Street, Suite 300, Washington, DC 20005 (202-452-0109; http://www.aamft.org).

American Association of Christian Counselors (AACC) An interdisciplinary association of professional helpers, religious leaders, and lay counselors "committed to integrating biblical truth with practical counseling principles." AACC's address is P.O. Box 739, Forest, VA 24551 (800-526-8673; http://www.aacc.net).

American Association of Pastoral Counselors (AAPC) An association that represents and sets professional standards for pastoral counselors and pastoral counseling centers in the United States. Founded in 1963, AAPC is nonsectarian in nature and practice. AAPC is located at 9504-A Lee Highway, Fairfax, VA 22031-2303 (703-385-6967; http://www.aapc.org).

American Association of Retired Persons (AARP) A leading advocacy group for people ages 50 and above, AARP seeks to influence social and political activities that impact the aging and aged. The address is P.O. Box 199, Long Beach, CA 90848-9983 (800-515-2299; http://www.aarp.org/).

American Association of Sex Educators, Counselors, and Therapists (AASECT) A multidisciplinary organization dedicated to informing the public about and promoting healthy expressions of human sexuality and setting standards for counseling professionals who treat sexual dysfunction. AASECT's address is P.O. Box 238, Mount Vernon, IA 52314 (fax 319-895-6203; http://www.aasect.org).

American Association of State Counseling Boards (AASCB) An association of state counseling boards whose members meet regularly to coordinate efforts at uniformity and discuss issues pertaining to the regulation of counseling.

American College Counseling Association (ACCA) A divisional affiliate of the *American Counseling Association (ACA)* that fosters student development in higher education.

American College Personnel Association (ACPA) An association of professionals employed in the field of student affairs. ACPA is located at 1 Dupont Circle, Suite 300, Washington, DC 20036 (202-835-2272; www.acpa.nche.edu/index.htm).

American College Testing, Inc. (ACT) An independent, nonprofit organization that provides educational services to students and their parents, to high schools and colleges, to professional associations and government agencies, and to business and industry. ACT is best known for its college admissions testing program. The address is P.O. Box 168, 2201 North Dodge Street, Iowa City, IA 52243-0168 (319-337-1028, http://www.act.org/).

American Council of Guidance and Personnel Associations (ACGPA) A loose confederation of organizations that was concerned with educational and vocational guidance as well as other personnel activities. ACGPA operated from 1935 to 1952 and was a forerunner of the *American Counseling Association (ACA)*.

American Counseling Association (ACA) The largest professional counseling association in the world, founded in 1952. ACA is located at 5999 Stevenson Avenue, Alexandria, VA 22304 (800-347-6647; 703-823-9800; http://www.counseling.org/).

American Counseling Association Foundation (ACAF) A foundation that focuses on preserving and enhancing the counseling profession through work in advocacy, research, and professional standards. ACAF is located at 5999 Stevenson Avenue, Alexandria, VA 22304 (703-823-9800; http://www.counseling.org/aca_foundation/).

American Dance Therapy Association (ADTA) The primary association in the United States working to establish and maintain high standards of professional education and competence in the field of dance/movement therapy. ADTA is located at 2000 Century Plaza, Suite 108, 10632 Little Patuxent Parkway, Columbia, MD 21044 (410-997-4040; http://www.ADTA.org). See also *dance/movement therapy.*

American Family Therapy Association (AFTA) An association that was formed in 1977 by Murray Bowen and is identified as an academy of about 1,000 advanced professionals interested in the exchange of ideas in the field of family therapy.

American Group Psychotherapy Association (AGPA) A psychoanalytically oriented organization established by Samuel R. Slavson in 1943.

American Mental Health Counselors Association (AMHCA) An autonomous divisional affiliate of the *American Counseling Association (ACA)* that represents and advocates for mental health counselors in many behavioral health settings. AMHCA is located at 801 N. Fairfax Street, Suite 304, Alexandria, VA 22314 (800-326-2642; http://www.amhca.org/ home2.html).

American Music Therapy Association (AMTA) Founded in 1998, AMTA's purpose is the progressive development of the therapeutic use of music in *rehabilitation*, special education, and community settings. Predecessors of the American Music Therapy Association include the National Association for Music Therapy founded in 1950 and the American

Association for Music Therapy founded in 1971. AMTA's address is 8455 Colesville Road, Suite 1000, Silver Spring, MD 20910 (301-589-3300; http://www.namt.com/indexhtml). See also *music therapy*.

American Personnel and Guidance Association (APGA) Formed in 1952 as an interest group from the *American Council of Guidance and Personnel Associations (ACGPA)*, APGA operated from 1952 to 1984 as an evolving professional counseling association. APGA later was renamed the *American Association for Counseling and Development (AACD)* (1984–1992) and the *American Counseling Association (ACA)* (1992 to present).

American Psychiatric Association (APA) An association of medical specialists that includes physicians who specialize in the diagnosis and treatment of mental and emotional illnesses and substance use disorders. APA is located at 1400 NW K Street, Washington, DC 20005 (202-682-6000; http://www.psych.org).

American Psychoanalytic Association (APA) A professional organization of psychoanalysts located throughout the United States and a regional association of the International Psychoanalytical Association. APA is located at 309 E. 49th Street, New York, NY 10017 (212-752-0450; http://www.apsa.org).

American Psychological Association (APA) Founded in 1892, the American Psychological Association is the largest professional group for psychologists in the world. APA's address is 750 First Street, NE, Washington, DC 20002 (202-336-5500; http://www.apa.org).

American Rehabilitation Counseling Association (ARCA) An autonomous divisional affiliate of the *American Counseling Association (ACA)* that is devoted to enhancing the development of people with *disabilities* and promoting excellence in *rehabilitation counseling*. ARCA's address is 1835 Rohlwing Road, Suite E, Rolling Meadows, IL 60008 (847-788-0848; http://www.nchrtm.okstate.edu/ARCA/index.html).

American School Counselor Association (ASCA) An autonomous divisional affiliate of the *American Counseling Association (ACA)* that promotes excellence in professional *school counseling* and the development of all students. ASCA's address is 801 North Fairfax Street, Suite 310, Alexandria, VA 22314 (800-306-4722 [4SCA]; http://www.schoolcounselor.org/index.htm). See also *school counseling*.

American Society of Group Psychotherapy and Psychodrama (ASGPP) A professional group association established by Jacob L. Moreno in 1942. ASGPP is located at 301 North Harrison Street, Suite 508, Princeton, NJ 08540 (609-452-1339; http://www.ncata.com/psychodrama.html). See also *psychodrama*.

Americans with Disabilities Act (ADA) A law enacted by Congress in 1990 that heightened awareness of the needs of the over 40 million people in the United States with disabilities and increased national efforts in providing multiple services for those with mental, behavioral, and physical disabilities. This act extended to people with a *disability* the same protection and guarantees given to minorities in the Civil Rights Act of 1964.

AMHCA See *American Mental Health Counselors Association*.

amnesia The loss of memory—either total or partial.

amphetamine A *stimulant* that temporarily increases one's mental alertness, produces a sense of euphoria, and reduces fatigue. Amphetamines are also known as uppers, speed, and bennies. Amphetamines are addictive and can cause *anxiety*, restlessness, headaches, rapid heartbeat, and difficulty breathing.

amplify To emphasize statements made by the *protagonist* in a *psychodrama*. Examples include verbalizing nonverbal communications, questioning one's self, interpreting statements for what is being said and not said, contradicting feelings, self-observing, and denial.

AMTA See *American Music Therapy Association*.

anal stage   The second stage of Freud's stages of *psychosexual* development. In this stage, children (between the ages of 18 months and 3 years) obtain erotic pleasure from withholding and eliminating feces. Toilet training is a major experience during this time, and children's personalities are influenced by the ways in which their parents respond to them as they master this task.

analogies test   A type of test that requires respondents to complete sentences that compare different situations or things with each other. For example, a rose is to a bush, as a leaf is to a _____. The Miller's Analogy Test is the best known of this type of test.

analysis   **1.**   An abbreviated term for *psychoanalysis*.   **2.**   An evaluation of a concern in counseling such as to do an analysis of a client's problem.   **3.**   The interpretation of data through the use of statistical tests.   **4.** The first step in E. G. Williamson's *directive counseling* approach. It involves the collection of data on a client.

analysis of variance (ANOVA)   An *inferential statistics* procedure used to test the null hypothesis that the means of two or more populations are equal to each other. Often, these groups represent performance on a dependent variable as a result of treatment by one or more independent variables. ANOVA can be used to test the significance of mean differences among several groups simultaneously.

analyst   A practitioner of *psychoanalysis*.

analytical psychology   Carl Jung's approach to therapy that begins with an exploration of a client's *conscious* state and proceeds to explore and interpret a client's *unconscious* mind (e.g., dreams, fantasies).

androgyny   The coexistence and display of what are considered male and female characteristics in the same person. The flexible integration in a person of masculine and feminine characteristics.

anecdotal record   An informal notation about a person, group, family, or situation in which a standard record reporting form is not used.

angel dust   See *phencyclidine hydrochloride*.

anima   A Jungian *archetype* term for the feminine component of the male personality.

animus   A Jungian *archetype* for the masculine component of the female personality.

anomie   A state of normlessness or the elimination or reduction of values, mores, and norms, and codes of conduct. Anomie usually occurs in rapidly changing societies that are subject to much stress.

anorexia nervosa   An *eating disorder* that primarily affects young women; it involves an avoidance of food and severe weight loss based on a distorted perception of one's self as being fat or overweight. Physical harm such as malnutrition or even death result from untreated anorexia.

ANOVA   See *analysis of variance*.

Antabuse   The trade name for the drug disulfram. It causes nausea when introduced into the bloodstream of someone who has consumed *alcohol* and is used in recovery programs to discourage drinking in recovering alcohol abusers.

antecedent   An event that precedes a behavior and is thought to influence it.

antecedent-response-consequence (A-R-C) model of behaviorism   A behavioral model that proposes behavior is functionally related to its *antecedent* and *consequent* events. Behaviors become more frequent or are suppressed, depending on what precedes or follows them.

antideterministic   A *humanistic approach* that proposes that each person is able to change and become responsible for his or her own life. This view is the opposite of the psychoanalytic view that *psychosexual* influences determine people's behaviors.

antisocial personality disorder   A disorder characterized by irresponsible behavior, low tolerance for frustration, frequent conflicts, lack of remorse or acknowledged responsibility for one's actions, and a low level of socialization. Someone with this disorder is sometimes referred to as a *psychopath* or *sociopath*.

antiwork group See *"BA" (basic assumption) activity.*

anxiety Mental and physical nervousness and uneasiness, often resulting in increased tension, usually associated with pressure to please, fear of failure, or the unknown. Anxiety may be connected with concrete events or free floating and not attached to any one particular thing.

anxiety disorders Disorders characterized by a chronic state of tension, uneasiness, worry, and fear that is reoccurring and has no known source or cause. The *DSM-IV* classifies *phobias*, *compulsive disorder*, *panic disorders*, *post-traumatic stress disorder*, and *acute* and general *anxiety disorders* in this category.

APA See *American Psychiatric Association; American Psychoanalytic Association; American Psychological Association.*

APGA See *American Personnel and Guidance Association.*

applied behavior analysis The use of *reinforcement, punishment, extinction,* stimulus control, and other procedures derived from *laboratory research* to human interactions in a pragmatic way.

applied research Research conducted for the purpose of applying or testing a *theory* and evaluating its usefulness in solving specific client or system problems. It is the opposite of *basic research.*

approach reaction The tendency of an individual to move toward a situation or issue regardless of whether it is positive or negative. An approach reaction is a positive sign; people who display it tend to work through difficulties.

approach-approach conflict When a person must choose between two equally attractive options.

approach-avoidance conflict When a person must choose between an option that is attractive and one that is not.

appropriateness **1.** Behavior or conduct that is at an expected age or stage level. **2.** When factors extraneous to the purpose and nature of a test, such as testing conditions, have no influence on a client's performance or response to the test.

approval Support, usually given verbally by a counselor, of a client's behavior or action.

APT See *Association for Play Therapy.*

aptitude Specific capacities and abilities required of an individual to learn or adequately perform a job or task; the potential for acquiring a skill.

aptitude test A standardized measurement device used to assess the readiness of someone to learn and become proficient in a given area in the future. The *Armed Services Vocational Aptitude Battery (ASVAB)* and the *General Aptitude Test Battery (GATB)* are examples of aptitude tests.

A-R-C model of behaviorism See *antecedent-response-consequence (A-R-C) model of behaviorism.*

ARCA See *American Rehabilitation Counseling Association.*

archetypes A Jungian concept that refers to the inherited primordial images of the *collective unconscious* that have accumulated over generations of human experience. Major archetypes are the *anima* and *animus.* Other archetypes include the Great Mother, the Wise Old Man, the Trickster, the Divine Child, rebirth, wholeness, and God. Archetypes that influence the development of the personality include the *persona,* the *shadow,* the *animus,* the *anima,* and the *self.*

arithmetic mean The sum of a set of scores divided by the number of scores. See also *mean.*

Armed Service Vocational Aptitude Battery (ASVAB) A multiple *aptitude test* first developed in 1966 and revised periodically since.

a

The ASVAB measures aptitude for general academic areas and for military and civilian work. The test is used in Grade 11 and higher.

Army Alpha and Army Beta Tests   Two of the earliest *intelligence tests* created in the United States. These tests were used to screen recruits during World War I. The Alpha Test was given to recruits who were literate; the Beta Test was given to inductees who were illiterate.

art therapy   The systematic use of art media, images, and creative art processes as a primary or adjunct means to bring about therapeutic change. In order to conduct art therapy, counselors must receive specialized training in this area. See also *American Art Therapy Association (AATA)*.

as if   See *acting "as if."*

ASCA   See *American School Counselor Association.*

ASERVIC   See *Association for Spiritual, Ethical, and Religious Values in Counseling.*

ASGPP   See *American Society of Group Psychotherapy and Psychodrama.*

ASGW   See *Association for Specialists in Group Work.*

Asian American/Pacific Islander   A resident of the United States whose background and identity are with peoples of Asia and the Pacific Islands (e.g., the Chinese, Japanese, Filipinos, Vietnamese, Koreans, Samoans, Thais, and Indians). There is tremendous heterogeneity within this population. It is the third largest ethnic minority group in the United States.

asking the question   An *Adlerian counseling* intervention in which clients are asked the question, "What would be different if you were well?" The question is often asked during the initial interview in Adlerian counseling. See also *miracle question.*

asocial behavior   Behavior that is indifferent to people or social *norms* and *values.*

assertiveness   Asking for what one wants in a timely and appropriate manner. Assertiveness is in contrast to either passive or aggressive behaviors.

assertiveness training   Training designed to help either aggressive or passive people learn how to ask for what they want or need in a timely and appropriate manner. The major tenet of assertiveness training is that people should be free to express their thoughts and feelings appropriately without undue *anxiety* or anger. Assertiveness training involves *counterconditioning* through *role playing* and *modeling* as well as instruction.

assessment   Administering tests and evaluation instruments or utilizing behavioral observations in order to gain information and make decisions about the *diagnosis*, *treatment*, and possible outcome of a counseling situation.

assimilation   **1.** The process of becoming part of the *culture* in which one lives by adopting the *values* and *norms* of the majority population.   **2.** In Jean Piaget's theory, the incorporation of an experience in one's *environment* into an already existing thought structure. It is the opposite of *accommodation.*

Association for Adult Development and Aging (AADA)   A divisional affiliate of the *American Counseling Association (ACA)* that addresses concerns in counseling and development across the human *life span.*

Association for Advancement of Behavior Therapy (AABT)   A professional, interdisciplinary organization that is concerned with the application of behavioral and cognitive sciences in understanding and enhancing human behavior. AABT is located at 305 Seventh Avenue, 16th Floor, New York, NY 10001-6008 (212-647-1890; http://server.psyc.vt.edu/aabt/).

Association for Assessment in Counseling (AAC)   A divisional affiliate of the *American Counseling Association (ACA)*. As an organization of counseling professionals, it provides leadership, training, and research in the creation, development, production, and use of assessment and diagnostic techniques.

Association for Counselor Education and Supervision (ACES)   A divisional affiliate of the *American Counseling Association (ACA)* composed primarily of counselor educators. ACES emphasizes the need for quality education and supervision of counselors in all work settings.

Association for Counselors and Educators in Government (ACEG) A divisional affiliate of the *American Counseling Association (ACA)* that attends to counseling and educational concerns of professionals in local, state, and federal government and military-related agencies.

Association for Gay, Lesbian, and Bisexual Issues in Counseling (AGLBIC) A divisional affiliate of the *American Counseling Association (ACA)* that educates and promotes sensitivity among counselors on issues related to gay, lesbian, and bisexual clients.

Association for Humanistic Education and Development (AHEAD) See *Counseling Association for Humanistic Education and Development (C-AHEAD)*.

Association for Multicultural Counseling and Development (AMCD) A divisional affiliate of the *American Counseling Association (ACA)* that emphasizes leadership, research, training, and development of multicultural counseling professionals. AMCD focuses on racial and ethnic issues in counseling.

Association for Play Therapy (APT) An international organization dedicated to the advancement of *play therapy*. APT is interdisciplinary and *eclectic* in orientation. It defines play therapy as "a distinct group of interventions that use play as an integral component of the therapeutic process." APT's address is 2100 North Winery Avenue, Suite 104, Fresno, CA 93703-2884 (209-252-2APT; http://a4pt.org/).

Association for Specialists in Group Work (ASGW) A divisional affiliate of the *American Counseling Association (ACA)* that specializes in research and facilitating the practice surrounding counseling, psychotherapy, educational, and task groups.

Association for Spiritual, Ethical, and Religious Values in Counseling (ASERVIC) A divisional affiliate of the *American Counseling Association (ACA)* that is devoted to professionals who believe that spiritual, ethical, religious, and other human values are essential to the full development of persons and counseling.

ASVAB See *Armed Services Vocational Aptitude Battery*.

at-risk People most likely to develop problems because of their backgrounds and/or present behaviors are considered to be at-risk. At-risk individuals often have not finished high school or leave school without the necessary skills to be successful. Other internal factors (e.g., a negative attitude) and external variables (e.g., poverty) play a part in making some people more at-risk than others. Being at-risk rests on a continuum with minimal to high probability.

attachment The emotional bonds between people that develop because of dependence and attraction, especially important in early life, as in child/parent relationships.

attachment theory A theory that describes the processes infants go through in developing close emotional bonds and dependence on one or more adult caregivers.

attack on the leader When members of the group become hostile or rebellious in regard to a leader's authority or his or her conducting of the group. Underlying reasons for such attacks are subgrouping, fear of intimacy, and extra-group socializing.

attending skills Being with and communicating to a client a sincere acceptance of him or her. Physically attending behaviors such as smiling, leaning forward, making eye contact, gesturing, and nodding one's head are effective nonverbal ways of conveying to clients that the counselor is interested in and open to them. *Active listening* and the use of *minimal encouragers*, such as "Hmm" and "Yes," are other ways of attending. Attending skills processes can be summed up in the mnemonic device called *SOLER*. See also *SOLER*.

attention deficit disorder (ADD)   A disorder that includes specific symptoms of inattention. A related malady, *attention deficit hyperactivity disorder (ADHD)*, includes an additional list of symptoms of hyperactivity/impulsivity. Individuals with forms of ADD and ADHD may know what to do but do not consistently do what they know because of their inability to efficiently stop and think prior to responding, regardless of the setting or task. Characteristics of the disorder have been demonstrated to arise in *early childhood* for most individuals. ADD and ADHD are treated and managed through medication and behavior therapy.

attention deficit hyperactivity disorder (ADHD)   See *attention deficit disorder*.

attentiveness   The amount of verbal and nonverbal behavior shown to a client by a counselor in order to establish and continue *rapport* and show *care*. Attentiveness behaviors include probing, restating, summarizing, making eye contact, smiling, and leaning forward.

attitude   A relatively stable and enduring predisposition to respond positively or negatively to a person, object, situation, institution, event, and so forth. An attitude carries a strong emotional component; when generalized, it becomes a *stereotype*. Attitudes emerge from cultural, familial, and personal sources.

attractiveness   1. The physical and/or psychological similarity between a client and counselor and the appeal of that to either or both.   **2.** A multidimensional concept referring to group members positively identifying with others in the group.

audience   A term used for others who may be present during a *psychodrama*.

authenticity   The ability to be transparent, real, and genuine; to be the same inwardly as one is outwardly.

authoritarian   A person or environment characterized by a lack of democracy and a structure of power that is punitive for those who do not comply with requirements handed down.

authoritarian leaders   Leaders who envision themselves as experts and retain all decision-making power. These leaders interpret, give *advice*, and generally direct the movement of others much like a parent controls the actions of a child. They are often charismatic and manipulative. They feed off obedience and expect conformity.

autism   A developmental disorder that begins prior to 30 months of age. Major characteristics include a lack of responsiveness to people, severe language impairment, and strong resistance to change in routine or the environment.

autodrama   See *monodrama*.

automatic thoughts   Personal beliefs and ideas, specific to a stimulus, that are unexamined and *dysfunctional* (e.g., seeing a person that one has not met before and thinking that he or she is boring).

autonomy   1. Respecting freedom of choice, the promotion of self-determination, or the power to choose one's own direction in life.   **2.** A stage in life development between ages 1 and 2, as defined by Erik Erikson. The focus of the stage is on acquiring self-mastery. It is the opposite of *shame*.

autoplastic approach   An adjustment to a culturally different environment through changing oneself. It is the opposite of the *alloplastic approach*.

auxiliary   A person in counseling who assists a counselor or a client in an *enactment*, such as in family counseling or psychodrama, or who functions like a counselor in a group.

Avanta Network   An association that carries on the interdisciplinary work of training counselors in Virginia Satir's methods. The network is located at 2104 SW 152nd Street #2, Burien, WA 98166 (206-241-7566; http://www. avanta. net/home.html).

average A research term for *measures of the central tendency* of a group of numbers. An average is expressed in three different ways: *median*, *mean,* and *mode*.

aversive therapy Behaviorally based unpleasant interventions, such as *overcorrection* and *punishment*, that are intended to suppress or eliminate negative or undesirable behaviors so positive behaviors can be taught. Aversive therapy is used only as a last resort and with *informed consent*.

avoidance reaction The tendency of someone to withdraw from or avoid a situation or issue that might be threatening or adversarial. An avoidance reaction is a negative sign because people who display it tend to eschew problems and issues and refuse to work through them.

avoidance-avoidance conflict When a person tries to escape two equally unpleasant choices.

avoiding conflict **1.** A style of coping in which a person is free from the stress that comes with conflict because he or she minimizes or denies conflict and/or does not directly address it. **2.** The silencing of members who expose a group's shortcomings or disagree with what the majority of a group thinks.

awareness **1.** An ongoing process in counseling of recognizing and being cognizant and *conscious* of what one is thinking about as well as what one is doing, feeling, and sensing. **2.** A *gestalt therapy* term for a total organism response.

awfulizing When a client irrationally believes that an inconvenience or disappointment is awful, terrible, and a major catastrophe. Albert Ellis theorizes that many individuals awfulize to the point of making themselves and others miserable.

Axes of the DSM-IV The DSM-IV suggests making a *diagnosis* using a five axes system. Axis I includes clinical syndromes and other conditions that may be a focus of clinical attention. It is usually thought of as the axis on which a client's presenting problem and principal diagnosis appear. Axis II contains diagnostic information only on *personality disorders* and mental limitations. Axis III contains information about general medical conditions (e.g., chronic pain) of the client. Axis IV contains information on psychosocial and environmental problems that may affect the diagnosis, treatment, and prognosis of *mental disorders* (e.g., a lack of friends, inadequate housing). Axis V gives a global assessment of functioning (GAF) for the client on a scale from 0 to 100 (higher numbers on the scale indicate a better level of functioning). The assessment can be in relationship to the past or the present. When all of the axes are combined, the result might look like the following: Axis I—305.00, alcohol abuse, moderate; Axis II—317.00, mild mental retardation; Axis III—chronic pain; Axis IV—divorced, unemployed, no friends; Axis V—GAF = 30 (present). See also *multiaxial assessment*.

b

"BA" (basic assumption) activity A classification devised by Wilfred Bion for the emotional pattern of an antiwork group (as opposed to a "W" [work group]). BA groups can be broken down further into three subpatterns: BA dependency (in which members are overdependent on the group leader); BA pairing (in which members are more interested in being with each other than in working on a goal); and BA fight-flight (in which members become *b*

preoccupied with either engaging in or avoiding hostile conflict).

band-aiding   The premature insertion of and misuse of support; a process of preventing clients from fully expressing their emotional pain by overly assuring them everything will work out.

bar graph   A graph that depicts *data* through the use of parallel strips drawn from a common base.

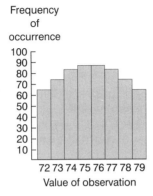

Frequency of occurrence

72 73 74 75 76 77 78 79
Value of observation

bar graph

barbiturates   *Drugs* that act as *sedatives* and are prescribed by physicians to facilitate sleep or control convulsions. Barbiturates are also popularly known as *downers, yellow jackets, red birds,* and *rainbows.* As a street drug, barbiturates produce a euphoric mood that can shift suddenly to one of sadness.

barbs   An abbreviated name for *barbiturates.*

basal age   The highest year level on an *intelligence test,* such as the *Stanford-Binet,* at which a person passes all *subtests.* It is the opposite of *ceiling age.*

baseline   A *research* term for the recording of the occurrence of targeted behaviors before an *intervention* is made. A baseline is usually a pretreatment procedure instituted so that the effectiveness of a counseling intervention can be measured.

basic encounter   See *encounter.*

basic encounter group   Also known as an *encounter group, personal growth group,* or *sensitivity group;* an approach to group work first established by Carl Rogers. It focuses on individuals' awareness of their own emotional experiences and the behaviors of others; emphasis is placed on the *awareness* of and *exploration* of intrapsychic and interpersonal

issues. The emphasis in this type of group is on personal development.

BASIC ID   An acronym for the fundamental concepts in Arnold Lazarus's *multimodal therapy.* The concepts are behavior, affect, sensation, imagery, cognition, interpersonal relations, and drugs.

basic mistakes   An *Adlerian counseling* concept for the myths, *irrational beliefs,* and self-defeating perceptions that are a part of a person's *lifestyle.* Basic mistakes include *overgeneralization,* false or impossible goals of security, misperceptions of life demands, denial of one's self-worth, and faulty *values.*

basic needs   The lower needs on Abraham Maslow's *hierarchy of needs.* At the base of the hierarchy are physiological needs followed by safety needs, belongingness and love needs, esteem needs, and *self-actualization.*

basic research   Research conducted for the purpose of *theory* development or refinement. It is the opposite of *applied research.*

battery   **1.** A group of several *tests* used to evaluate an individual or group. See also *test battery.*   **2.** *Abuse* that involves physical force.

battle for initiative   A process by which a counselor gets a client to become motivated to make needed changes through stressing the need and urgency for doing so. Clients must "win" the battle for initiative if counseling is to be effective.

battle for structure   The struggle to establish the parameters under which counseling is conducted (e.g., time limits, frequency of sessions). Counselors must "win" the battle for structure if counseling is to be effective.

BDI   See *Beck Depression Inventory.*

Beck Depression Inventory (BDI)   A 21-item self-report measure of *depression.* It is easily administered, scored, and interpreted, with high *reliability* and *validity* components. The Internet address is http://www.beckinstitute. org/.

becoming   Gordon Allport's term for the human tendency to move toward growth and *self-actualization.*

before-after design An experimental design in which both *the experimental group* and *control group* are given a pretest and then an aftertest.

behavior Any action or response by an individual or group.

behavior modification A general term for behavioral methods used in altering behaviors especially through the use of *conditioning*. Behavior modification is most often applied in educational environments or with clients undergoing treatment.

behavior therapy an approach that focuses on the collective behaviorist point of view. The emphasis of behavior therapy is on the removal or elimination of *dysfunctional* behaviors and the instilling of new functional behaviors.

behavioral counseling An approach to counseling based on *learning* principles; the approach focuses on dealing with clients' behaviors directly in order to produce *change*.

behavioral determinist A *counselor* or *helping professional* who emphasizes learning as the primary determinant of human actions. B. F. Skinner is a prime example of a behavioral determinist.

behavioral family counseling A school of family therapy that is primarily nonsystemic and that stresses the importance of *learning*. Behavioral family counseling emphasizes the importance of family *rules* and skill training and the belief that behaviors are determined by *consequences* rather than *antecedents*. The goals of behavioral family counseling are specific, and work is usually limited to three main areas: *behavioral parent education,* behavioral marriage counseling, and treatment of *sexual dysfunctioning*.

behavioral groups Either interpersonal or transactional groups, depending on the purposes of the leader and members. *Interpersonal groups* are highly didactic and involve specified goals that usually center on self-improvement. *Transactional groups* are more *heterogeneous* and focus on broader, yet specific, goals.

behavioral objective A specific behavioral *outcome* that is observable and that is agreed upon beforehand to be the target of an *intervention*.

behavioral parent education An approach associated with direct change and manipulation. Parents are trained to be *change agents* and to record and reinforce certain behaviors in their children.

behavioral rehearsal Procedures that involve practicing a desired behavior until it is learned and performed the way one wishes. The process consists of gradually *shaping* a behavior and getting corrective *feedback*.

behaviorism A school of thought that began in the United States with the work of John B. Watson. Behaviorism emphasizes the role of environmental stimuli and the importance of *reward* in the *learning* and *conditioning* of *behavior*.

behaviorist A *clinician* who ascribes to the tenets of *behavior therapy* and who usually emphasizes overt behavior techniques and processes, such as changing of maladaptive actions, over other techniques and processes.

being A *humanistic* and *existential* term for the individual's concept of *self*.

bell-shaped curve A curve obtained by plotting the frequency of a *normal distribution*.

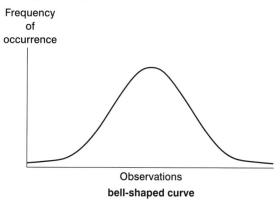

bell-shaped curve

belonging An innate *need* or drive in human life to associate with others. Belonging leads individuals to seek out relationships and involvement with fellow human beings.

Bender Gestalt Test   An evaluative test, officially named the *Bender Visual Motor Gestalt Test,* in which clients are asked to copy on a blank sheet of paper nine cards containing abstract designs. The test was designed to measure visual-motor integration and function in children ages 5 to 11. Aspects of *personality,* such as impulsivity, *anxiety,* and aggression are also revealed in the test.

Bender Visual Motor Gestalt Test   See *Bender Gestalt Test.*

beneficence   An *ethical principle* that stresses promoting the good of others.

benzodiazepines   A group of prescriptive *drugs* that are widely used in the treatment of *anxiety* and insomnia; they include diazepam (Valium), chlordiazepoxide (Librium), and triazolam (Halcion). Benzodiazepines can be addictive. They often are used as street drugs to treat the adverse effects of *cocaine, heroin,* and *alcohol.*

bias   **1.** *Prejudice* or a negative *attitude* toward an individual, idea, or group.   **2.** A systematic, as opposed to a random, error in *research* (e.g., improper sampling or the misuse of statistics).

bibliotherapy   A term derived from the Greek words "biblion" meaning book and "therapeio" meaning healing. Bibliotherapy is generally understood to be the reading of selected literature in order to help individuals gain a better understanding of themselves and others as well as to produce at times a healing or helpful *catharsis.* See also *scriptotherapy.*

bimodal distribution   A *frequency distribution* in which two values occur at the same frequency.

binge drinking   The consumption of five or more drinks of alcohol for men or four or more drinks of alcohol for women at one sitting.

binuclear family   A postdivorce family structure in which ex-spouses reside in separate but interrelated households. The two interrelated family households comprise one family *system.*

biofeedback   A *behavioral therapy* process that involves the training of individuals to control or *change* automatic responses (e.g., heart rate, blood pressure, and brain wave activity) once thought to be involuntary. In biofeedback therapy, mechanical instruments provide information about a client's physiological processes; the client then controls these processes through self-monitoring, even though he or she may be unsure as to how these processes are being modified.

biographic inventory   A *questionnaire* used to obtain information about a person's background and experiences.

bipolar disorder   Formerly known as *manic-depressive illness;* a disorder (with several variations) characterized by maladaptive mood swings that vary from being manic (e.g., hyperactive, euphoric) to being depressed (e.g., low in self-esteem, sad).

birth order   The position a child occupies in a *family.* Five ordinal positions are emphasized in *Adlerian counseling:* firstborns, children born second, middle children, youngest children, and the only child. Adler believed birth order was a determinant of *personality* and that individuals with the same birth order had more in common (in regard to experiences and approaches to life) than siblings.

birth trauma   The shock of birth described by Otto Rank as being the basis for all other human anxieties.

bisexual   A person who is sexually attracted to both males and females.

Black   A term sometimes used in the United States for descendants whose ancestry was African. See also *African American.*

blamer   A person, according to Virginia Satir, who attempts to place blame on others and not take responsibility for what he or she is doing.

blended family   See *stepfamily.*

blind self   One of the four quadrants in the *Johari Awareness Model.* The blind self is known to others but not known to self.

blocking **1.** The *suppression* of painful feelings and thoughts by a client. **2.** In group or family counseling, the technique of protecting vulnerable members in which the leader intervenes to stop counterproductive behavior. This intervention can be done verbally or nonverbally through hand signals or other behaviors.

blocking role An antigroup member role. Individuals who take this role act as aggressors, dominators, recognition seekers, and self-righteous moralists.

body dysmorphic disorder A *somatoform disorder* characterized by an imagined flaw in one's appearance.

body language Nonverbal communication (e.g., hand tapping) associated with body posture and movement. Body language is emphasized in many counseling approaches, such as *gestalt therapy.*

Bogust v. Iverson A 1960 case ruling that a counselor with a doctoral degree could not be held liable for the *suicide* of one of his clients because counselors were "mere teachers" who received training in a department of education. It was not until 1971 in an *Iowa Law Review Note* that counselors were legally recognized as professionals who provided personal as well as vocational and educational counseling.

bonding A process that occurs between a mother and a child early in the baby's life. Bonding may be physical or emotional. A failure to bond may lead to *neglect* or *abuse.*

borderline personality A *personality disorder* characterized by impulsive, unpredictable, and often self-destructive behaviors, intense mood swings, chronic boredom, manipulation of others for short-term gain, uncontrollable anger, and maladaptive patterns of relating to others.

boundaries **1.** The physical and psychological factors that separate people from one another and organize them. **2.** The parameters under which counselors operate their sessions, such as starting and ending on time.

Bowen family therapy An approach that focuses on differentiation of one's thoughts from one's emotions and oneself from others. Techniques in this approach focus on ways to differentiate oneself from one's extended *family of origin.* In the process, there is an attempt to create an individuated person with a healthy *self-concept* who will not experience undue *anxiety* when relationships become stressful. Ways of achieving this goal include assessment of self and family through a *genogram* and a focus on cognitive processes, such as asking content-based questions of one's family. The therapeutic interaction takes place with both spouses together or with an individual.

brainstorming A way to stimulate divergent thinking. It requires an initial generating of ideas in a nonjudgmental manner within a group. The premise of this approach is that creativity is often held back because of the critical evaluation of ideas and actions.

brief therapy An approach to working with clients that generally requires 10 sessions or less. However, brief therapy has to do more with the clarity about what needs to be changed rather than time. A central principle of brief therapy is that one evaluates which solutions have so far been attempted (without success) and then tries new and different solutions to the problem, often the opposite of what has already been attempted.

bubblegummers An informal term that refers to middle school children between the ages of 10 and 14.

bubbles An informal term for the flaws found in all *research* methods.

Buckley Amendment See *Family Educational Rights and Privacy Act (FERPA).*

bulimia An *eating disorder* characterized by periods of binge eating followed by purging.

burnout A gradually intensifying pattern of physical, psychological, and behavioral responses to a continual flow of *stressors* in which a person becomes physically and emotionally exhausted. Burnout is characterized by apathy, fatigue, anger, and conflict.

Buros Institute of Mental Measurements An institute set up by Oscar and Lucella Buros at the University of Nebraska-Lincoln to continue their work in advancing the field of measurement. The Buros Institute encourages improved test development and measurement research. The institute publishes important works in the measurement field, including the *Mental Measurement Yearbook* and *Tests in Print (TIP)* (published by the University of Nebraska Press, 312 North 14th Street, P.O. Box 880484, Lincoln, NE 68588-0484 (http://www.unl.edu/buros/subburos.html).

C

C group A type of *Adlerian* parent education group. Each component of the group—collaboration, consultation, clarification, confrontation, concern, confidentiality, and commitment—begins with the letter "c." The group is primarily *psychoeducational.* It emphasizes developmental and preventive aspects of parenting.

CACREP See *Council for Accreditation of Counseling and Related Educational Programs.*

caffeine A mild *stimulant* that dissipates drowsiness or fatigue, speeds up one's heart rate, raises blood pressure, and irritates the stomach. Caffeine is found primarily in coffee, tea, cola beverages, and chocolate. Caffeine can be addictive.

C-AHEAD See *Counseling Association for Humanistic Education and Development.*

California Achievement Test (CAT) A battery of tests used to evaluate children's academic achievement in Grades 2 through 12. The CAT is a widely used *achievement test* in the schools.

California Psychological Inventory (CPI) A pencil-and-paper *personality inventory* for ages 12 through 70 designed to diagnose and understand interpersonal behavior, such as sociability, tolerance, and responsibility, within normal populations. The CPI is sometimes called the sane person's *MMPI.*

camera check A *rational self-analysis* technique in which the client is asked to envision a situation the way a camera would. The idea behind the technique is to objectify events so that they do not become contaminated with emotional content and can thus be handled cognitively.

cannabis A controversial stimulant *drug* in the United States that can be smoked, eaten, or drunk. Cannabis is known by many names (e.g., hashish, *pot,* grass, *dope,* and *marijuana*). See also *marijuana.*

capping The process of easing out of emotional interaction and into cognitive reflection, especially useful during *termination* of counseling.

care A genuine concern for and interest in others and their well-being.

career The activities and positions, both remunerated and nonremunerated, involved in work-related roles and leisure over the course of one's life.

career change group A type of group for adults, usually in *midlife,* that is both *psychoeducational* and psychotherapeutic in nature.

career counseling Counseling that focuses on career choices, especially the relationships between the needs of clients and their vocational development over the *life span.*

career development The process of choosing, entering, adjusting to, and advancing in an occupation. It is a lifelong process that interacts dynamically with other life roles.

career-development assessment and counseling (C-DAC) model A model based on

Donald Super's theory of *career development* that views a client as an individual in a constantly changing *environment*. It assesses career maturity and identifies *values* placed on work and occupational careers using a *battery* of tests and *interest inventories*. Clients high in career salience and ready for career decision-making activities work with a counselor to objectify their interests, abilities, and values. They then take the final step of subjectively assessing life themes and patterns they can identify. The C-DAC model is employed over the life span and incorporates culturally based variables such as work-role importance and values.

career fairs   A *career guidance* activity, often found in educational settings, in which practitioners in a number of fields are invited to explain their jobs and/or employment.

career guidance   All activities that seek to disseminate information about present or future *vocations* in such a way that individuals become more knowledgeable about and aware of who they are in relationship to the world of *work*. Guidance activities can take the form of *career fairs,* library assignments, outside interviews, computer-assisted information experiences, *career shadowing,* didactic lectures, and experiential exercises such as *role playing.*

career information   Information related to the world of *work* that can be useful in the process of *career development,* including educational, occupational, and *psychosocial* information related to working (e.g., availability of training, the nature of work, and status of workers in different *occupations*).

Career Occupational Preference System (COPS)   A career *interest inventory* composed of three parts designed to measure interests and present a *profile* in 14 areas.

career problems   Difficulties that include but are not limited to career indecision and undecidedness, unsatisfactory work performance, *stress* and *adjustment,* incongruence of the person and work environment, and inadequate

or unsatisfactory *integration* of life roles (e.g., parent, friend, citizen).

career shadowing   Also known as shadowing; a *career guidance* activity in which an individual follows a worker around on his or her daily routine in order to learn more about a given profession.

caregiver   A person who provides for the physical, emotional, and social needs of another who is dependent and who cannot provide for his or her own needs.

caring days   A behavioral marital procedure devised by Richard Stuart in which one or both marital partners act as if they care about their spouse regardless of the other's action(s). This technique embodies the idea of a *positive risk.*

Carl D. Perkins Vocational Act   Federal legislation that amended the Vocational Education Act of 1963 and mandated that *career guidance* and counseling must be made accessible to all segments of the population.

case conference   A clinical conference with other helping specialists for the purpose of presenting circumstances surrounding a client and reviewing *treatment* and recommending *interventions.*

case law   The type of *law* determined by decisions of courts at all levels from state to federal.

case notes   Notes written (in each session) by a counselor that document a client's progress toward stated *goals.*

case study   An attempt to understand one unit, such as a person, group, or program, through an intense and systematic investigation of that unit longitudinally. Some case studies rely on a *self-report research format;* others involve *natural observation,* in which the study extends over a period of time.

CASS   See *Educational Resources Information Center/Counseling and Student Services Clearinghouse (ERIC/CASS).*

castration anxiety   During the *Oedipal complex,* the fear a boy has that his father will castrate him in retaliation for the boy's wish to possess his mother.

CAT　See *California Achievement Test.*

catastrophizing　A *cognitive distortion* in which a negative event becomes exaggerated so that it becomes more important than it actually is. For example, if a person makes a mistake at work, the person may think he or she is going to be fired. Albert Ellis popularized this term in his *rational emotive behavioral therapy (REBT).*

catatonia　A *mental disorder* in which a person appears in a stupor seemingly detached from reality and his or her *environment.* Catatonics may occasionally become excited and uncontrollable.

catching oneself　An *Adlerian counseling* term for when clients learn to become aware of self-destructive behaviors or thoughts.

catharsis　The release of pent-up or repressed emotions such as anger or joy that once expressed provide the client relief. Catharsis is sometimes used as a synonym for *abreaction.*

cathexis　A *psychoanalytic* term for emotional attachment to an idea, person, or object.

CCMHC　See *Certified Clinical Mental Health Counselor.*

C-DAC model　See *career-development assessment and counseling model.*

ceiling　The upper limit of a particular ability as measured by a *test.*

ceiling age　The year level on a test, such as the *Stanford-Binet,* at which a person fails all *subtests.* It is the opposite of *basal age.*

Center for Play Therapy　A center at the University of North Texas, established by Garry L. Landreth. Its mission is to encourage the unique *development* and emotional growth of children through the process of *play therapy.* The center's address is P.O. Box 311337, Denton, TX 76203-1337 (940-565-3864; http://www.coe.unt.edu/cpt/).

centrifugal　**1.** Directed away from a center. **2.** A tendency to move away or disengage from a family, either physically or emotionally (i.e., family disengagement). At points in the *family life cycle,* centrifugal movement is con-sidered appropriate, such as during *adolescence,* when teens are attracted more toward their peers than their parents.

centripetal　**1.** Directed toward a center.　**2.** A tendency to move toward family closeness. At points in the *family life cycle,* centripetal movement is considered appropriate and healthy, such as after the birth of a baby.

certification　The process by which an agency, government, or association officially grants recognition to an individual for having met certain professional qualifications that have been developed by the profession. Certification in counseling is voluntary at the national level (e.g., the *National Board for Certified Counselors [NBCC]*), but it is mandatory for some school counselor positions at the state level.

Certified Clinical Mental Health Counselor (CCMHC)　A specialized certification in mental health counseling that is obtained after a professional becomes a *national certified counselor (NCC).*

Certified Rehabilitation Counselor (CRC)　A counselor certified by the Commission of Rehabilitation Counselor Certification (CRCC). Counselors must complete *CORE*-accredited programs and specific courses and satisfy experience requirements.

CEU　See *continuing education units.*

chain　A *group* arrangement in which people are positioned or seated along a line, often according to their rank. *Communication* is

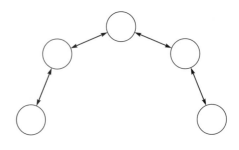

chain

passed from the person at one end of the configuration to the person at the other end through those in between the two. The chain is a popular way to run some group organizations, such as the armed forces. Disadvantages of the chain include the indirectness of communication, the lack of direct contact with others, and the frustration of relaying messages through others.

chaining   Specific behavioral response sequences used in *shaping* behavior.

CHAMPUS   See *Civilian Health and Medical Program of the Uniformed Services.*

change   A process, whether gradual or dramatic, that involves shifts in how one behaves, thinks, or feels. Change is at the heart of counseling.

change agent   A counselor or other *helping professional* who attempts to improve conditions for clients through actions that foster changes in society.

changing questions to statements   A *gestalt therapy* procedure that requires a person who raises a question to make it into an *"I" statement.* For example, "Don't you think you should act differently" would be changed to "I think you should act differently."

character disorder   A behavioral disorder characterized by immaturity and the general inability to cope with the challenges of adult life. Persons with character disorders are frequently in trouble in society either through self-imposed means, such as alcohol abuse, or through breaking laws.

charting   A procedure that involves asking clients to keep an accurate record of problematic behaviors. The idea is to get clients to establish a *baseline* from which *interventions* can be made and to show clients how the *changes* they are making work.

checklist   A list of adjectives, phrases, or other descriptors of *behaviors.* Individuals are asked to check the presence or absence of each item and sometimes the degree (e.g., always, often, sometimes, seldom, never) to which it is present or displayed in their lives.

chemotherapy   The use of prescriptive drugs or chemicals in the treatment of *mental disorders.*

Chi Sigma Iota (CSI)   The international honor society for counselors-in-training, counselor educators, and professional counselors. CSI's mission is to promote scholarship, research, professionalism, leadership, and excellence in counseling and to recognize high attainment in the pursuit of academic and clinical excellence in the field of counseling. The society can be reached at the School of Education, UNCG, P.O. Box 26171, Greensboro, NC 27402-6171 (336-334-4035; http://www.csi—net.org/).

chi square test   A *nonparametric statistical* test used to determine whether two *variables* are statistically independent, that is, whether a set of observed frequencies differ significantly from a set of hypothesized expected frequencies by chance alone.

Chicano   A term sometimes used to describe citizens of the United States who are of Mexican birth or heritage.

child   An individual who has not yet reached maturity. A term usually used to designate a person between birth and puberty.

child custody evaluator   A counselor who acts on behalf of a court to determine what is in the best interest of a *child* in a custody arrangement.

child ego state   A *transactional analysis* concept describing one of three ego states in persons. The child ego is divided into two parts: the *adaptive child,* who conforms to the rules and wishes of the *parent ego state* within the self and others, and the *free child* (or natural child), who reacts more spontaneously and intuitively and takes care of his or her needs without regard for others.

childhood   The period in the human life cycle from birth to puberty (i.e., around age 12). Childhood is often divided into two periods: *early childhood* (up to age 6) and *middle childhood* (age 6 up to puberty). This time of life is characterized by rapid physical, cognitive, and social growth.

choice   A decision-making process about behaviors over which individuals have some control (e.g., whether to use drugs). Much of life involves learning how to make good choices. The concept of *guidance* revolves around helping individuals learn to make choices.

choice theory   A theory that underlies William Glasser's *reality therapy*. In choice theory, the idea is that people have mental images of their needs and behave accordingly; thus, individuals are ultimately self-determining (i.e., they choose). Individuals can choose to be miserable or mentally disturbed. They may also choose to determine the course of their lives in positive ways and give up trying to control others.

Choosing a Vocation   A book written by Frank Parsons and published a year after his death in 1909. It outlines Parson's systematic method for obtaining employment and was the forerunner of *trait-and-factor theory.*

choreography   A process in which clients symbolically enact a pattern or a sequence involving a *relationship,* often with family members. This process is similar to mime.

chronic   Problems, situations, or conditions that have developed and persisted over an extended period of time.

chronological age   A person's actual age in years and months.

circle   A group configuration in which all members have direct access to each other and implied equality in status and power. The circle is probably the best way to ensure group members have an opportunity to express themselves.

circular causality
Also known as nonlinear causality and nonlinear thinking. Circular causality is based on the idea that causality is nonlinear. Actions are a part of a causal chain within a context and within a network of interacting loops, each

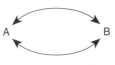

circular causality

reciprocally influencing and being influenced by the other. Circular causality is at the heart of *systems theory*. It is the opposite of *linear causality.*

circular counseling   An unproductive type of counseling in which the same ground is covered over and over again.

circular questioning   A *Milan family therapy* technique of asking questions that focus attention on family connections and highlight differences among family members. This procedure is done through framing every question so that it addresses differences in perception about events or relationships by various family members.

civil law   Law dealing with acts offensive to individuals. The remedy in most civil law cases is compensation for the victim. Most of the law involving counselors pertains to civil law, for example, *divorce* law.

civil liability   Responsibility for acting wrongly toward another or for failing to act when there is a recognized duty to do so.

Civilian Health and Medical Program of the Uniformed Services (CHAMPUS)   A federally funded health insurance company that provides benefits for active and retired U.S. military personnel.

clarification   A counselor technique that attempts to focus on and understand the *content* or intent of a client's statement and at the same time help the client better comprehend what was said. For example, the counselor might state "I'm having difficulty understanding what you are saying. Repeat your last thoughts in either the same or different words."

clarifying the purpose   When group leaders remind members and the group as a whole what behavioral interactions or foci are appropriate in the group and why.

classical conditioning   A theory developed by Ivan Pavlov; also known as *respondent conditioning.* It is the oldest form of *behaviorism.* In classical conditioning, a *stimulus* that was previously neutral (conditioned) is repeatedly paired up with another stimulus (unconditioned) that elicits a natural *response* (unconditioned) so that it comes to elicit the same response (conditioned). For example, the neutral stimulus of a green Ford Taurus might be paired with the unconditional stimulus of food so that every time a person sees the car, his or her mouth waters (an unconditioned natural response to the food).

classroom guidance   See *guidance.*

clear boundaries   *Rules* and habits that allow people to enhance their *communication* and relationships with one another because they allow and encourage *dialogue.*

client   A person, group, family, or community receiving help from the counselor. Analogous words for client are *helpee* or *counselee.* In the medical model, a client is known as a *patient.*

client records   See *records.*

client-centered therapy   A theory developed by Carl Rogers. It falls somewhere between the original name of *nondirective counseling* and the more modern name of *person-centered counseling.* The idea of the approach is that the client, not the counselor, should direct the counseling process in terms of focus.

clinic   A place where people can receive needed medical or mental *treatment.* The word "clinic" is often the last word in the names of mental health facilities (e.g., mental health clinic).

clinical counseling   E. G. Williamson's directive approach to counseling, developed in the 1930s. See also *counselor-centered counseling; directive counseling.*

clinical psychology   A mental health treatment branch of psychology that focuses on and specializes in working with persons who are experiencing *distress* and *disorders.*

clinician   A helping professional who works with *clients.*

closed   **1.** A term used to signify that a client case has been terminated.   **2.** The psychological stance of a person in counseling who

refuses to consider different perspectives or options for his or her life.

closed groups   Groups that do not admit new members after their first session.

closed system   A *system* that is self-contained with impermeable boundaries, not open to forces outside of it. Closed systems are prone to increased disorder over time.

closed-ended questions   Queries that can be answered in a few words and are generally used to gather information. See also *open-ended questions; questioning.*

closure   **1.** A *gestalt therapy* term for the completion of unfinished experiences by a client. Closure helps a person gain *insight* or resolve a situation.   **2.** The *termination* of a counseling case.

coaching   **1.** A technique for helping individuals, couples, or families make appropriate responses by giving them verbal instructions.   **2.** A method used for helping test takers answer specific types of questions and improve their test performance. This type of coaching is sometimes known as *teaching to the test.*

coalition   An alliance found in groups and families in which two persons team up against a third person. There are two types of coalitions: a *stable coalition* and a *detouring coalition.*

COAMFTE   *See* Commission on Accreditation for Marriage and Family Therapy Education.

cocaine   A *drug* derived from the leaves of the coca plant that produces a feeling of euphoria, energy, alertness, and heightened sensitivity in users when *snorted* (i.e., taken through the nostrils), injected, or *freebased* (i.e., smoked). Cocaine is also known as *coke* or *snow.* With continuous use, it produces a marked deterioration in the nervous system as well as general physical deterioration and maladaptive disorders, such as *hallucinations, paranoia,* and *depression.*

code of ethics   A set of standards and principles that organizations create to provide guidelines for their members to follow in working with the public and each other.

codependent   A mutually dependent but often emotionally unhealthy relationship in which two people meet each others' needs and rely on each other to the point of being inseparable. This term is often used in regard to a marriage relationship in which one spouse is an *alcohol* or *substance* abuser and the other (the codependent) is the long-suffering spouse who takes care of the abuser at the expense of taking care of *self.*

cognition   A *thought,* idea, or *conscious* intellectual process involved in knowing.

cognitive approaches to human relations   Approaches based on the *theory* that how one thinks largely determines how one feels and behaves.

cognitive behavioral theory   An approach to counseling in which interventions make use of both cognitive and behavioral treatment techniques that are direct, structured, goal oriented, and time limited in nature. Examples of cognitive behavioral techniques include *cognitive restructuring, shame attacks, stress inoculation, and thought stopping.*

cognitive bypass   The belief of the client that an experience directly causes feelings.

cognitive counseling   Approaches to counseling that emphasize working with clients in modifying their thought processes so that they do not *overgeneralize* or distort cognitive messages in a *dysfunctional* way. Aaron Beck's cognitive therapy emphasizes modifying thought processes as the primary means of bringing about change.

cognitive disputation   A technique used in Albert Ellis's *rational emotive behavior therapy* and Maxie Maultsby's *rational behavioral therapy* that involves the use of direct questions, logical reasoning, and *persuasion* in order to dispute *irrational thoughts* and *irrational beliefs.*

cognitive dissonance   Leon Festinger's theory that people have a strong need or drive toward consistency (i.e., consonance). Therefore, when two ideas are inconsistent at the same time, individuals have a need to resolve them (i.e., make them consistent). They can do so by changing either their actions or beliefs. For example, if a person pays a high fee for mental health services but does not think he or she received much for the money, the person will either reevaluate the service upward or quit the therapeutic process.

cognitive distortion   A pervasive and systematic error in reasoning (e.g., believing that people do not like you unless they meet your needs).

cognitive restructuring   A cognitive therapeutic process for coping with stress that involves replacing stress-provoking or irrational thoughts with more constructive or rational thoughts.

cohesiveness   The togetherness or closeness of a group; "we-ness." Cohesiveness in a group can be increased through friendly interaction, *cooperation,* increased group status, an outside threat, or democratic (as opposed to authoritarian) leadership.

coke   A slang term for *cocaine.*

coleader   A professional or a professional-in-training who undertakes the responsibility of sharing the leadership of a group. The use of coleaders usually occurs when group membership is 12 or more.

collective counseling   Alfred Adler's form of *group counseling.*

collective unconscious   Carl Jung's term for that part of the *unconscious* that is universal in human beings and contains inherited psychic functions, such as *archetypes,* that are passed on genetically from one generation to another (e.g., the *anima* and *animus*).

College Adjustment Scale   An important *assessment* instrument for *college counseling* centers to use in deciding what services and programs they will emphasize. This test screens college students for common developmental and psychological problems using nine scales that measure psychological *distress* in the following areas: *anxiety, depression,* suicidal ideation, *substance abuse, self-esteem* problems, interpersonal problems, family problems, academic problems, and career problems.

college counseling   Counseling that focuses on the needs and development issues of both traditional students (ages 18 to 22) and nontraditional students (ages 25 years and higher) enrolled in colleges and universities. See also *American College Counseling Association (ACCA).*

commission   A term used in connection with malpractice for doing something that should not have been done.

Commission on Accreditation for Marriage and Family Therapy Education (COAMFTE) A specialized accrediting body that accredits the master's, doctoral, and postgraduate clinical training programs in marriage and *family therapy* throughout the United States and Canada. Since 1978, the COAMFTE has been recognized by the U.S. Department of Education (USDE) as the national accrediting body for the field of marriage and family therapy. COAMFTE is located at 1133 NW 15th Street, Suite 300, Washington, DC 20005-2710 (202-452-0109; http://www.aamft.org/about/ accred. htm).

commitment   **1.** A dedication to counseling and the process of *change.*   **2.** An involuntary institutionalization of a person who is mentally disturbed to a mental health facility.

common law   *Law* derived from tradition and usage. Most common law in the United States is based on British common law.

communication   The verbal and nonverbal exchange of information or messages.

communication stance   An experiential/humanistic family therapy procedure of Virginia Satir's in which family members are asked to exaggerate the physical positions of their roles in order to help them "level." See also *leveling.*

communications theory   An approach to working with families originated by Virginia Satir. It focuses on the *clarification* of verbal and nonverbal transactions among family members. Much communication theory work has been incorporated into *strategic family therapy.*

community counselor   A term coined by Judith Lewis and Michael Lewis in the 1970s to describe a counselor who can function in multidimensional roles regardless of employment setting.

Community Mental Health Centers Act (1963)   A congressional act in 1963 that authorized the establishment of 2,000 community mental health centers in the United States. These centers opened up opportunities for counselor employment outside educational settings.

commuter marriage   A marriage in which each partner maintains a separate household, usually in a different city, in order to pursue a *career.* Holidays and weekends are times that individuals in commuter marriages usually spend together.

comparative research studies   Studies (also called *correlational studies*) that form a link between *case study* methods and *experimental design* and *quasi-experimental design.* They make directional and quantitative comparisons between sets of data. Such studies are non-manipulative. They simply note similarities in variations among factors with no effort to discern cause-and-effect relationships.

compensation   An *Adlerian counseling* term for the act of making up for a deficiency in one area by excelling in a different but related activity.

competency   A person's ability to function adequately in his or her *environment.*

competency test   **1.** A test that assesses an individual's level of knowledge or skill in a particular domain.   **2.** A test or tests given to determine if a person who claims or is claimed to be mentally disturbed or deficient is competent to stand trial.

complainers   One of three types of *clients* classified by Steve deShazer. These clients are characterized by their expectation that they will find some solution to their problems through the process of *therapy*. They are given observational and thinking tasks by deShazer to combat *resistance*. See also *customers; visitors*.

complementary relationship   A *relationship* in which family member *roles* are specifically and even rigidly different from each other (e.g., one being dominant and the other submissive). If members fail to fulfill their roles, such as that of a decision maker or a nurturer, other members of the family are adversely affected.

complementary transaction   A communicative process in *transactional analysis* in which both persons are operating either from the same *ego state* (e.g., child to child, adult to adult) or from complementary ego states (e.g., parent to child, adult to parent). Responses are predictable and appropriate. For example, an adult-to-adult transaction might transpire as follows: Person 1—"What time is it?" Person 2—"It is 7 o'clock."

compliment   A written message used in *brief family therapy* designed to praise a family for its strengths and build a "yes set" within it. A compliment consists of a positive statement with which all members of a family can agree. For example, the counselor might say "Most families would have folded under the pressure you have faced, but you didn't."

composite score   The direct sum or weighted sum of the scores on two or more tests or subsections of tests.

compulsion   A repetitive behavior (usually as the result of an *obsession*), for example, washing one's hands every few minutes.

compulsive disorder   A disorder that involves repetitive behaviors, often performed in a ritualistic manner.

computer or rational analyzer   According to Virginia Satir, a person who interacts in a family primarily on a cognitive or intellectual level.

computer-assisted career guidance systems   Computer-based systems that offer career information and help individuals sort through their *values* and interests or simply find job information.

computer-assisted counseling   The use of computers and technology to help clients in the counseling process.

computer-assisted testing   Testing that is done on a computer rather than in a test booklet.

computer-based interpretation   The use of computers to score and interpret *standardized tests*. In this process, narrative descriptors about results are usually provided in addition to the scores themselves.

con words   Expressions used by clients, such as "try" or "maybe," that are not specific to a designated *behavior* or *outcome* objective. Such expressions usually result in clients failing to achieve a *goal*.

conclusions   Generalizations about a phenomenon made as a result of *research* or clinical observations.

concrete operations   The third phase in Jean Piaget's four stages of cognitive development. In concrete operations, children (from ages 7 to 11) learn to mentally manipulate objects and apply logic to specific observations. Children master the idea of *conservation* at this phase but cannot think abstractly. They are literal minded.

concurrent marriage counseling   A session in which the married couple is counseled separately.

concurrent validity   A type of *validity* that compares a test with a criterion available at the time of testing, such as an independent measure of the same construct. Concurrent validity is usually reported in terms of a *correlation coefficient*.

condemning questions   Questions that put people down and prevent them from seeing situations more honestly and openly (e.g., "Don't you think you should feel differently?").

conditioned response   A learned *response*. In *classical conditioning*, a learned response comes about because of being paired repeatedly with a *conditioned stimulus*.

conditioned stimulus   A term in *classical conditioning* for when a neutral stimulus becomes associated with a positive stimulus and an organism learns to respond to the neutral stimulus in the same way it responds to the positive stimulus.

conditioning   A process of learning that involves stimuli and responses becoming paired through association or training. The two primary types of conditioning are *classical conditioning* and *operant conditioning.*

confidentiality   The professional, ethical, and legal obligation of counselors that they not disclose client information revealed during counseling without the client's written consent. Confidentiality must be broken when a client is potentially dangerous to self or others. See also *duty to warn.*

confirmation   A *transactional analysis* technique in which the counselor points out to the client that a previously modified behavior has occurred again. Only when the client has a firmly established *adult ego state* can this technique be effective.

confirmation of a family member   A process that involves using a feeling word to reflect an expressed or unexpressed feeling of a family member or using a nonjudgmental description of an individual's behavior. For example, in the latter situation, a counselor might say to a father "You seem to be very active today."

conflict   **1.** An intrapersonal struggle in making a decision between two or more *choices.* **2.** An interpersonal striving by two or more parties to achieve opposite or mutually exclusive *goals.*

confrontation   Verbally challenging clients to look at the discrepancies and incongruencies between their words and actions. For example, "I hear you want to meet new people, yet I understand you watch television at home every night." The purpose of confrontation is to promote *awareness* of self-contradictions and to promote *change.*

congruence   **1.** A consistency between the way people feel and the way they act.   **2.** A key concept, also known as *genuineness,* in the theory of Carl Rogers. According to Rogers, congruence is one of the *core conditions* necessary in counseling if *treatment* is to be successful.

conjoint family drawing   A procedure in which families are initially given the instructions to "draw a picture as you see yourself as a family." Each member of the family makes such a drawing and then shares through discussion the perceptions and insights that emerged from doing the activity.

conjoint family therapy   A session in which two or more members of a family are counseled together at the same time. Conjoint family therapy was pioneered and promoted by Virginia Satir in the 1960s.

conjoint marriage counseling   A session in which the married couple is counseled together at the same time.

conscience   **1.** In *psychoanalysis,* the part of the *superego* that induces guilt when persons act against ways they have been taught.   **2.** An internal set of *rules* that governs a person's behavior.

conscious   A term in *psychoanalysis* for that part of the mind that is attuned to events in the present, to an *awareness* of the outside world.

consciousness   A total *awareness* of oneself.

consciousness-raising group   A group that is set up to help its participants become more aware of the issues they face and the wide variety of *choices* they have within their *environment.*

consent   To give approval or permission; to agree. In counseling, written consent on the part of the client is necessary in some situations (e.g., for the transfer of client records), and verbal consent on the part of the client is necessary in other situations (e.g., when trying a technique).

consequences   The results of a *behavior.* In *Adlerian counseling,* consequences are either *natural consequences* or *logical consequences.*

conservation   A Piagetian concept that deals with an understanding that physical properties of objects do not change even when appearances change. For example, children cannot understand that changing the shape of the object that water is poured into does not change the volume of the water. The concept of conservation is typically acquired around the age of 7, when a child reaches the stage of *concrete operations.*

construct validity   The degree to which a test measures an intended construct (i.e., that which it was constructed to measure).

constructional interpretation   A level of *interpretation* that focuses on thought patterns and the way clients express themselves. See also *interpretation.*

constructivism   A philosophy that proposes that reality is subjective in nature, a reflection of observation and experience, not an objective entity. Some counseling theories, such as *narrative therapy,* are based on constructivism.

consultant   A resource person with special knowledge who assists individuals and groups in resolving difficulties they have not been able to resolve on their own.

consultation   A voluntary relationship between a professional helper and an individual or group that needs help. In such a relationship, the *consultant* provides assistance by helping to define and resolve a *problem* or potential problem of the client. Consultant relationships are described as triadic (i.e., client, consultant, problem) and are content based, goal directed, and process oriented.

contact   A term used in *gestalt therapy* to refer to the sensory and motor immediacy that may be experienced when a client meets the *environment* directly.

contaminating variables   Factors that invalidate an *experimental research* study, such as one group of clients being healthier than another.

contamination   **1.** In *transactional analysis,* the intrusion of the *parent ego state* and/or the *child ego state* into the boundaries of the *adult ego state.*   **2.** In research, *variables* that invalidate an *experimental research* study, such as comparing two unequal groups.

content   The actual ideas discussed in counseling between a counselor and client. Content is the substance or the "what" of counseling and is the opposite of *process.*

content analysis   The analysis of a client session to see what themes emerge.

content validity   The degree to which a *test* measures intended content (i.e., a specific body of knowledge). Content validity is determined judgmentally and not through the use of statistical procedures. Content validity is especially applicable to *achievement tests.*

contingency contract   A written *treatment plan* that defines *goals,* procedures, and expected *outcomes,* as well as the identification of *rewards* if the client performs the expected *behaviors.* One action is contingent (i.e., dependent) on another.

Week 1
(must earn 5 points for a reward)

	make bed	clean room	hang up clothes	pick up toys	Goal
George	✓	✓		✓	Pizza
Will		✓		✓	Baseball game
Ann	✓	✓	✓	✓	Spend-the-night party

contingency contract

continuing education unit (CEU)   Credit for participating in professional educational programs that update one's knowledge. CEUs are often required for continuing a counselor's licensure and/or certification.

continuous reinforcement   The constant rewarding or reinforcement of a behavior. Continuous reinforcement is often used to establish a behavior. It is the opposite of *intermittent reinforcement.*

contract   A formal agreement between counselors and clients, often in writing, about what behavioral changes will be made and when; there are built-in *rewards* for behaving in a certain manner.

control group   A comparison group that is treated equivalent to the *experimental group* except that they are not exposed to *the independent variable.* Thus, researchers can determine whether the experimental group would have changed significantly without the manipulation of the independent variable.

control theory   A complete system for explaining how the brain works. Control theory was integrated into *reality therapy* by William Glasser from the late 1980s to the late 1990s, when it was replaced with *choice theory.*

conventional stage   The second of three major stages of Lawrence Kohlberg's stages of *moral development.* The conventional stage contains two levels. At the first level, morality is based on what other people think. At the second level, morality is based on what authorities say. According to Kohlberg's research, most people do not get past the conventional stage of moral development.

conversion reaction   A *defense mechanism* in which feelings that a person is unable to express are converted into physiological symptoms, such as blindness, loss of feeling, or paralysis.

cooperation   Individuals, especially in groups, working together for a common purpose or good.

cooperative learning groups   *Study groups* established so that assigned tasks can be divided and accomplished; members are responsible for meeting regularly and teaching each other what they have learned.

coping skills   The skills and behaviors people use to adjust to their *environments* and avoid *stress* (e.g., a person may obtain certain information in order to learn to control his or her emotions).

COPS   See *Career Occupational Preference System.*

CORE   See *Council on Rehabilitation Education.*

core conditions   The necessary personality qualities a counselor must possess and show for effective counseling to take place. These conditions, as outlined by Carl Rogers, are *empathy, unconditional positive regard* (i.e., *acceptance*), and *congruence* (i.e., *genuineness*).

core mechanisms of group leadership   The essential conditions necessary in a group in order for it to properly function (e.g., there must be emotional stimulation, caring, meaning attribution, and executive function).

correctional counseling   Counseling that is conducted in correctional or prison settings and often referred to as *offender counseling.*

correlation   The statistical relationship between two *variables,* for example, a *score* on an *ability test* and the relationship of that score to an actual skill. Correlation does not deal with cause and effect but with dependence.

correlation coefficient   A numerical index of the relationship between two *variables,* ranging from +1.00 (perfect positive relationship) to -1.00 (perfect negative relationship). An index of .00 indicates an absence of a relationship.

correlational research   Research that examines the correlation between two variables (e.g., height and leadership). Neither variable is said to cause a change in the other.

correlational studies   See *comparative research studies.*

Council for Accreditation of Counseling and Related Educational Programs (CACREP)   An affiliate organization of the *American Counseling Association (ACA).* CACREP, formed in 1981, standardized counselor education programs for master's and doctoral programs in the areas of school, community, mental health, and marriage and family counseling, as well as for personnel services for college students. CACREP is located at 5999 Stevenson Avenue, Fourth Floor, Alexandria, VA 22304 (800-347-6647, ext. 301; http://www.counseling.org/CACREP/main.htm).

Council on Rehabilitation Education (CORE)   The accrediting agency of institutions of higher education that offers *rehabilitation counseling.* CORE's address is P.O. Box 1788, Champaign, IL 61824-1788 (217-333-6688; http://www.core—rehab.org/).

counselee   Another name for a *client.*

counseling   "The application of mental health, psychological or human development principles, through cognitive, affective, behavioral or systemic interventions, strategies that address wellness, personal growth, or career development, as well as pathology" *(American Counseling Association).*

Counseling and Human Development   A monograph on current issues in counseling published nine times a year by Love Publishing Company, 9101 East Kenyon Avenue, Suite 2200, Denver, CO 80237 (303-221-7333).

Counseling and Student Services Clearinghouse (CASS)   See *Educational Resources Information Center/Counseling and Student Services Clearinghouse (ERIC/CASS).*

Counseling Association for Humanistic Education and Development (C-AHEAD)   A divisional affiliate of the *American Counseling Association (ACA)* that advocates positive attitudes toward self and others through diversified learning and developmental processes. Until 1999, C-AHEAD was known as the Association for Humanistic Education and Development (AHEAD).

counseling psychology   A psychological specialty also referred to as *Division 17* of the *American Psychological Association (APA)* (see their brochure at www.siu.edu/~div17/brochure.html). Its aim is to facilitate personal and interpersonal functioning across the *life span.* Its focus is on emotional, social, vocational, educational, health-related, develop-

mental, and organizational concerns. It encompasses a broad range of practices that help people improve their well-being, alleviate distress and maladjustment, resolve crises, and increase their ability to live more highly functioning lives.

counseling specialty   A narrowly focused entity in counseling (e.g., *career counseling*) requiring advanced knowledge and experience and often *certification* or *licensure.*

Counseling Today   The monthly newsletter published by the *American Counseling Association (ACA).*

counseling/interpersonal problem-solving groups   Groups that focus on each person's *behavior* and growth or *change* within the group in regard to a particular *problem* or concern.

counselor   A *helping professional* who has obtained a master's or doctorate in counseling and who has passed *competency tests* on a general and/or specific level in the field of counseling. Counselors who are licensed by states are often referred to as *licensed professional counselors.*

Counselor in a Changing World   A landmark book in the history of counseling, written by Gilbert Wrenn and published in 1962. The book proposed a blueprint for *school counseling* and for school counselors and broached the subject of *multicultural counseling* in an influential way.

Counselor Preparation   A national comprehensive study, published every 3 years, of programs, faculties, and trends in the field of counseling. Now in its 10th edition and published by the *National Board for Certified Counselors,* the study was first published by Joseph Hollis and Richard Wantz in 1971.

counselor-centered counseling   A term used to describe E. G. Williamson's *theory* of counseling. See also *directive counseling.*

counterconditioning   The process of unlearning paired associations, with new ones taking their place; a key component of *systematic desensitization.*

counterscript A term in *transactional analysis* for temporarily taking on a *role* that is the opposite of one's *life script*. The individual takes on the role because of a *conflict* between two of his or her *ego states*.

countertransference A term in *psychoanalysis* for the positive or negative wishes, fantasies, and feelings that the counselor unconsciously directs or transfers to the client, stemming from his or her own unresolved conflicts.

couple group counseling A form of counseling developed by John Bell in which counselors see more than one couple at a time in a group setting. Treatment is conducted in the group by having couples discuss their problems in front of other couples. The advantages of this approach are that group members see that some problems are universal, they can identify appropriate and inappropriate behaviors and expectations of others, they can develop insight and skills through observing other couples, they can receive group feedback and support for the ventilation of feelings and changed behavior, and they can share the cost.

couples counseling The counseling of either *heterosexual* or *homosexual* couples about dynamics within their relationship.

courage An *Adlerian counseling* term for the ability to take a risk without knowing the outcome.

court order A *subpoena* to appear in court at a certain time with regard to a specific case.

court ordered witness A person ordered to appear before a court to testify in behalf of or against someone else.

covert rehearsal A *cognitive behavioral* technique in which individuals learn new information or behaviors through practicing them repeatedly by themselves. It is the opposite of *overt rehearsal*.

covert sensitization A *behavioral* technique in which undesired behavior is eliminated by associating it with unpleasantness. It is used in treating clients who have problems in such areas as smoking, obesity, substance abuse, and sexual deviation.

CPI See *California Psychological Inventory*.

crack A highly addictive form of *cocaine*.

CRC See *Certified Rehabilitation Counselor*.

creative arts therapies Clinical use of the creative arts (e.g., music, writing, drama) as a primary or adjunct way of bringing about *change*. See also *National Coalition of Arts Therapies Associations (NCATA)*.

creative imagery A *warm-up* technique that consists of inviting *psychodrama* participants to imagine neutral or pleasant objects and scenes that are not present. The idea is to help participants become more spontaneous.

criminal liability Responsibility for a criminal act. For example, a counselor can be held legally liable (or accountable) for working with a client in a way that the *law* does not permit.

crisis An emergency or urgent situation. A crisis may be developmental and expected, or it may be situational and unexpected.

crisis counseling A special type of counseling that is often directive in nature and that focuses on helping a client find ways to respond productively and constructively in the midst of a chaotically urgent or acute emotionally disturbing situation, such as a hurricane or earthquake.

criterion A standard, norm, or judgment used as a basis for quantitative and qualitative comparison.

criterion-referenced A type of referencing related directly to the dimension (e.g., skill or ability) being measured. It is the opposite of *norm-referenced*.

criterion-related validity The predictability of test scores with other criteria, such as a person's actual performance of a certain skill across time and situations.

critical incident in life An event such as marriage or an automobile accident that has the power to positively or negatively shape or influence a person.

critical parent A term in *transactional analysis* that describes the negative aspect of the *parent ego state* in which the negative behaviors (e.g., scolding) of parents are displayed.

critical period   A developmental term that describes a time period within children's lives in which they are optimally ready to learn certain behaviors, such as reading or speaking a foreign language.

cross cultural counseling   Counseling between individuals from different cultural backgrounds. If conducted properly, such counseling transcends or bridges the differences of specific cultures and leads to therapeutic results. See also *multicultural counseling*.

cross validation   Readministering a test that has been found to be valid with one group to a second group to determine whether it is valid with that group.

crossed transaction   A communication pattern described in *transactional analysis* in which an inappropriate *ego state* is activated producing an unexpected response.

Person 1:	Can you help me carry these bags? They must weigh a ton.
Person 2:	Those bags weigh approximately 20 pounds, and you are capable of carrying them.

cross-generational alliance (coalition)   An inappropriate family alliance that contains members of two different generations within it (e.g., a parent and child).

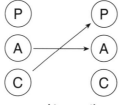

crossed transaction

cross-sectional study   A *research* approach in which large numbers of representative *variables* are studied at a given period in time. A cross-sectional study is frequently the basis for the establishment of normative data. It is the opposite of a *longitudinal study.*

crystallization   A *transactional analysis* technique that consists of an adult-to-adult transaction in which the client comes to an *awareness* that individual game playing may be given up if so desired. Thus, the client is free to do as he or she chooses, and the therapeutic process is virtually complete.

crystallized intelligence   Mental skills and abilities accumulated through experience and education that continue to increase with age (e.g., knowledge of world events). It is the opposite of *fluid intelligence.*

CSI   See *Chi Sigma Iota.*

cue   A *stimulus* (e.g., a word or a gesture) that is intended to communicate information (e.g., a yawn).

cultural diversity   The existence within a society of a number of varied groups with distinct values and lifestyles. Cultural diversity is also known as *cultural pluralism.*

cultural pluralism   See *cultural diversity.*

culturally encapsulated counselors   A term coined by Gilbert Wrenn for counselors who treat everyone the same and in so doing ignore important cultural differences.

culture   The shared *values,* beliefs, expectations, *worldviews, symbols,* and appropriate behaviors of a group that provide its members with norms, plans, and *rules* for social living.

culture shock   The experience of being temporarily confused, anxious, disoriented, and depressed when entering another *culture* in which one is uncertain of the *rules* and customs.

culture-fair test   A test that has been normed on various cultural groups and attempts to be fair to all cultural groups by not penalizing any group because of a lack of relevant experience.

culture-specific treatment   Approaches in counseling designed especially for the needs or concerns of specific cultural groups.

curative factors   Eleven factors first researched and described by Irvin Yalom that contribute to the betterment of individuals in a group. These eleven factors are instillation of *hope,* universality, imparting of information, *altruism,* corrective recapitulation of the primary family group, development of socialization techniques, imitative behavior, interpersonal learning, group *cohesiveness, catharsis,* and *existential factors.*

custody The assignment of children to one or both parents after a *divorce,* along with stipulations concerning living arrangements and visitation rights.

customers Steve deShazer's classification for the type of client who wants to do something about his or her situation. Such clients are given behavioral tasks. See also *complainers; visitors.*

cut off To physically or psychologically distance oneself from others.

cutoff score A *score* chosen by a test administer below which individuals fail.

cutting off **1.** Making sure that new material is not introduced too late in a counseling session to be adequately dealt with. **2.** Preventing clients from rambling when speaking. **3.** Removing oneself either physically or psychologically from others or an *environment.*

cybercounseling See *Internet counseling.*

cybernetics The study of methods of *feedback* control within a system, especially with regard to the flow of information.

cyclotherapy process The idea that a group continues to evolve and can be conceptualized as forever forming, with certain issues returning from time to time to be explored in greater depth.

d

dance/movement therapy The use of dance and movement as a primary or adjunct way of bringing about therapeutic outcomes. Dance/movement therapy is defined by the *American Dance Therapy Association (ADTA)* as "the psychotherapeutic use of movement as a process which furthers the emotional, cognitive and physical integration of the individual." See also *American Dance Therapy Association (ADTA).*

DAT See *Differential Aptitude Test.*

data Bits of information gathered on some characteristic of a group or object under study; facts or *statistics.*

DCT See *developmental counseling and therapy.*

death instinct A term in *psychoanalysis* for the *unconscious* drive toward destructiveness and death. The death instinct is usually manifested in human behavior through unnecessarily risky or dangerous behavior. Death instinct is the opposite of *life instinct.*

decile Ranking *percentiles* according to tenths (e.g., 10th percentile, 20th percentile, etc.).

decision A cognitive process of choosing to take an action and close out other possibilities. Making a decision is an important part of counseling (e.g., substance abusers must decide to stop their destructive behavior and dry out before they can be rehabilitated).

decision-redecision methods A *transactional analysis* technique emphasized by Robert and Mary Goulding. In this technique, clients reexamine decision moments in their childhoods based on parental *injunctions* (negative messages that begin with don't, e.g., "Don't be that way") that limit personal interactions. They then choose to redecide whether to continue acting in accordance with these messages or to *change.*

defamation Injury to a person's character or reputation either through verbal means *(slander)* or written means *(libel).*

defense mechanism A psychological response that helps protect a person from *anxiety* and other negative emotions accompanying *stress.* Defense mechanisms originate in the *unconscious* and include *repression, displacement, projection, reaction formation, regression, rationalization, denial, undoing,* and *identification.*

delayed-entry women   See *late-entry women.*

delinquency   Antisocial or *illegal* activity. When such behavior is connected with a teenager, the action is called *juvenile delinquency.*

delirium, dementia, and amnesic and other cognitive disorders   A diagnostic category in the *DSM-IV* that deals with types of permanent or transient damage to the brain.

delirium tremens   Severe *withdrawal* symptoms, such as *hallucinations,* that sometimes follow heavy and prolonged alcohol abuse.

delusion   A false but strongly held belief despite a lack of support for it. The two most common forms of delusions are those of grandeur and persecution.

dementia   The deterioration of mental processes such as memory loss. The onset of dementia is usually due to physical causes such as a stroke.

dementia praecox   An historically antiquated name for *schizophrenia.*

democratic leader   A leader in a group who trusts others to develop their own potential and that of others. Such a leader serves as the *facilitator* and not as a director, thereby cooperating, collaborating, and sharing responsibilities.

denial   A *defense mechanism* in which a person ignores or disavows unacceptable thoughts or acts as if an experience does not exist or never did.

density of time   Lee Combrinck-Graham's model of family relationships. The model outlines the natural tendencies of three-generational families to be close or distant from each other over time. The fullness of time in regard to events and relationships is greatest during certain periods of the *family life cycle,* such as the birth of a child.

dependency   **1.** A client who presents himself/herself as helpless and incapable but refuses to accept constructive *feedback* or try new ways of behaving. Such clients are help-rejecting complainers and encourage the behavior of *advice giving.*   **2.** A descriptor of a *relationship* in which one person cannot or will not function without the aid or input of another.   **3.** The relatedness of two scores in *research.*

dependent variable   **1.** In *experimental research,* the behavior or *outcome* that is measured as a result of manipulating the *independent variable.*   **2.** In *correlational research,* the measure being predicted; also called the criterion variable.

depersonalization disorder   A condition in which a person experiences the feeling that his or her body is unreal.

depressants   Drugs with an effect similar to that of *alcohol.* Small doses can produce calmness and relaxed muscles; large doses can cause respiratory depression, coma, and death. Types of depressants are *barbiturates* and *tranquilizers.* Slang names for depressants include *downers, barbs, yellow jackets, red birds,* and *ludes.*

depression   A common as well as major *disorder* characterized by sadness, dejection, lack of energy, hopelessness, and loneliness. Depression may be *chronic* or *acute,* mild or severe.

derived score   A test score, such as a *percentile, stanine,* or *standard score,* that has been converted from a raw score through some type of mathematical operation.

descriptive statistics   Numbers that summarize, organize, and/or graph characteristics of a group of scores or a pool of research data. *Measures of the central tendency* (i.e., *mean, mode, median*) as well as variability measures (e.g., *standard deviation*) are descriptive statistics. Descriptive statistics are the opposite of *inferential statistics.*

desensitization   See *systematic desensitization.*

desensitized   To become less sensitive to a *stimulus* because of repeated exposure to it.

designer drugs   *Illegal* drugs that have had their molecular structure modified to produce analogs that may be several times stronger than the drugs they were designed to imitate.

despair   An inability in old age to find meaning in one's life. Despair is the opposite of Erik Erikson's virtue of *integrity.*

detachment   Physical or psychological separateness from others.

determinism   The view that factors beyond people's control, such as biology, determine their future. Determinism underlies much of the theory of *psychoanalysis* and can be summed up in the phrase "biology is destiny."

detouring coalition   A coalition in which the pair holds a third member responsible for their difficulties or conflicts with one another. See also *coalition.*

detoxification   The process of removing a harmful *drug* from a person's body through the withholding of the toxic substance and providing that person with rest, a proper diet, exercise, health care, and so on. Detoxification is typically completed in an *inpatient* setting under medical care.

detriangulated   The process of being in contact with others and emotionally separate from them. It is the opposite of *triangulate.*

Developing Understanding of Self and Others (DUSO)   A commercial classroom guidance program based on *Adlerian counseling* theory.

development   Predictable physical, mental, and social changes over the *life span* that occur in relationship to the environment.

developmental counseling   A counseling approach that emphasizes that human *personality* develops based on the interaction between the person and the environment. In this approach there is an emphasis on growth, age-appropriate *intervention,* and *prevention.*

developmental counseling and therapy (DCT)   A comprehensive clinical mental health approach originated by Allen Ivey for the treatment of individuals from a nonpathological, positivistic perspective. DCT suggests that the way clients understand and operate in the world is based on two main interacting systems: their levels of *cognitive development*

and the implications of larger social units in which clients are involved (e.g., family, community, culture).

developmental crises   Times of change in the *life span* often accompanied by turmoil and new opportunity. Examples of developmental crises are marriage, birth, and aging.

developmental disability   A *disability* that is the result of a disease, genetic disorder, or impaired growth pattern that occurs before *adulthood.* Developmental disabilities continue indefinitely and may require specific and lifelong care. Examples of developmental disabilities are *mental retardation,* cerebral palsy, and Down's syndrome.

developmental factors   Variables such as the age, gender, and maturity level of clients.

developmental group counseling   Counseling that takes place in a *psychoeducational group.* It is often used for teaching basic *life skills.*

developmental stages   Growth and behavioral organization categories in an individual, group, or family. Each new stage, compared to a preceding one, is qualitatively different, novel, and more comprehensive. Developmental stages occur in a fixed sequence of maturation and are often age- and maturity-related.

developmental tasks   Important skills and *achievements,* such as walking, talking, and reading, that children must master at certain ages if they are to function in a healthy way.

deviation IQ   A *score* on an IQ test that compares a person with his/her age or grade group. The fixed mean is usually 100 with a standard deviation of 15.

diagnosis   An interpretation, derived from the use of *assessment* information, about a person's condition (e.g., his or her level of functioning). The *DSM-IV* and *ICD-10* are often used in making a diagnosis because of the criteria they have established in regard to diagnostic categories.

Diagnostic and Statistical Manual (DSM-IV)   The fourth edition of a manual published *d*

by the *American Psychiatric Association* that codifies psychiatric disorders. The DSM-IV contains 400 different categorical classifications of *disorders.* It is compatible to the *International Classification of Diseases (ICD-10)* manual, published by the World Health Organization. See also *Axes of the DSM-IV.*

diagnostic test   A *test* that is used to help in the *diagnosis* of a client. Almost any test can be used as a diagnostic instrument, depending on what the evaluator is seeking to assess.

dialogue   1. Honest and genuine communication between oneself and others or between different aspects of oneself.   **2.** A primary therapeutic tool in counseling.   **3.** An essential ingredient in an existential "I-Thou" relationship.

dichotomous thinking   Thinking that categorizes experiences and people in extremes, with no middle ground (e.g., all women think alike).

Dictionary of Occupational Titles (DOT) A U.S. government publication, first published in 1939. Often used in *career counseling,* it provides information and descriptions of current *occupations* within the United States.

Differential Aptitude Test (DAT)   A multi-aptitude *battery* composed of eight subtests used for vocational and educational purposes in Grades 7 through 12 and with adults.

differential diagnosis   The process of choosing which *diagnosis* to make when coexisting diagnoses, such as *addiction* and another *mental disorder,* exist together.

differentiation of self   A level of maturity that enables one to separate his/her rational and emotional selves. The individual is thus able to separate from his/her family. Differentiation is the opposite of *fusion.*

diffuse boundaries   Physical and/or psychological arrangements that do not allow enough separation between family members, resulting in some members becoming fused and dependent on other members.

DINKS   An acronym for double-income-no-kids families.

directive   An instruction from a family counselor for a family to behave differently. A directive is to *strategic family therapy* what *interpretation* is to *psychoanalysis* (i.e., it is the basic tool of the approach).

directive counseling   A counseling theory developed by E. G. Williamson in which the counselor functions as a teacher and/or advisor. The theory is sometimes referred to as *counselor-centered counseling, trait-and-factor counseling,* and the *Minnesota Point of View.*

director   The person who guides the *protagonist* in the use of a *psychodrama* method in order to help that person explore his or her problem. The director is roughly equivalent to the group leader in other theoretical approaches but serves also as a producer, a *facilitator,* an observer, and an analyzer.

Directory of Counselor Educators   The first study of counselor preparation conducted in the United States. This directory was initially published in 1962 by the U.S. Department of Health, Education, and Welfare. Several other editions of the directory were published until Joseph Hollis and Richard Wantz began their more thorough publication, *Counselor Preparation,* in 1971.

dirty game   A term used in Milan family therapy to describe a power struggle between generations sustained by symptomatic behaviors (e.g., schizophrenia).

disability   A physical, behavioral, or a mental condition that limits a person's activities or functioning. A disability may be either temporary or permanent.

disassociation   A *defense mechanism* in which part of an individual's *personality* appears to split off from the rest and take on an existence of its own. Disassociation is the basis for *multiple personality disorder.*

discontinuous change   A dramatic leap to a new level of functioning with *change* occurring in a startling and sudden way. Periods of *stress* and disruption are often preludes to this type of transformation. In families, discontinuous change is more likely to occur around stages in the *family life cycle.* In individuals, discontinuous change is manifest in such acts as falling in love.

discount A term in *transactional analysis* for either a lack of attention or negative attention that is hurtful. Discounts carry an ulterior put-down.

DISCOVER A program widely used in the United States for career planning. DISCOVER consists of four components: (1) self-assessment (Self-Information), (2) identification of occupational alternatives (Strategies for Identifying Occupations), (3) reviewing occupational information (Occupational Information), and (4) identification of educational alternatives (Searches for Educational Institutions).

discrimination 1. *Prejudice* actions against a person or a group. 2. The ability to distinguish between two slightly different stimuli.

discussion team The dividing of a large *group* into four or five *teams* in order to get group members involved with one another and a topic under consideration.

disease model of alcoholism A model held by many *substance abuse counselors* and mental health professionals that *alcoholism* is a disease that can best be treated by emphasizing total abstinence.

disengaged Psychologically isolated from others.

disidentification The process in which a counselor becomes emotionally removed from the client.

disorder A disease or condition of dysfunctionality. See also *mental disorder.*

disorders usually first diagnosed in infancy, childhood, or adolescence A diagnostic category of the *DSM-IV* that includes *mental retardation,* learning disorders, motor skills disorder, communication disorder, pervasive development disorder (such as *autism*), *attention deficit* and disruptive disorders, feeding and *eating disorders,* tic disorders, elimination disorders (*encopresis* and *enuresis*), and others (e.g., *separation anxiety disorder*).

displaced homemakers Women who have lost their source of economic support and are forced back into the workforce after spending a number of years at home caring for their families.

displacement A *defense mechanism* in which, on an *unconscious* level, energy is channeled away from a threatening object to an alternative safe target. For instance, a person who has had a hard day at the office may come home and yell at the dog instead of yelling at his/her boss.

disputing irrational thoughts A technique of *rational emotive behavior therapy (REBT)* in which a client's *irrational beliefs* about an event are challenged by a counselor.

dissociative amnesia See *amnesia.*

dissociative disorders Disorders that involve an alteration in *consciousness,* such as memory loss or alternate personality states, that is not organic or psychotic in nature. The *DSM-IV* classifies *dissociative identity disorder* (formerly known as *multiple personality disorder*), *dissociative fugue,* dissociative *amnesia,* and *depersonalization disorder* in this category.

dissociative fugue See *fugue.*

dissociative identity disorder See *multiple personality disorder.*

dissonance The lack of blending or fusing of two aspects of an experience, resulting in discrepancies and discomfort. Dissonance may occur in a number of situations, such as when an inner and outer experience do not fit together well.

distancing Isolated separateness of family members from each other either physically or psychologically.

distractor 1. Virginia Satir's term for a person who relates by saying and doing irrelevant things. 2. Any of the incorrect alternatives on a multiple choice item.

distress Being overcome or overwhelmed by *stress* to the point of not being able to function adequately or being impaired.

distribution   The frequency with which a given *variable* occurs in a research *graph.*

diversity   Differences, unlikeness, variety. To be competent, counselors must learn to deal effectively with diversity in a number of areas (e.g., culture, age, gender).

Division of Rehabilitation Counseling (DRC)   Established in 1958, a forerunner of the *American Rehabilitation Counseling Association (ARCA).*

Division 17 (American Psychological Association)   The Counseling Psychology division of the *American Psychological Association.* Founded in 1946, this division of the APA came into existence when the association's Counseling and Guidance Division dropped the term *guidance.* Part of the impetus for the division's formation came from the Veterans Administration. The focus of members of the division is in working with a more "normal" population than the one seen by clinical psychologists. Division 17's Internet address is http://www.div17.org/.

divorce   The legal dissolving of a marriage. Most divorces occur in stages, both legally and emotionally.

divorce mediation   A nonadversarial form of arbitration in which two parties, such as a divorcing couple, meet with a counselor trained in *mediation* to negotiate a mutually satisfactory settlement, on important matters such as child custody, before entering into legal arrangements to end their marriage.

door in the face technique   A counseling technique in which the counselor asks the client to do a seemingly impossible task followed by a request that the client perform a more reasonable task.

dope   A slang term for *marijuana.*

DOT   See *Dictionary of Occupational Titles.*

double standard of mental health   A standard of *mental health* that basically depicts adult female behavior as less socially desirable and healthy. Such a perspective lowers expectations for women's behavior and sets up barriers against their advancement in nontraditional roles.

double-bind theory   The Gregory Bateson research group's hypothesis regarding the origin of *schizophrenia.* The theory states that two seemingly contradictory messages may exist at the same time on different levels and lead to confusion, if not schizophrenic behavior, on the part of an individual who cannot comment on or escape the relationship in which this is occurring. For example, a mother may tell her child that she loves him or her while discouraging or rejecting any show of affection from the child.

doubt   See *shame.*

downers   The street or slang name for any *depressant* drugs such as *barbiturates* or *tranquilizers.*

drama therapy   The systematic use of drama and theater techniques as a primary or adjunct means to bring about therapeutic *change.* In order to conduct drama therapy, counselors must take specialized training in this area. See also *National Association for Drama Therapy (NADT).*

drama triangle   See *Karpman Triangle.*

Draw-a-Person Test   A *projective test* of *intelligence* and *personality* in which children are asked to draw a person of their choosing.

drawing out   The opposite of *cutting off* or *blocking;* the process whereby group leaders purposefully ask more silent members to speak to anyone in the group, or to the group as a whole, about anything on their minds.

dream analysis   A psychoanalytic technique in which dreams are explored according to *manifest content* or *latent content.*

dream work   A technique based on an idea of Fritz Perls that dreams are the royal road to *integration.* In this procedure, clients recreate and relive their dreams in the present. By doing so, these individuals become all parts of the dream. They may work alone or in a group. When working in a group, members act out different parts of the dream (i.e., dream work as theater).

drug abuse   See *substance abuse.*

drugs   Chemical substances that have a marked physiological and often psychological impact on persons.

DSM-IV   See *Diagnostic and Statistical Manual* (fourth edition).

dual career family   A family in which both marital partners are engaged in work that is developmental in sequence and to which they have a high commitment.

dual diagnosis   The identification of more than one aspect of *personality* that is open to *diagnosis,* giving the client two diagnoses (e.g., a substance abuser may be impulsive or depressed in addition to being addicted).

dual nature of human beings   The idea that individuals have both rational and *irrational beliefs,* a key concept proposed by Albert Ellis as a part of *rational emotive behavioral therapy (REBT).*

dual personality   The simplest form of a *multiple personality disorder,* sometimes referred to as a Jekyll and Hyde personality.

dual relationship   A *relationship* that is not built on mutuality and is usually unethical because the counselor assumes a second role with a client (e.g., that of friend, business associate, or sex partner) in addition to that of therapist. Whenever possible, dual relationships should be avoided. The reason is that even if a dual relationship seems harmless, a conflict of interest almost always exists, and a professional counselor's judgment is likely to be negatively affected because of a loss of objectivity. Also, clients may be placed in situations in which they cannot be assertive and take care of themselves.

dual therapy   A term devised by Carl Whitaker for conjoint couple therapy.

DUD   An informal and cruel counseling acronym for people perceived as dumb, unintelligent, and disadvantaged.

DUSO   See *Developing Understanding of Self and Others.*

duty to care   A legal obligation on the part of health providers to not act negligently. This legal precedent was set in a 1994 California court, when Gary Ramona sued his daughter's *therapist* for implanting in her mind false memories of sexual abuse. Ramona won, and the therapist was found negligent.

duty to warn   The *legal* responsibility a counselor has to warn others if a client is potentially dangerous to self or others. This legal precedent was set as a result of the *Tarasoff v. Board of Regents of the University of California.*

dyad   A one-to-one *relationship* between two people.

dyadic effect   Reciprocal *self-disclosure* between counselor and client. See also *self-disclosure.*

dyscalculia   A *learning disability,* specifically a difficulty in doing math.

dysfunctional   Impaired; *abnormal;* unable to function adequately.

dysfunctional thoughts   Thoughts that are nonproductive and unrealistic; a key concept in the therapeutic approach of Aaron Beck.

dysgraphia   A *learning disability,* specifically a difficulty in writing.

dyslexia   A *learning disability,* specifically a difficulty in reading.

e

EAP   See *Employee Assistance Program.*

early childhood   The period in the human life cycle from birth to age 6.

early recollections   Memories from childhood used in *Adlerian counseling* to assess a person's initial outlook on life and how these memories influence present interactions with others.

eating disorders   *Maladaptive* eating patterns in which clients starve themselves through eating too little or purging food they have consumed because of obsessive and distorted ideas they have in regard to thinness and body image. The two most prevalent eating disorders are *anorexia nervosa* and *bulimia.*

eclectic counseling   Employing concepts from various theoretical systems in the treatment of a client rather than restricting oneself to a single theoretical approach. Eclecticism occurs on several levels—*syncretism, traditional eclecticism,* theoretical integrationism, *and* technical eclecticism.

ecosystemic thinking   A focus on the interconnectedness of the individual, family, and *culture.*

ecstasy   A synthetic designer *drug.* Ecstasy's structure is similar to that of the *hallucinogen* mescaline and the stimulant *amphetamine.* It is usually swallowed as a pill but may be inhaled or injected. Ecstasy increases energy and sensuality; it also raises heart rate and blood pressure, causes confusion and severe *depression,* impairs memory, and masks fatigue.

ECT   An abbreviation for *electroshock therapy.*

Education of All Handicapped Children Act   See *Public Law 94-142.*

Education Resource Information Center/ Counseling and Student Services Clearinghouse (ERIC/CASS)   A national information system that provides ready access to an extensive body of education-related literature. ERIC/CASS was established by Garry R. Walz in 1966 and has been in continuous operation since its beginning. Its scope includes *school counseling,* school social work, school psychology, *mental health counseling, family counseling, career counseling,* and student development, as well as parent, student, and teacher education in the human resources area. The address of ERIC/ CASS is School of Education, University of North Carolina at Greensboro, Greensboro, NC 27412-5001 (800-414-9769; http://www. uncg.edu/edu/ ericcass).

Edwards Personal Preference Schedule (EPPS)   A pencil-and-paper, forced-choice *personality test* developed by Henry Murray and designed to measure 15 important needs, such as *autonomy* and *achievement.*

ego   A concept in *psychoanalysis* that describes the *conscious* part of the *personality* responsible for decision making. The ego is sometimes called the "executive of the mind"; it mediates disputes between the *id* and the *superego.* The ego works according to the *reality principle.* A strong ego is necessary for a healthy personality to develop. Otherwise, neurotic tendencies set in because of the unabated conflict between the id and the superego.

ego analysis   An analysis of how the ego functions, especially how it deals with and resolves *conflict.*

ego ideal   A part of the *superego* that rewards those who follow parental and societal dictates and do what they have been taught. For example, children who have been taught by their parents that neatness is a virtue feel good when they keep a neat room.

ego states in transactional analysis (TA)   A system of feelings accompanied by a related set of behavior patterns. There are three basic ego states in *transactional analysis:* parent, adult, and child. See also *adult ego state; child ego state; parent ego state.*

ego strength   The ability of persons to maintain a strong ego so that they are in contact with reality and free of mental disturbances.

egocentric   **1.** Preoccupation with oneself and one's importance. **2.** In Piaget's theory, the normal state of a child under age 6, who believes everyone sees the world from his or her perspective.

egogram   A term in *transactional analysis* for a *bar graph* showing how people structure their time in six major ways: *withdrawal, ritual, pastimes, work, games,* and *intimacy.*

egoistic Concerned with one's own needs and interests while being indifferent and unresponsive to others.

elasticity A term in *gestalt therapy* for the ability to move from one set of *needs* to another and back.

elder hostel A place where older individuals live and study together for a select period of time.

elderly Persons who are 65 years of age and older.

Electra complex The female version of the *Oedipus complex*. According to Freud's theory, during the *phallic stage* (ages 3 to 5) of *psychosexual* development, girls have sexual feelings for their fathers and accompanying hostility toward their mothers. This complex is eventually resolved when girls identify with their mothers.

electroshock therapy A treatment involving electrically induced grand mal seizures that is used for select patients with severe depression who have not responded to a pharmacological form of therapy.

elegant REBT An emphasis in *rational emotive behavioral therapy (REBT)* on the beliefs of clients and a focus on their taking responsibility for their own feelings and not blaming others. Clients realize in the process that success in everything is not essential and that catastrophe is not the result of every unfulfilled want.

elementary school counseling A relatively recent development in the field of *school counseling* in which counselors in schools work in preventative and remedial ways with children in kindergarten through fifth grade. Elementary school counselors are a vanguard in the *mental health* movement. No other profession has ever been organized to work with individuals from a purely preventive and developmental perspective. Overall, the elementary school counselor is charged with facilitating optimal development of the whole child.

ELIZA An early reflective software counseling program with a large vocabulary and the ability to formulate a virtually unlimited number of responses. ELIZA's Internet address is http://www.sky.net/~williamj/ai/eliza/index.html.

emic approach A perspective that assumes that counseling approaches must be designed to be culturally specific. This approach is sometimes criticized for placing too much emphasis on specific techniques as the vehicle for client change. It is the opposite of the etic approach. See also *etic approach*.

emotion A strong *feeling* of any kind (e.g. joy, anger). The so-called "Big Four" feeling words counselors search for are anger, sadness, fear, and joy.

emotional ambivalence Feelings of loss, sadness, and separation mixed with those of hope, joy, and accomplishment.

emotional anatomy The recognition and understanding by clients of the way in which feelings and thoughts are attached (i.e., feelings influence behaviors and vice versa).

emotional cutoff A Murray Bowen concept that describes the avoidance by family members of each other, either physically or psychologically, because of an unresolved emotional *attachment*.

emotional deadness A condition in which *affect* is seemingly absent or at a minimum in clients because they have either *suppressed* their feelings or are unaware of them (e.g., clients who always give cognitive answers).

emotional impact of separation The processes involved in a separation event that include dealing with loss, putting the separation in perspective, becoming aware of the limited value of searching for causes of separation, becoming more cognizant of systems interactions (family, work, social network), using the past as a guide to the future, and moving from a dyadic to a monadic identity.

emotional overinvolvement The *fusion* of family members with each other. In this process, individuals experience undifferentiated emotional togetherness and lose a sense of who they and others are.

emotional response of separation   The continuing relationships a person has with an ex-spouse, including the influence of the separation on family, friends, and children, working and dating, and sexual adjustment.

empathize   To put oneself in another's place in regard to subjective perception and emotion and yet to keep one's objectivity. Empathizing demands a suspension of judgment and a response to another person that conveys sensitivity and understanding. It communicates understanding, fosters *trust,* and encourages deeper levels of client *self-exploration.*

empathy   The counselor's ability to see, be aware of, conceptualize, understand, and effectively communicate back to a client the client's feelings, thoughts, and frame of reference in regard to a situation or point of view. Empathy operates on at least two levels: *primary empathy* and *advanced empathy.* Empathy is one of the *necessary and sufficient conditions for change,* along with *unconditional positive regard* and *congruence,* according to Carl Rogers.

Employee Assistance Program (EAP)   A program set up by an employer for employees. EAPs offer *mental health* services or referrals to employees to assist them in meeting personal or family needs.

empowerment   A way of promoting self-efficacy by encouraging and supporting clients to think and take action in a positive way.

empty chair technique   A *gestalt therapy* technique designed to help group members deal with different aspects of their personalities (e.g., a person may be given an opportunity to *role play* and speak to a missing person with whom he/she has *unfinished business*).

empty nest   A term that describes a stage in the *family life cycle* in which couples have launched their children and are without child rearing responsibilities.

enabler   **1.** An individual who makes things possible.   **2.** In counseling, someone who helps another person continue *dysfunctional* behaviors, such as alcohol abuse.

enactment   **1.** A client's actively exhibiting to a counselor problematic behavioral sequences instead of just talking about them (e.g., having an argument instead of talking about one).   **2.** Jerome Brunner's belief that children represent their world by the activities they perform.

encopresis   A lack of bowel control that results in inappropriate defecation. There are emotional and organic causes.

encounter   An *existentialist* concept that involves total physical and psychological contact between persons on an intense, concrete, and complete basis in the here and now.

encounter group   See *basic encounter group.*

encouragement   **1.** The verbal supporting of a client as he or she struggles in making changes.   **2.** An *Adlerian counseling* technique of having clients take a risk without knowing what its final outcome will be.

enmeshment   The loss of *autonomy* within a family due to overconcern and overinvolvement of family members with each other either physically or psychologically. Enmeshment makes individual autonomy impossible.

entropy   The tendency of a *system* to become disorganized.

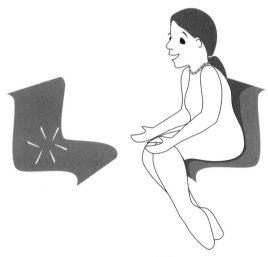

the empty chair

enuresis   A lack of bladder control that results in the involuntary release of urine, such as in bed-wetting. The cause can be either emotional or organic.

environment   The significant aspects of an individual's surroundings either in the present or the past, including significant events and experiences that influenced a person's *development.*

environmental fit   A state in which an environment is conducive to helping people grow and resolve *crises.* When the environment does not "fit," people regress or deteriorate.

epistemology   The study of knowledge (i.e., how we know what we know).

EPPS   See *Edwards Personal Preference Schedule.*

equifinality   The idea that similar *outcomes* may result from different origins.

equitability   The proposition that everyone is entitled to have his or her welfare interests considered in a way that is fair from a multilateral perspective. Equitability is the basis for relationship *ethics.*

equivalence   The extent to which two versions of a *test* or measurement instrument yield the same or similar results. See also *reliability.*

ERIC/CASS   See *Educational Resources Information Center/Counseling and Student Services Clearinghouse.*

erogenous zones   Sigmund Freud's term for those areas of the body that are most receptive to sexual stimulation.

eros   Freud's term for the life force of the *id,* sometimes equated with the *libido.* Eros is the opposite of *thanatos.* See also *thanatos.*

erotic   Having to do with sexual passion, pleasure, or love.

Esalen Institute   A facility devoted to the human potential movement. The address is Highway 1, Big Sur, CA 93920-9616 (831-667-3000; http://www.esalen.org/).

esteem   The value one attributes to oneself or another. See also *self-esteem.*

estimation   A form of *inferential statistics* in which sample *data* is used to estimate the qualities of the *population* as a whole.

e-therapy   See *Internet counseling.*

ethical principles   Principles related to a counselor's choices and activities as they pertain to *beneficence, nonmaleficence, autonomy, justice, fidelity,* and the like.

ethics   **1.** The moral principles from which individuals and social groups determine *rules* for right conduct.   **2.** Suggested standards of conduct based on a set of professional *values.*   **3.** The study and evaluation of moral beliefs and actions of counselors within certain professional domains.

ethnicity   A group classification in which members believe that they share a common origin and a unique social and cultural heritage such as language or religious belief.

etic approach   The perspective that there are universal qualities in counseling that generalize across *cultures.* The etic approach can be criticized for not taking important cultural differences into account. It is the opposite of the *emic approach.* See also *emic approach.*

European American   Americans who are descendants from European ancestors. As a group, European Americans have blended together more than other cultural groups. Reasons include a history of intergroup marriages and relationships that have simultaneously influenced the group as a whole and made it more *homogeneous.*

evaluation   The process of collecting, analyzing, and judging *data* in order to make a decision. In counseling, such a decision usually involves a *treatment plan.*

executive function   Management by a leader of a group as a social system that allows the members to achieve specific *goals.*

exercises   *Structured activities* that clients do for a specific purpose (e.g., to gain *awareness*).

exhibitionism   **1.** The tendency of someone to show off his or her *traits* or talents to gain the attention of others.   **2.** The displaying of one's genitals to others in unacceptable and antisocial ways.

existential counseling   An approach to counseling that emphasizes a philosophy about the importance of *anxiety, values,* freedom, and responsibility in human life and finding meaning in one's existence. Irvin Yalom, Rollo May, Clemmont Vontress, and Victor Frankl are prominent clinicians who have embraced *existentialism.*

existential factors   As defined by Irvin Yalom, such factors as accepting responsibility for one's life in basic *isolation* from others and recognizing one's own mortality as well as the capriciousness of existence.

existential isolation   Inevitable separation from others and the world. Existential isolation can be reduced but not completely eliminated.

existential vacuum   A feeling one has of having no value.

existentialism   A philosophical approach that deals with existence. Existential philosophers believe that existence is the only knowable reality because individuals cannot know about their origin or eventual end. Existentialism stresses the importance of *authenticity* and responsibility, the primacy of the here and now, and the use of experience in the search for knowledge.

exit interview   A final *interview* that takes place when a person is terminating counseling. The purpose is to assess the *outcome* of *treatment.*   **2.** A final interview that takes place when a person leaves a counseling situation prematurely. The purpose is to find out the reasons for leaving and to assist the person with future life transitions. See also *premature termination.*

experience near research   Research that closely approximates what is done in the counseling office.

experiential symbolic family therapy   An approach to working with families developed by Carl Whitaker. Its major premise is that individuals in families are not aware of their emotions. Therapists therefore emphasize expressing feelings in the here and now. They also use their own personalities, spontaneity, and creativity during *treatment* to promote *change.*

experiment   A scientific procedure of investigation that involves the manipulation of some aspect of an *environment* in order to determine what effect the manipulation had.

experimental design   A global term for the procedures used to conduct an *experiment* (e.g., pairing up subjects between comparison groups so that persons are matched along some relevant variable).

experimental group   A group that undergoes experimental manipulation (i.e., some aspects of their *environment* is changed in order to observe its effect).

experimental research methods   Procedures used to describe, compare, and analyze *data* under controlled conditions. Experimental methods used in counseling *research* have their origin in the natural sciences. The purpose of using these methods is to determine the effect of one *variable* on another by controlling other factors that might explain the effect. In other words, researchers who use this method are seeking to determine causation.

experiments   Experiences that occur spontaneously in a *gestalt therapy* session.

expert witness   A person who is asked to testify in a court of law about a particular subject because he or she possesses superior knowledge on a matter due to education or experience. The purpose of the expert witness is to assist a jury or judge in understanding complicated and technical subjects that are relevant to a legal case or issue.

exploration   The process of discovering or uncovering new materials and insights related to a client's concern(s) so that ideas may be clarified and *goals* generated.

expressive arts therapies   See *creative arts therapies.*

extended family **1.** A family composed of three generations or more. **2.** A family that includes immediate and distant relatives.

externalizing problems A narrative family therapy method of treating a problem in which the problem becomes a separate entity outside of a client. Such a *process* when applied to families helps them reduce their arguments about who owns the *problem,* form *teams,* and enter into *dialogue* about solving the problem.

extinction The process of lowering the rate at which a *behavior* occurs through withdrawing the *reinforcers* that have been maintaining it so that the targeted behavior will stop altogether and be eliminated.

extrovert A Jungian concept that describes an individual's basic orientation to the external world and things outside of himself or herself. An extrovert tends to be an outgoing and gregarious person. Such a person is the opposite of an *introvert.*

F ratio A statistical technique in which the larger sample variance is divided by the smaller one. When the researcher is conducting an ANOVA (one of several statistical procedures that yields an F ratio), the between-groups mean square is divided by the within-groups mean square. The resulting statistic, known as F, is interpreted for statistical significance using an F distribution table. Larger F values are more likely to be significant than smaller F values.

face validity The degree to which a *test* appears to measure what it is supposed to measure.

facilitate To help client's open up and talk about their concerns.

facilitator A *helping professional* who serves as a catalyst, especially in a group situation, by aiding members in choosing and accomplishing *goals.*

factor A dimension, *trait,* or characteristic that is discovered through the process of *factor analysis.*

factor analysis A statistical method of analyzing the intercorrelation among a set of *variables,* such as test *scores,* in order to determine the minimum number of factors or dimensions that explain the intercorrelation. Factor analysis is used to discover the essential variables that underlie and summarize information in a larger set of *data.*

fading The gradual cessation of *reinforcement* in regard to a client's behavior so that the behavior eventually disappears.

failure identity A concept from *reality therapy* that describes a person characterized by a lack of confidence and a tendency to give up easily.

fallible human being A term used by Albert Ellis in *rational emotive behavioral therapy (REBT)* to describe all persons, because no one is perfect. By using the term, clients avoid the temptation to judge or label themselves in overly critical or negative ways.

false memory syndrome The memory of an event that did not happen.

family A group of two or more persons related by birth, marriage, or adoption and residing together in a household (per the Census Bureau).

family constellation An *Adlerian counseling* term for the *birth order* of children in a family (e.g., firstborns, those born second, middle children, youngest children, and the only child). Adlerians believe that individuals who share a birth order in a family may have more in common with each other than they do with their siblings.

family council   A form of family group meeting designed to open up communication between family members. Alfred Adler introduced the idea.

family counseling   See *family therapy/counseling.*

Family Educational Rights and Privacy Act (FERPA)   An act, also known as the *Buckley Amendment,* passed by Congress in 1974. The statute gives students access to certain records that educational institutions have kept on them.

family group therapy   A treatment approach formulated by John Bell that conceptualizes family members as strangers in a group. Members become known to each other in stages similar to those found in groups.

family homeostasis   The tendency of the family to remain in its same pattern of functioning and resist change unless challenged or forced to do otherwise. See also *homeostasis.*

family life cycle   A sociological term used to describe the various *developmental stages* within a family over time (e.g., newly married, family with young children).

family life fact chronology   Virginia Satir's *family reconstruction* technique in which the *"star"* creates a listing of all significant events in his or her life and that of the extended family that have had an impact on the people in the family.

family map   Virginia Satir's *family reconstruction* technique of producing a visual representation of the structure of three generations of the *"star's"* family, with adjectives to describe each family member's personality (see diagram on page 49).

family mapping   A symbolic representation of a family's structure used by *structural family therapists* to plan their *interventions.*

family mediation   The *process* of helping couples and families settle disputes or dissolve their marriages in a non-adversarial way. See also *mediation.*

family of origin   The *family* a person was born or adopted into.

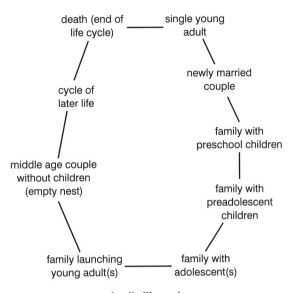

family life cycle
(based on a middle-class family with children)

family of procreation   The *family* a couple creates through marriage.

family reconstruction   A therapeutic innovation developed by Virginia Satir to help family members discover *dysfunctional* patterns in their lives stemming from their *families of origin.*

family rules   The overt and covert *rules* families use to govern themselves (e.g., that you must only speak when spoken to).

family sculpting   See *sculpting.*

family secrets   Overt events and covert fantasies or thoughts that are not talked about by a family or family members. Family secrets consume the family's energy because members must always be on guard to not disclose information.

family systems theory   See *systems theory.*

family therapy/counseling   The treatment of a family as the client through a number of theoretical approaches, including *psychoanalytic, Bowen, structural, experiential, strategic, systemic* (i.e., *Milan*), *solution-focused,* and *narrative.* In most family *treatment,* the family is seen together.

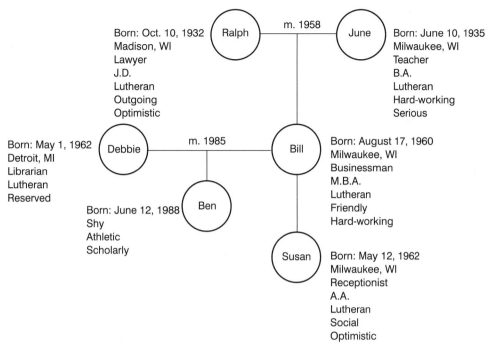

Born: Oct. 10, 1932
Madison, WI
Lawyer
J.D.
Lutheran
Outgoing
Optimistic

Ralph — m. 1958 — June

Born: June 10, 1935
Milwaukee, WI
Teacher
B.A.
Lutheran
Hard-working
Serious

Born: May 1, 1962
Detroit, MI
Librarian
Lutheran
Reserved

Debbie — m. 1985 — Bill

Born: August 17, 1960
Milwaukee, WI
Businessman
M.B.A.
Lutheran
Friendly
Hard-working

Born: June 12, 1988
Shy
Athletic
Scholarly

Ben

Susan

Born: May 12, 1962
Milwaukee, WI
Receptionist
A.A.
Lutheran
Social
Optimistic

basic family map of a star

fantasy   A form of daydreaming in which a person uses his or her imagination to create mental pictures of desired objects, people, or places.

fantasy exercises   A method used in *gestalt therapy* group work to help group members (1) to be more concrete in assessing their feelings, (2) to deal with catastrophic experiences, (3) to explore and express feelings of *guilt* and *shame,* and (4) to become more involved in the *group.* It is not necessary that group members live out their fantasies.

farewell-party syndrome   A syndrome in which group members at *termination* emphasize only the positive aspects of what has occurred in the group, instead of what they have learned. This type of focus tends to avoid the pain of closure.

faulty logic   Irrational ideas that clients think and believe and that are the basis of their problems in living and relating to themselves and others (e.g., "Susie spoke to Jim but not to me; therefore, Susie does not like me and I am no good").

feedback   1. The reinsertion of results of past performances back into a *system.*   **2.** The sharing of perception of a behavior and relevant information with a client or a group member so that the person can make decisions as to whether he or she would like to *change.* Feedback information should be given in a clear, concrete, succinct, and appropriate manner. See also *negative feedback; positive feedback.*

feedback loops   Circular mechanisms for the continuous reintroduction of information about a system's output back into the *system.*

feeling   *Emotion; affect.* Unexpressed or *repressed* feelings are viewed as the cause of *distress* and some *mental disorders.* The expression of feeling in some counseling theories (e.g., *psychoanalysis, gestalt*) is considered therapeutic.

felony   A serious criminal charge or act such as assault, rape, homicide, and burglary.

feminist counseling   Counseling from a feminist perspective that is based on the idea that women's problems are inseparable from societal problems that socialize women to assume inferior *roles*. Therefore, counseling focuses on issues such as the development of *androgyny* and the sharing of *power* between men and women, accepting one's body as is, and a focus on non-sex-biased careers. *Techniques* in feminist counseling vary but include techniques that are *behavioral* and *cognitive behavioral* such as *modeling, assertiveness training,* and *cognitive restructuring.*

feminist movement   A social movement dedicated to removing the prejudicial treatment of women in society and advancing women's issues in general.

feminist theory   An attitude and body of ideas concerning gender hierarchy, *socialization,* and *power* and their impact on conducting counseling. Feminists recognize the overriding importance of *sexism* as a factor in the problems women have in society and how important it is to eliminate sexist practices that are detrimental to women in particular and society in general.

FERPA   See *Family Educational Rights and Privacy Act.*

fetish   An *erotic* attraction to inanimate objects (e.g., shoes, clothing) or parts of the body (e.g., hair, the neck). A fetish can become a sexual disorder known as fetishism when it becomes an *obsession.*

fiction   An *Adlerian counseling* concept that describes the subjective *evaluations* people have of themselves and their *environments.*

fidelity   An *ethical principle* encompassing faithfulness and honoring commitments.

field study   *Qualitative research* that involves spending considerable time in a setting under study and collecting as much relevant information as possible. Field study is the opposite of *laboratory research.*

field theory   Kurt Lewin's approach to *groups* that emphasizes the interaction between individuals and their *environments.* It is based on the ideas of *gestalt therapy,* in which there is an interdependence of part/whole relationships.

figure/ground   A *gestalt therapy* term used to describe focus. Figure in one's personal life is composed of experiences that are most important. Ground is composed of experiences that are less pressing.

filial therapy   Bernard and Louise Guerney's approach in which parents function as counselors and play therapists for their children.

first-degree games   A *transactional analysis* term for the least harmful games, in which minor faults are highlighted. See also *games.*

first-order change   The process whereby someone unable to adjust to new circumstances often repetitiously tries the same solutions as before or intensifies nonproductive behaviors. First-order change does not alter the nature or structure of a *system.* For example, a person may try raising his or her voice if another person does not respond to a request spoken in a normal tone; the request remains the same regardless.

fishbowl procedure   See *group observing group.*

fixation   A term in *psychoanalysis* for the cessation of *psychosexual* development at a certain stage due to too much or too little gratification at that stage. In fixation, there is a tendency to cope with the outside world in a manner similar to that employed in the earlier stage in which one is stuck. To overcome fixation requires that people *regress* to that earlier time and come to terms with themselves and significant others who were involved in the fixation process.

flashback   A mental picture of a historic scene or earlier experience that comes to a person's mind unexpectedly. Flashbacks can be disturbing or comforting. When they occur frequently, they are often the source of *distress* and may be symptoms of other disorders.

flat affect   Lack of *emotion;* sometimes a symptom of *depression* or *schizophrenia.*

flexibility   The ability to adjust to new conditions and circumstances. Emotionally mature people and competent counselors are flexible.

floating hot seat   A *gestalt therapy* technique in which interaction is promoted by encouraging group members to work on exploring their own personal issues when someone else in the group touches on an issue that has personal relevance for them.

flooding   A *behavioral therapy* concept that describes the presentation to a fearful person of an imagined *anxiety*-producing scene that does not have dire *consequences*.

fluid intelligence   A person's inherited ability to think and reason, including the processes of perceiving relationships, reasoning inductively, and solving problems. It is the opposite of *crystallized intelligence.*

focus group   A group composed of a representative sample of individuals concerned with issues, products, and/or outcomes. Focus groups are being utilized increasingly by businesses and politicians.

focus on exceptions   A technique utilized by *brief therapists* to help people realize that their symptoms are not always present and that they have some *power* over what they are presently doing to make changes.

focused approach to multicultural counseling   A view that sees multiculturalism in the United States as focusing on four visible ethnic minority groups: *Native Americans, African Americans, Asian Americans,* and *Hispanics/ Latinos(as).* It is the opposite of the *universal approach to multicultural counseling.*

focused imagery   When a client actually practices a *behavior* or imagines doing more of a task than he or she had done previously.

follow-up   Reconnecting with clients after they have left counseling and had enough time to *process* what they experienced and work on their *goals* and objectives.

foot in the door technique   A counseling technique in which the counselor asks the client to comply with a minor request and then later follows with a larger request. It is the opposite of the *door in the face technique.*

forced-choice item test   An *objective test* in which each question has several choices and a person is required to select at least one of the items. A forced-choice format prevents the development of a certain response set.

forensic psychiatry   A psychiatric specialty that deals with determining the mental competency of individuals in court cases.

formal operations   The last of Jean Piaget's four stages of cognitive development. The formal operations stage usually begins around age 11 or 12. Formal operations is characterized by the increasing ability to use logical thought processes and abstract reasoning, and to develop symbolic meaning.

forming   The first stage of *group development,* which is characterized by initial caution associated with any new experience. During this time, there is an attempt by group members to avoid being rejected by others, the leader, or even themselves.

fourth force   A term used by Paul Pedersen to describe *multicultural* approaches to counseling. The first, second, and third forces are *psychoanalysis, behaviorism,* and *humanism.*

frame   A mental perception or opinion that organizes one's interactions.

framework   The structure surrounding the *process* of counseling, such as a specific time and place where it will occur. Having a framework promotes the development of counseling.

free association   A *psychoanalysis* technique, especially useful in uncovering *repressed* thoughts and feelings, in which the client reports everything that comes to mind as soon as it occurs. Through such a process, *conflicts* and disturbances from the *unconscious* surface and can be therapeutically dealt with.

free child   See *natural child.*

freebasing   The smoking of a drug such as cocaine.

frequency distribution A tabulation of *data* that indicates the number of times something occurred in a study.

frequency distribution of math scores

test score	frequency
78	2
85	5
89	4
94	7
99	2

frustration A negative emotional reaction to being blocked or thwarted in achieving one's goals.

fugue A relatively long period of *amnesia* during which a person takes flight by leaving his or her immediate *environment.* Described in the *DSM-IV* as *dissociative fugue.*

fully functioning person A term originated by Carl Rogers to describe an individual who is using his or her abilities to the fullest extent possible.

functional autonomy A concept introduced by Gordon Allport to explain why some human motives have no biological need behind them. According to Allport, some acquired motives come to function independently (autonomously) although they may have originally been means to an end. For instance, a college student who studies a subject in college because it was required may later come to read in the subject for the pleasure of it.

functional family therapy A type of *behavioral family therapy* that is basically systemic in nature.

functional fixity Seeing things in only one way or from one perspective or being fixated on the idea that a particular situation or attribute is the issue.

fusion **1.** In *family therapy,* the merging of intellectual and emotional functions together so that an individual does not have a clear sense of *self* and others. It is the opposite of *differentiation.* **2.** In *existential therapy,* an attempt to become part of another person or group in an effort to reduce feelings of *isolation.*

g

G factor See *generalized intelligence.*

GA See *Gamblers Anonymous.*

Gamblers Anonymous (GA) A *mutual help group,* similar to *Alcoholics Anonymous,* composed primarily of compulsive gamblers. GA's address is P.O. Box 17173, Los Angeles, CA 90017 (213-386-8789; http://www.gamblersanonymous.org/).

game analysis An examination in *transactional analysis* of destructive and repetitive behavioral patterns and their payoffs. Such an analysis involves an exploration of the *ego states* and types of *transactions* involved.

games **1.** A *Milan family therapy* concept that stresses how children and parents stabilize around disturbed behaviors in an attempt to benefit from them. **2.** In *transactional analysis,* an ongoing series of complementary *ulterior transactions* progressing to a well-defined, predictable outcome. Games are played on three levels (*first-, second-, and third-degree games*), and almost all of them are destructive and result in negative payoffs (i.e., *rackets*). People who play games operate from three distinct positions: *victim, persecutor,* and *rescuer.* See also *first-degree games; persecutor; rescuer; second-degree games; third-degree games; victim.*

gang A *group* that arises out of children's needs to be independent from their parents and to be with their peers. Members are obligated to participate in the group's activities; outsiders are excluded. Gangs may have secret passwords, explicit or implicit *rules* of conduct, and *rituals* such as initiation rites.

GATB See *General Aptitude Test Battery.*

gay   A term used to describe a *homosexual* male.

gender identity disorder   A disorder under *sexual and gender identity disorders* in the *DSM-IV* that is characterized by a strong and persistent cross-gender identification, coupled with a discomfort about one's own assigned sex. Such disorders are treatable if client motivation is strong.

gender roles   The characteristics and behaviors assigned to individuals because of their sex. For example, females may be expected to be nurturing and men competitive. Gender roles often prove untrue for individuals because of their interests, abilities, and temperament. See also *sex roles.*

General Aptitude Test Battery (GATB)   A career *aptitude test* battery composed of 12 speed tests published by the U.S. Department of Labor and administered in state employment services, community colleges, and some high schools. The *battery* yields nine aptitude scores on cognitive, perceptual, and psychomotor factors.

general systems theory   A *theory* that emphasizes *circular causality* as opposed to *linear causality* and focuses on the interconnectedness of elements within all living organisms.

generalization   The extent to which conclusions, *rules,* principles, and other behaviors are applicable in *environments* outside of where they were originally learned.

generalized intelligence (G factor)   The factor that is measured in most *intelligence tests.*

generativity   A goal of *midlife,* according to Erik Erikson, in which people seek to be creative in their lives and work for the benefit of others and the next generation. Generativity is the opposite of *stagnation.*

genital stage   The last of Sigmund Freud's *psychosexual* stages of development. The genital stage begins around age 11 or 12 and lasts until about age 18 or 19. If all has gone well previously, each gender takes more interest in the other, and heterosexual patterns of interaction appear. If there were unresolved difficulties in any of the first three psychosexual stages (collectively known as the *pregenital stages*), the person may have difficulty adjusting to the adult responsibilities that begin at the genital stage.

genogram   Murray Bowen's visual diagram of a person's family tree over at least three generations depicted in geometric figures, lines, and words. It is used to trace reoccurring patterns within a family (see diagram on page 54).

genuineness   Also known as *congruence,* a quality that is one of the *necessary and sufficient conditions for change,* according to Carl Rogers. Genuineness is characterized by openness, transparency, *self-disclosure, authenticity,* and a lack of pretense.

gerontological counseling   Counseling that centers around working with the aged.

gerontology   The study of *aging,* including biological, mental, psychological, and social components.

gestalt   A German word meaning "whole figure"; an integrated whole.

gestalt therapy   A form of treatment originated by Fritz Perls and based on the assumption that clients' problems arise when they behave according to other people's expectations rather than to their own true feelings. The aim of gestalt therapy is to help the client become more aware of self and emotion and to act in the *now.* The approach is aimed more at doing rather than talking and uses a number of both *exercises* and *experiences.*

gifted   A person with exceptional talents or mental abilities. This term is often used in educational settings to describe students who are above average in one or more areas and who could benefit from special instruction.

glass ceiling phenomenon   A term used to describe the barriers to advancement of women or minorities in organizations. The lack of advancement is not due to an organization's official policy but is simply a failure by the organization to promote women and minori-

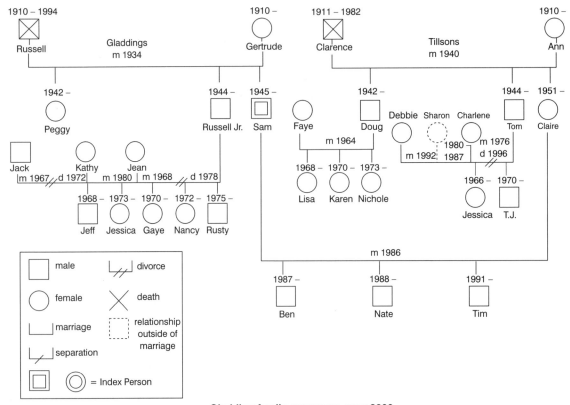

Gladding family genogram, year 2000

ties to top-level executive duties even when they are equal to or better qualified than those who are promoted.

goals   Specific objectives that individuals wish to accomplish in counseling. Goals are mutually agreed on by clients and counselors and may change over the lifetime of a counseling relationship.

goal-setting   A strategy used in counseling to help clients clarify what they wish from the *process* and define the steps they need to take to reach their objectives.

going home again   A Bowen technique in which the family counselor instructs an individual to return home in order to better get to know the family in which he/she grew up. By using this type of information, individuals can *differentiate* themselves more clearly.

good enough mother   A mother who lets an infant feel loved and cared for and thereby helps the infant develop *trust* and a true sense of *self.*

go-rounds   See *rounds.*

grade equivalent score   A score, usually on an *achievement test,* that is translated into the grade level regardless of the age of the individual.

Graduate Record Exam (GRE)   An *aptitude test* used to predict success in advanced graduate work. Test results are reported along three dimensions: verbal, quantitative, and analytical.

graph   A visual representation of a set of *data* (e.g., *pie charts, histograms*).

GRE   See *Graduate Record Exam.*

Greek chorus   Observers/consultants of a family treatment session (i.e., the team). The chorus members debate the merits of what a therapist is doing to bring about *change*. They send messages about the process to the therapist and family. The family is helped through this process to acknowledge and feel their ambivalence.

grief An intense emotional response to a loss characterized by sorrow and *distress*.

grief work A series of stages people in *grief* must go through in order to resolve their deep feelings of sorrow. Among these stages are reminiscing, expressing emotions, accepting, adjusting to newness, and forming new relationships.

group A collection of two or more individuals who meet in face-to-face interaction, interdependently, with the *awareness* that each belongs to the group and for the purpose of achieving individual and/or mutually agreed-upon *goals*.

group analysis A term first applied to the *treatment* of individuals in psychoanalytically oriented groups by Trigant Burrow, who emphasized that social forces affect individuals' behaviors.

group casualties Members of a *group* who drop out or become worse because of the experience.

group cohesiveness The degree of togetherness in a *group* expressed in a feeling of "we-ness."

group collusion Cooperating with others unconsciously or consciously to reinforce prevailing *attitudes, values, behaviors,* or *norms.* The purpose of such behavior is self-protection, and its effect is to maintain the status quo in the *group.*

group counseling Groups that focus on *prevention,* growth, and remedial issues that are both intrapersonal and interpersonal in nature. Sometimes these groups are known as *interpersonal problem-solving groups.*

group development The stages that groups move through over time, such as *forming, storming, norming, performing,* and *adjourning/mourning.*

group dynamics A term originally used by Kurt Lewin to describe the interaction among members in a *group.*

group guidance The process of using educational methods to help group members acquire information and develop needed skills. One type of group guidance is *life-skills* training.

group interaction The way members relate to each other with nonverbal and verbal behaviors and the *attitudes* that go with them. Group interaction exists on a continuum, from extremely nondirected to highly directed.

group marathon An extended, one-session group experience that breaks down defensive barriers that individuals may otherwise use. It usually lasts for a minimum of 24 hours.

group observing group The situation that occurs when a *group* breaks up into two smaller groups and the outer group observes the inner group function for a set amount of time. It is sometimes referred to as a *fishbowl procedure.*

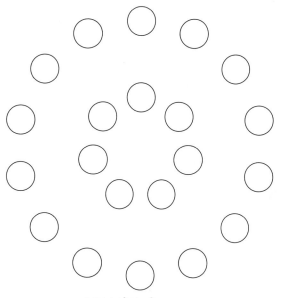

group observing group

group process The interactions of *group* members as the group develops. See also *process.*

group processing A situation that occurs when a neutral third party (a *group processor*) observes and gives *feedback* to the *group* concerning the interactions between members and in the group itself, in regard to both *content* and *process.*

group processor See *group processing.*

group psychoanalysis A model that emphasizes that the whole group is the *client* and that *group dynamics* are an essential feature to analyze.

group psychotherapy A *group* treatment that specializes in *remediation* or *personality* reconstruction. It is meant to help people who have serious psychological problems of a long-term duration. As such, this type of group is found most often in mental health facilities such as clinics or hospitals.

group setting The group's physical *environment,* for instance, where the group room is located and how the room is arranged.

group structure Both the way a group is set up physically as well as the way group members interact or structure themselves in relationship to others.

group techniques *Exercises,* such as *icebreakers,* that are structured in such a way as to get group members to interact with one another.

group test A paper-and-pencil test given to a large number of people at one sitting. A group test has an advantage in its ease of administration and cost, but it does not pick up the subtleties of an *individual test.*

group therapy See *group psychotherapy.*

group work The giving of help or the accomplishment of tasks in a group setting. It involves the application of group *theory* and process by a capable professional practitioner in order to help an interdependent collection of people reach their mutual goals; the goals may be personal, interpersonal, or task related. According to the *Association for Specialists in Group Work (ASGW),* group work is a broad professional practice.

grouping A statistical procedure for combining individual scores into categories or ranking them, such as in *percentiles.*

groupthink A group situation in which there is a deterioration of mental efficiency, reality testing, and moral judgment that results from in-group pressures. The end result is usually a bad decision.

growing times Times at which fresh learning occurs on an individual and interpersonal level.

guidance A point of view in education that emphasizes the total *development* of individual students and utilizes instructional services to help students develop their abilities and learn to cope. Guidance also deals with helping individuals learn to make *choices.*

guidance counselor A term sometimes used to describe a *school counselor* or a counselor in an educational setting who provides clients with guidance activities related to problem solving, career decision making, and work or study habits.

guidance hour Also known as *guidance room;* the term used in the 1930s for time in a homeroom at school that was devoted to guidance. The homeroom teacher's responsibilities were to establish friendly relationships with students, discover their abilities and *needs,* and develop right *attitudes* with them toward school, home, and the community.

guidance room See *guidance hour.*

guidance/psychoeducational group Groups that were originally developed for use in educational settings, specifically public schools. The primary function of the *group* is the *prevention* of personal or societal *disorders* through the conveying of information and/or the examining of *values.* Guidance/psychoeducational groups stress growth through knowledge. *Content* includes but is not limited to personal, social, vocational, and educational information.

guilt An emotional response to having done something wrong or having failed to do something. Guilt is the opposite of initiative in Erik Erikson's *psychosocial* stages of development. See also *initiative.*

h

habilitation   The education of clients who have had *disabilities* since early life and who have never been self-sufficient.

halfway house   A supervised group home for individuals who are making a transition from any type of *treatment* or *rehabilitation* to society.

hallucinations   Imagined perceptions of an object, sound, or phenomenon that is not present in reality. Hallucinations are often *symptoms* of severe *disorders* such as *schizophrenia.*

hallucinogen   A substance, such as *lysergic acid (LSD),* mescaline, *phencyclidine (PCP),* or peyote, that when ingested induces *hallucinations.* The user may experience panic, confusion, suspicion, *anxiety,* and loss of control. Delayed effects, or *flashbacks,* can occur in some cases, even after use has ceased.

halo effect   The tendency to evaluate individuals in a positive light, according to initial impressions or past performances that may be inaccurate in the present. It is the opposite of the *horn effect.*

handicap   A mental or physical limitation of a person with a *disability.* Such limitations are exacerbated by the presence of various barriers.

hangover   The negative aftereffect of abusing *drugs* or *alcohol.*

happenstance   A chance event that is unpredictable. Happenstance sometimes plays a part in the *development* of people's friendships, careers, lifestyles, and so forth.

Hawthorne effect   A social research phenomenon in which changes in human behavior occur as a result of observing or manipulating a person's *environment.*

health   An interactive process involving one's mental, physical, spiritual, and social well-being and associated with positive relationships and outcomes.

health maintenance organization (HMO)   A comprehensive health care organization that provides health services to its members for a specific fee or cost over a period of time. See also *managed care.*

hedonistic   Oriented toward or seeking pleasure for its own sake.

help line   A telephone crisis or referral *hot line* usually staffed by trained volunteers to provide assistance to those in *need.* See also *hot line.*

helpee   See *client.*

helping   The process of assisting individuals in their times of *need.*

HELPING   An acronym for *health, emotions, learning,* personal interactions, imagery, need to know, and *guidance.* HELPING is Donald Keats's multimodal framework for *helping.*

helping profession   Any profession in which the primary responsibility is to assist individuals in *need.* Examples of helping professions include counseling, nursing, social work, psychiatry, marriage and family therapy, and psychology.

heroin   An opiate related to morphine, heroin produces a feeling of profound well-being, followed by drowsiness, nausea, and vomiting. Heroin works on the pain and pleasure centers in the brain. It can be injected, smoked, or snorted. Heroin is physically addictive and can cause convulsions, coma, and death. Heroin is also called smack, horse, junk, and brown sugar.

heterogeneous group   A group composed of dissimilar persons. Such groups can broaden members' horizons and enliven interpersonal interactions.

heterosexual   A person who is orientated toward sexual relationships with someone of the opposite sex.

hidden agenda   Covert, as opposed to overt, agendas or *goals.* For instance, a person may seek counseling with the hope that a court of law may look more favorably upon her or him in an upcoming trial.

hierarchy of needs Abraham Maslow's *theory* that human *needs* occur in ascending order; physical needs must be fulfilled first, followed by safety needs, belonging needs, *self-esteem* needs, and, finally, *self-actualization* needs.

Maslow's hierarchy of needs

Hispanic/Latino(a) A generic label for people from Spanish backgrounds whose origins are in Latin America or the Caribbean Islands. This group is the fastest growing minority population in the United States.

histogram A *bar graph* that provides a description of the distribution of the frequency of *scores*. The horizontal axis of a histogram is marked off in limits of score intervals; the vertical axis is marked off in frequencies.

historical time The era in which people live. It consists of forces that affect and shape humanity at a particular point in time, such as in economic depression or war.

histrionic personality disorder A *personality disorder* characterized by all or some of the following: an overreaction to minor events, tantrums, overly dramatic behavior, a craving for excitement and attention, manipulation of others, lack of depth or genuineness, and suicidal threats. Individuals with this disorder are sometimes referred to as *hysterics.*

HIV See *human immune deficiency virus.*

HMO See *health maintenance organization.*

holding the focus Concentrating on a specific topic for a set length of time.

holistic The view of humans as complete entities rather than individuals made of separate parts. A holistic perspective is the underlying basis of such helping approaches as *existentialism, gestalt therapy,* and *person-centered counseling.*

home-based therapy A method of *treatment* in which counselors spend time with families before attempting to help them. This type of approach is appropriate in working with select families (e.g., some Native American families) unfamiliar with the helping process.

homeostasis The tendency of a *system* or organism to remain static and to strive to restore balance if disturbed. This tendency results in resisting *change* and keeping circumstances in a state of equilibrium. Homeostasis is one factor affecting clients in the process of making changes in their lives.

homework Assignments given clients to work on outside of or between counseling sessions in order to help them practice or refine skills learned in counseling or try new behaviors.

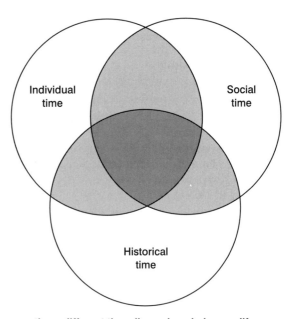

three different time dimensions in human life

homogeneous group   A group composed of persons with similar backgrounds.

homophobic   Excessive fear of associating with homosexuals or being *homosexual.*

homosexual   A person who has a preference for sexual activities with members of his or her own sex.

hope   An experience that is important to client progress both cognitively and emotionally. Cognitively, hope is the belief that what is desired is also possible and that events will turn out for the best. Emotionally, hope is the feeling that what one believes will occur. The importance of hope is that it energizes and directs clients.

horizontal stressors   Stressful events in a person's life related to the present, some of which are developmental, such as *life cycle* transitions (e.g., aging), and others of which are *happenstance* (e.g., accidents).

horn effect   The tendency to evaluate individuals in a negative light, according to initial impressions or past performances that may not be accurate in the present. It is the opposite of the *halo effect.*

hospice   A philosophy and a program of caring for the terminally ill in a nonhospital, homelike atmosphere in which family, relatives, and friends can be with the person who is dying.

hot cognition   A powerful and highly meaningful idea that produces a strong emotional reaction.

hot line   A crisis phone line managed by helping specialists and specially trained volunteers. See also *help line.*

hot seat   The place in *gestalt therapy* groups where the person who wants to work sits in a chair facing the counselor or leader while the rest of the *group* serve as a kind of *Greek chorus* in the background. The chorus members resonate and empathize with the person who is working and gain insights into themselves and others through the process of *identification.*

HOUND   A cruel but sometimes used counseling acronym to describe a client perceived as homely, old, unintelligent, nonverbal, and disadvantaged.

House-Tree-Person (HTP) test   A projective *personality test* in which a person is asked to draw a house, a tree, and a person, in that order. Both *conscious* and *subconscious* dimensions of *personality* are assessed.

how   The process in *gestalt therapy* of actually promoting *change* in a client through structure and behavior. One of the two legs on which gestalt therapy is based, the other being *now.*

HTP   See *House-Tree-Person test.*

human immune deficiency virus (HIV)   A virus that is transmitted by direct exposure to blood and blood derivatives, certain acts of sexual intercourse, or transfer from an infected mother to her fetus or infant. HIV causes a chronic, progressive, immunologic deficiency disorder called HIV disease, which is linked to immune system malfunctions. HIV infection ultimately results in the condition known as *acquired immune deficiency syndrome (AIDS),* although a person may be initially asymptomatic. Some people live for many years with HIV infection and with AIDS. See also *acquired immune deficiency syndrome (AIDS).*

human relations training   See *sensitivity training.*

human-development consultation   A model emphasizing the primary role of the *consultant* as that of educator and facilitator in affective and cognitive processes.

humanism   A philosophy that is primarily concerned with humanity (i.e., the worth of humans as individuals).

humanistic approach   The collective *treatment* approaches in *counseling* and *psychotherapy* that distinguish humans from other animals. Theorists associated with the humanistic approach include Abraham Maslow, Carl Rogers, and Gordon Allport. Humanistic psychotherapy is sometimes called the *third force (psychoanalysis* is the first force and *behaviorism* the second force).

humor The ability to laugh at oneself and one's circumstances in a therapeutic and non-defensive way.

hyperactivity See *hyperkinesis.*

hyperkinesis A term synonymous with hyperactivity and used by many professionals in place of *attention deficit hyperactivity disorder (ADHD).*

hypersomnia A *sleep disorder* characterized by excessive sleeping or fatigue.

hypnosis An induced state of altered *consciousness* in which a person's suggestibility is heightened. Hypnosis is sometimes used as a complementary treatment to counseling in order to recover *repressed* memories or to help clients become more relaxed.

hypnotherapy The treatment of disorders through *hypnosis.*

hypochondriasis A *somatoform disorder* characterized by a preoccupation with the idea of having a serious illness.

hypothesis An educated guess or explanation for the occurrence of a *phenomenon.*

hypothesizing A technique central to the *Milan family therapy* approach. Hypothesizing involves a meeting of the treatment *team* before the arrival of a family in order to formulate and discuss aspects of the family's situation that may be generating a *symptom.* Through hypothesizing, team members prepare themselves for treating the family.

hysteria An historical term for a *conversion reaction.*

hysteric A term used by Sigmund Freud to describe patients he worked with who displayed many of the *symptoms* of what is today known as a *histrionic personality disorder.*

"I" statements The expression of feelings and thoughts, using the first person singular "I," in a way that encourages others to express their personal opinions and beliefs.

IAAOC See *International Association of Addictions and Offender Counseling.*

IAC See *International Association of Counseling.*

IAMFC See *International Association of Marriage and Family Counselors.*

ICD-10 See *International Classification of Diseases* manual.

icebreaker An *activity* or *exercise* designed to promote initial *communication* between two or more people especially in a *group (*e.g., having people talk about their favorite color or movie).

id A term in *psychoanalysis* for the part of the *personality* present at birth and expressed as biological urges that strives continually for gratification. The id is where human instincts reside. It is amoral and functions according to the *pleasure principle.* The id contains the psychic energy *(libido)* of the person.

ideal self A *person-centered* term originated by Carl Rogers to describe what the person is striving to become as opposed to the *real self* (what the person is). The further the ideal self is from the real self, the more alienated and maladjusted a person becomes.

identification 1. A "normal" developmental process in which individuals see themselves as similar to others. 2. A *defense mechanism* in which a person takes on the *role* and *attitudes* of someone more powerful than himself or herself.

identified patient (IP) A family member who is identified as the *presenting problem* or for whom *treatment* is sought and who carries a family's *symptoms.*

identity   **1.** The sense of oneself as a unique person.   **2.** A virtue that is part of the fifth stage of *psychosocial* development conceptualized by Erik Erikson. Identity occurs between ages 12 and 18 and is the period at which adolescents establish a clear idea of who they are in regard to *values* and *roles* in life. Identity is the opposite of *role confusion* (which often leads to an *identity crisis).*

identity crisis   Confusion and doubt over one's role in life. An identity crisis is most likely to happen during *adolescence.*

ideographic   Geared toward or focused on an individual person. Much of counseling has traditionally been ideographic.

IEP   See *individualized educational program.*

illegal   An action or behavior that is in violation of the *law.*

illicit drug   An unlawful drug, such as *cocaine, an opiate,* and *marijuana.*

illusion   A misperception due to physical or psychological reasons.

image   **1.** A mental picture created in one's mind.   **2.** An impression one has of a person, place, or thing.

imagery techniques   *Techniques* that help people imagine other people, scenes, smells, *feelings, thoughts,* and *behaviors* as vividly as possible. Arnold Lazarus is one of the more noted authorities in devising imagery techniques.

imaginal disputation   A *rational emotive behavioral therapy (REBT) technique* that has participants see themselves in *stressful* situations and examine their *self-talk.*

Imago (Image) Relationship Therapy   An eclectic approach to couple work that includes elements of *psychoanalysis, transactional analysis, gestalt therapy, cognitive therapy,* and *systems theory.*

imitation   Learning new knowledge and *behavior* by observing other people and events without engaging in the behavior itself and without any direct *consequences* to oneself. Imitation is also known *as observational learning, social modeling,* and *vicarious learning.*

immanent justice   The idea, especially in young children, that *punishment* for a wrong doing is absolute and inevitable.

immediacy   **1.** The ability of the counselor to discuss with the client the quality of their *relationship* and current interactions.   **2.** A response by a counselor to something that just took place in a counseling session.

impaired   Unable to function adequately.

impasse layer   A term in *gestalt therapy* for a client who is adrift in a sea of helplessness and dread without any sense of direction.

implosive therapy   A form of *behavioral counseling* in which the client is taught to *image* vividly the things that he or she most fears through a process called *flooding.* As a result, the client becomes *desensitized* to and less anxious about previously feared stimuli.

in loco parentis   A Latin phrase that means "acting in the place of the parent." In loco parentis is a theoretical model in which parents entrust others to act in their place. This model is sometimes used in educational institutions.

inappropriate affect   *Emotions* that are not appropriate to the situation at hand, such as laughing at the death of a loved one. Inappropriate affect is a *symptom* of a *mental disorder.*

incapacitated   Unable to take care of oneself because of diminished physical or mental functioning.

incest   Sexual relationships, specifically intercourse, between close relatives, such as a father and daughter or two siblings.

incompetent   A legal term for the inability of a person to make *legal* decisions or to stand trial.

incongruence   Disparity between two things that are supposed to be in harmony, such as words and actions. Counselors and clients do not make progress when things are incongruent in the counseling *process.*

independent variable   A term used in a *research* experiment for the factor, experience, or *treatment* that is under the control or manipulation of the experimenter and that is expected to have an effect on the subjects as assessed by changes in the *dependent variable.*

individual counseling   One-on-one counseling between a counselor and a client. See also *ideographic.*

individual differences   The differences among people regarding *traits* and quantifiable factors, such as height or weight, that make them unique and distinguishable from others.

individual psychology   1. The name given to Alfred Adler's approach to *counseling* and *psychotherapy.* See also *Adlerian counseling.*   **2.** The branch of psychology that investigates differences between individuals.

individual test   A test administered to only one person at a time. Often these tests are measures of *intelligence* (such as a *Wechsler*) or *personality* (such as a *Rorschach*). It is the opposite of *group test.*

individual time   The span of life between one's birth and death. Notable individual achievements are often highlighted in this perspective, for example, being recognized as "teacher of the year."

individualized educational program (IEP)   An educational program tailored to the specialized needs of a certain child. Counselors, especially in schools, engage in either direct *interventions* or support services with students for whom IEPs are drawn up.

individuation   The *process* by which an individual comes to understand himself or herself as an indivisible and integrated whole person who is different from others.

inductive reasoning   A form of logical analysis that moves from specific observations to a *generalization.*

industry   A virtue that is a part of the fourth stage of *psychosocial* development conceptualized by Erik Erikson. Industry occurs between ages 6 and 12 and is conceptualized as the setting and attaining of personal *goals.* It is the opposite of *inferiority.*

infancy   The period in human life that begins a few weeks after birth and lasts for approximately 2 years.

inferential statistics   A set of procedures for making *generalizations* about a *population* by studying a *subset,* or *sample,* of the population. Sample *surveys* use inferential statistics (e.g., the Gallup Poll).

inferiority   1. The opposite of Erik Erikson's concept of *industry.* Inferiority occurs between ages 6 and 12 if children come to feel that they are inferior to others and fail to set and attain *goals* because they think they cannot.   **2.** An *Adlerian counseling* concept for feelings of inadequacy that stem from being born with a physical or mental defect, being pampered by parents, or being neglected. The *feelings* must be corrected and inappropriate forms of *behavior* stopped. To do so, the counselor assumes the role of teacher and interpreter of events.

inferiority complex   An *Adlerian counseling* concept denoting the unresolved feeling of inadequacy and insecurity a person has in regard to others. An inferiority complex may lead to *overcompensation.*

infliction of mental distress   Outrageous and inappropriate behavior toward a client by a therapist that causes undue mental anguish and suffering.

information giving   Providing a *client* with information needed in order to help make a decision. For example, in *career counseling* specific information may help a client decide on a *vocation.*

informed consent   A document clients sign acknowledging that they have been informed of the activity they are about to participate in and are entering it voluntarily (see diagram on page 63).

inhalant   A toxic vapor found in such products as glue, gasoline, nail polish remover, aerosols, anesthetics, cooking sprays, and organic nitrites that when inhaled gives their users a quick high with a minimal *hangover.* Inhalants damage the nerves that control breathing, and sniffing them can lead to a coma or death. Yet, inhalants are readily available, inexpensive, and *legal.*

inherent inferiority An *Adlerian counseling* concept that refers to the belief that everyone is born with a built-in feeling of inferiority because of their helplessness and dependency as an infant. This inferiority is a motivator for people to achieve.

inherited cultures Identification based on groupings such as *ethnicity* or *religion.*

initiative A virtue that is a part of the third stage of *psychosocial* development conceptualized by Erik Erikson. Initiative occurs between ages 3 and 5 and emphasizes the child achieving a sense of competence and initiative through encouragement to discover, experiment, and learn. The opposite of initiative is *guilt* (i.e., a sense of badness that results in passivity because of rejection, punishment, and restriction).

injunction **1.** A *transactional analysis* concept for negative messages in an individual's *life script,* such as parent commands (e.g., "Do as you are told") recorded by the child that call for the child to adopt certain roles. Injunctions often begin with the word "don't" (e.g., "Don't be that way") and limit personal interactions. **2.** A *legal* term for a court process that forbids taking a particular action.

inpatient A person who is treated in a residential setting such as a hospital. Inpatient is the opposite of *outpatient.*

insane A *legal* term for a person with a severe *mental disorder.*

insight Self-understanding and increased *awareness* about one's problems and the factors that are influencing one's behaviors. Insight often occurs during or after the experience of *catharsis.* It is sometimes sudden. Insight comes about as a result of reorganizing ideas and *perceptions.* See also *aha reaction.*

insomnia The inability to sleep, especially when such an inability is *chronic.*

inspection A process whereby a state agency periodically examines the activities of a profession's practitioners. In doing so, the agency ascertains that the practitioners are practicing in a fashion consistent with the public safety, health, and welfare. Many state agencies that employ counselors, such as mental health centers, are subject to having their personnel and programs regularly inspected.

instinct Inborn tendencies to act in a certain way; a natural tendency or ability. Instinct is the opposite of learning.

Institute for Family Counseling An early *intervention* program at the Philadelphia Child Guidance Center for community *paraprofes-*

i

Informed Consent Statement
(for group counseling)

I, _____, acknowledge that group counseling is an activity that involves my being open, honest, and willing to participate with others as I strive, with them, to reach personal and group goals. I may experience negative, as well as positive, feelings in this process. I am entering this relationship voluntarily and pledge to work hard in the group in collaboration with the group leader and other members.

_____
date

_____
group member signature

_____
group leader signature

sionals. It proved to be highly effective in providing *mental health* services to the poor.

Institute for Rational-Emotive Therapy   See *Albert Ellis Institute.*

Institute for Reality Therapy   A center that William Glasser established in California to train *counselors* and other *helping professionals* in the *theory* and *techniques* of *reality therapy.* The institute's address is Lassen Street, Suite 118, Chatsworth, CA 91311 (800-899-0688; http://www.wglasserinst.com/).

institutional barrier   Institutionalized inconveniences minority populations must endure to receive *mental health* services, such as an inconvenient clinic location, the use of a language not spoken by one's family, and the lack of diversified practitioners.

intake interview   The initial *interview* a client undergoes to screen or *diagnose* his or her situation and determine whether he or she is a good candidate for counseling. Usually intake interviews involve taking a history of the person and his or her *presenting problem.*

integration   **1.** The ability of a person or group to bring together ideas into a unified whole.   **2.** The bringing together of different *ethnic* or social groups into harmonious relationships.   **3.** The last phase of *psychodrama,* which involves discussion and *closure.*

integrity   A virtue in Erik Erikson's eighth and last stage of *psychosocial* development that can occur from age 65 on. Integrity describes the total integration of life experiences into a meaningful whole. It is the opposite of *despair* (i.e., the feeling that one's life has been meaningless).

intellectualization   A *defense mechanism* that is characterized by an emphasis on abstraction with a minimal amount of *affect;* it is as if a person used thoughts and a sophisticated vocabulary to avoid dealing with personal feelings.

intelligence   Higher level thought processes, including the ability to learn from experiences,

problem solve, remember, and successfully manipulate the environment. There are multiple forms of intelligence and a number of individual and group *intelligence tests.*

intelligence quotient (IQ)   The score of an intelligence test that defines a person's relative standing in a group. An intelligence quotient may be derived by a ratio or deviation method. In the *ratio IQ* method, IQ equals a person's *mental age* divided by one's *chronological age* times 100 (IQ=MA/CA x 100). In the *deviation IQ* method, one's IQ is computed according to how far one's score deviates from the *mean* score obtained by individuals of the same chronological age. The deviation method assumes a *normal distribution* of scores for each age group.

intelligence test   A standardized way of assessing a person's current mental ability given either on a group or an individual level.

intensity   A *structural family therapy* method of changing *maladaptive* transactions by having the counselor use strong *affect,* repeated *intervention,* or prolonged pressure with a family.

intentional civil liability   Intentional violations of a person's civic rights through *battery, defamation, invasion of privacy,* and *infliction of mental distress.*

interest inventory   A *test* or *questionnaire* that records an individual's preference for, interest in, or *motivation* for various activities. Interest inventories are often used as part of *career counseling;* some have *norms* from individuals who work in select *occupations.*

interlocking pathology   A term created by Nathan Ackerman to explain how families and certain of their members stay *dysfunctional.* In an interlocking pathology, there is an unconscious process that takes place between family members that keeps them together.

interlocking triangles   Murray Bowen's idea that the most stable and basic unit within a family relationship consist of three-person sets of interactions (e.g., father/mother/child).

intermittent reinforcement A *schedule of reinforcement* that varies over time and that is used once a behavior has been established through *continuous reinforcement.*

internal consistency analysis A form of *reliability* in which the scores of two randomly selected halves of a *test* are compared.

internalization **1.** The process of taking in *thoughts* and *behaviors* from others and making them one's own. **2.** The process of incorporating the *norms* from one's *culture* and making them one's own.

International Association of Addictions and Offender Counseling (IAAOC) A division within the *American Counseling Association.* Founded in 1972, IAAOC was formerly the *Public Offender Counselor Association.* The association is composed of counselors who have an interest in or work in settings that counsel with addicts and those convicted of crimes.

International Association of Counseling (IAC) An international organization of counselors from throughout the world who meet for a conference annually.

International Association of Marriage and Family Counselors (IAMFC) A division of the *American Counseling Association.* IAMFC, founded in 1989, is composed of counselors who work with families and couples. IAMFC's Internet address is www.iamfc.org/.

International Classification of Diseases (ICD-10) manual A manual, now in its 10th edition, published by the World Health Organization, that codifies psychiatric disorders. The ICD is the parallel publication to the *DSM-IV.* See also *DSM-IV.*

International Transactional Analysis Association (ITAA) An association that was founded by Eric Berne, the creator of *transactional analysis.* It is a professional organization that helps advance the theory, methods, and principles of transactional analysis and offers *certification* and training in various categories. ITAA's address is 450 Pacific Avenue, Suite 250, San Francisco, CA 94133-4640 (415-989-5640; http://www.itaa-net.org/index.html).

Internet counseling A controversial but prevalent form of individual, group, and family counseling in which clients use computers to interact with counselors via e-mail, chat rooms, and video on the Internet. Sessions are for fixed periods of time for a fee. *Nonverbal cues* and messages are difficult, if not impossible, to process. Empirical evidence of effectiveness is scarce. However, clients may benefit from being able to express their thoughts and feelings at any time, not just at appointed times. Persons with limited mobility or who live in isolated regions may benefit too. There is also a healing quality to writing. Counselors may also have time to consult with colleagues prior to responding. Internet counseling is also known as *cybercounseling, web counseling, e-therapy,* and *therap-e-mail.* See also *scriptotherapy.*

internship A clinical training experience in a counselor education program following a *practicum,* in which the counselor-in-training essentially works full time in a clinical setting under the *supervision* of a more experienced counselor, both on-site and at the institution from which the counselor is receiving his or her degree.

interpersonal Between two or more people.

interpersonal problem-solving groups See *group counseling.*

Interpersonal Process Recall An approach to *supervision* originated by Norman Kagan. It utilizes *feedback* to the counselor through the use of videotaped playbacks.

interpretation A verbal technique that focuses on helping clients gain insights into their past or present *behavior.* Interpretation offers possible explanations for certain behaviors, feelings, or thoughts, usually from a theoretical perspective, such as psychoanalysis. When used successfully, interpretation helps a client explain or understand a situation better, develop insight, and become more open to *change.* There are three levels of interpretation: *constructional, situational, and thematical.* See also *constructional interpretation; situational interpretation; thematical interpretation.*

interval scale   A *measurement* scale that can be used to classify and order measurements. An interval scale does not have a true zero point but does have score points that are of equal distance from each other. An IQ test is an example of an instrument based on an interval scale.

intervention   *Treatment* initiated by a counselor that is aimed at disrupting and/or alleviating client *problems* (e.g., giving a *directive* to a client to do the opposite of what he or she has been doing).

interview   A method of seeking research *data* or clinical information that involves two-way verbal *communication* between the interviewer and the interviewee.

intimacy   A virtue in Erik Erikson's sixth stage of *psychosocial* development that occurs between ages 18 and 35. The emphasis in intimacy is on achieving intimate interpersonal relationships. Intimacy is the opposite of *isolation* (i.e., facing life alone).

intrapersonal   A synonym for *intrapsychic;* literally "within the person."

intrapsychic   Within the mind of the person.

intrinsically neutral   An approach that views individuals as neither positive nor negative (i.e., without a predetermined set of responses).

introjection   A *defense mechanism* in which a person internalizes messages from another person, such as a parent, and applies them to his or her life.

introspection   The process of examining one's *thoughts.*

introvert   A Jungian concept for a person who tends to direct his or her life energy inward rather than toward the *environment.* Introverts are more concerned with their own *thoughts* and *feelings* than with others. Introvert is the opposite of *extrovert.*

invariant prescription   A specific kind of *ritual* in Milan family therapy given to parents with children who are psychotic or anorexic in an attempt to break up the family's *dirty game.* An invariant prescription requires parents to unite so that children cannot manipulate them as "winners" or "losers" and thereby side with them.

invasion of privacy   A violation of the right to be left alone.

inventory   A list of questions, statements, or words to which an individual responds (e.g., agrees or disagrees). Inventories are designed to measure a dimension of *personality,* interest, *aptitude,* or other behavioral characteristic.

investment syndrome   A situation that occurs when counselors are reluctant to work with older adults because they feel their time and energy are better spent working with younger people who may eventually contribute to society. Professionals who display this attitude are banking on future payoffs from the young and may well be misinformed about the possibilities for change in older adults.

invisible loyalty   An *unconscious* commitment that a grown child makes to help his or her *family of origin,* especially his or her parents (e.g., phoning to see how the parents are doing or sending money).

involuntary client   A client who is ordered to receive counseling. Such clients are usually *reluctant* (referred by a third party and unmotivated to seek help) or *resistant* (unwilling or opposed to *change*).

Iowa Law Review Note   A 1971 ruling that legally recognized counselors as professionals who provided personal as well as vocational and educational counseling. This legal ruling was among the first to view counseling as a profession separate from other helping specialties.

Iowa Test of Basic Skills   A *battery* of *achievement tests* covering kindergarten through Grade 8. The tests are designed to measure basic educational skills and include reading, math, language, and study skills.

IQ See *intelligence quotient.*

irrational belief (IB) The generation of an upsetting and disturbing *thought.* Albert Ellis classifies irrational beliefs under three main headings dealing with *self,* others, and the *environment.* All contain the word "must" and when believed lead to various kinds of emotional disturbance.

irrational thinking A concept associated with Albert Ellis's *rational emotive behavioral therapy (REBT)* that describes how illogical thinking of clients is based on wants and desires (e.g., "I must have all of my wishes filled"). See also *awfulizing; musturbation.*

isms The suffix of many words that have an impact on counselors and clients. Negative isms include *sexism* and *racism.* Positive isms include *altruism.*

isolation **1.** A style of living in which a person is disconnected socially and emotionally from others. **2.** It is the opposite of *intimacy* in Erik Erikson's sixth stage of *psychosocial* development. If a person does not achieve intimate relationships, he or she becomes socially isolated. **3.** A *defense mechanism* that people employ to separate an idea from its emotional content.

ITAA See *International Transactional Analysis Association.*

item A task or question of which a *test* is composed.

item analysis The examination of test questions to determine the effectiveness of each one as a discriminating item.

I-Thou relationships An *existential* term originated by Martin Buber to describe relationships that focus on the persons in them rather than things (e.g., as in I-It relationships).

j

Jaffee v. Redmond The 1996 U.S. Supreme Court decision that held that communications between licensed *psychotherapists* and their *patients* are privileged and do not have to be disclosed in cases held in federal court.

JCD See *Journal of Counseling and Development.*

job A definite piece of work undertaken for a fixed price.

job analysis A procedure used to determine the factors or tasks that make up a *job.*

Johari Awareness Model (Johari Window) A representative square with four quadrants that, when the process works well, is often used in *counseling* to show what happens with an individual or in group interactions. If the group works well, the first three quadrants (the *public self,* the *blind self,* and the *private* self) grow, and the last one (the *unknown self*) shrinks.

joining The process of "coupling" that occurs between the counselor and the client, leading to the development of a therapeutic *relationship* and *change.*

joint custody A *legal* term for the right of both parents to share in making certain major decisions for their children.

Jonah complex A term coined by Abraham Maslow for a defense that involves a person trying to run away from his or her responsibilities, potential, and talents, just as the biblical character Jonah tried to escape his fate.

journal Also known as a *log;* the writings of one's reactions to a counseling session or daily events. This process enables clients and counselors to spot patterns, *thoughts,* and themes more quickly than otherwise. See also *scriptotherapy.*

Journal of Counseling and Development (JCD)   The flagship journal of the *American Counseling Association (ACA).*

Journal of Counseling Psychology   The flagship journal of the Counseling Psychology division *(Division 17)* of the *American Psychological Association (APA).*

Journal of Marital and Family Therapy   The flagship journal of the *American Association for Marriage and Family Therapy (AAMFT).*

justice   An *ethical principle* encompassing fairness and referring to the equal treatment of all people. This virtue implies that everyone's welfare is promoted and that visible differences in people, such as gender or race, do not interfere with the way they are treated.

juvenile   **1.** A general term for a young person who is under age 18 and not considered an *adult.*   **2.** A *legal* term for a young person who has not reached the age at which he or she would be tried as an adult in a court of law.

juvenile delinquency   See *delinquency.*

K-ABC   See *Kaufman Assessment Battery for Children.*

KAIT   See *Kaufman Adolescent and Adult Intelligence Test.*

Karpman triangle   Also known as the *drama triangle;* a way of conceptualizing game interactions in *transactional analysis* for the three positions (*victim, persecutor,* or *rescuer*) people assume during transactional analysis *games.* To keep games going there is often a switch-off, in which people assume new roles. For example, in the game "Why Don't You/Yes, But," one person plays the rescuer, responding to a complaint by the victimized other person by saying, "Why don't you . . . ?" The victim answers, "Yes, but . . . [I've tried]." After this game becomes tiresome, the rescuer may switch to a more punishing, persecuting role. When the victim complains, the persecutor may respond sarcastically, "Ain't it awful," until the game ends. See also *games.*

Kaufman Adolescence and Adult Intelligence Test (KAIT)   An individually administered *intelligence test* for use with adolescents and adults. The KAIT provides three broad measures of *intelligence:* a crystallized scale, a fluid scale, and a total score. See also *crystallized intelligence; fluid intelligence.*

Kaufman Assessment Battery for Children (K-ABC)   An individually administered measure of *intelligence* and *achievement* containing 16 subtests of mental and processing skills for children 2 years 6 months to 12 years 6 months.

kleptomania   A neurotic *compulsion* to steal.

KOIS   See *Kuder Occupational Interest Survey.*

Kuder Occupational Interest Survey (KOIS)   An activity-preference, item-type, untimed, forced-choice, triad-response interest test, in which a person is asked to respond to each triad by picking his or her least and most preferred activity. There are six forms of the Kuder, which was first published in 1939 and has continued to evolve. Scores on the Kuder correlate highly with commonly expressed interests of select career groups and college majors. The test's 10 broad career areas are social services, persuasive, clerical, computational, musical, artistic, literary, mechanical, outdoor, and scientific.

Kuder Preference Record-Vocational   An instrument that measures interest in 10 career areas: outdoor, mechanical, computational, scientific, persuasive, artistic, literary, musical, social service, and clerical.

l

labeling   The use of a label, such as a *diagnosis,* to characterize or name a client's *behavior.*

labile   A tendency for abrupt changes in *mood* or emotion.

laboratory research   Investigation within a controlled *environment,* such as a counseling laboratory, in which the researcher has control over experimental and environmental conditions.

latchkey children   Children who let themselves into their houses each day after school and are unsupervised for a period of time because their parents are at *work.*

late-entry women   Also known as delayed-entry women; women who decide to enter the job market after considerable time at home.

latency   A period between ages 6 and 12 in which there is little manifest interest in sexuality, according to Sigmund Freud. Instead, energy is focused on peer activities and personal mastery of cognitive learning and physical skills.

latent content   The symbolic features of the dream that escape first analysis (e.g., water as a *symbol* for life). Sigmund Freud believed that in dreams, the presumed true meaning is hidden behind the *manifest content.* See also *dream analysis.*

Latino(a)   A person from Latin America who stresses his or her Latin American heritage. See also *Hispanic/Latino(a).*

law   A body of *rules* recognized by a nation, state, or community as binding on its members.

Law of Triviality   An axiom that states that the time spent discussing an issue is in inverse proportion to the *consequences* of the issue. The Law of Triviality is important in attending to the *content* of a group.

layers of neurosis   A *gestalt therapy* term for aspects of people's lives that keep them from being healthy (e.g., the *phony layer,* the *pho-* bic layer, and the *impasse layer*). See also *impasse layer; phobic layer; phony layer.*

leader-centered group   An autocratic group in which the leader instructs the followers. The leader-centered group is based on obedience from followers.

leaderless group   A group that rotates the leadership role among its members (e.g., *a self-help group*).

leading   A term coined by Francis Robinson to describe certain deliberate behaviors counselors engage in for the benefit of their *clients.* Leads vary in length, and some are more appropriate at one stage of counseling than at another. Robinson used the analogy of a football quarterback and receiver to describe a lead: A good quarterback anticipates where the receiver will be on the field and throws the ball to that spot. The same is true of counselors and clients. Counselors anticipate where their clients are and where they are likely to go and then respond accordingly. If there is misjudgment and the lead is either too far ahead (i.e., too persuasive or direct) or not far enough (i.e., too uninvolved and nondirect), the counseling relationship suffers.

learned helplessness   Martin Seligman's idea that when people have been in situations in which they were not able to control their environment (e.g., in dire poverty), they will fail to take initiatives to influence their surroundings when they are in circumstances in which that is possible because they have learned to be helpless (i.e., they do not think they can make a difference in improving their lot in life).

learning   A general term referring to processes that lead to relatively permanent changes in *behavior* resulting from past experiences. Learning can occur on a number of levels (e.g., overt or covert, *conscious* or *unconscious*). Although there are multiple theories on how learning takes place, there is general agreement on what learning entails.

learning curve A graphic presentation of the changes in *learning* over time. Although learning curves differ, a classic learning curve is steeper when beginning new tasks and then, after a time, plateaus.

learning disability A term for a child of average or above average *intelligence* who has difficulty *learning*. Specific difficulties are *dyslexia* (reading difficulty), *dysgraphia* (writing difficulty), and *dyscalculia* (math difficulty).

learning theory The idea that all human *behavior* is learned; the foundation for *behavior therapy*. It is the opposite of *instinct*.

least restrictive environment A mandate from *Public Law 94-142* that states that persons with *disabilities* must be placed in the most normal situation possible.

legal The *law* or the state of being lawful.

leisure *Activities* that are a part of a person's self-expression and that one does for enjoyment and relaxation when not engaged in *work*. Leisure is a part of career life planning.

lesbian A term used to describe a homosexual female.

leveling A term used by Virginia Satir to describe a *congruent communication*, in which the straight, genuine, and real expression of one's feelings and wishes are made in an appropriate context.

liability A *legal* term that involves issues concerning whether counselors have caused harm to clients. Liability may be *civil* (e.g., for failing to perform one's duties as required by *law*) or *criminal* (e.g., for failing to report suspected child abuse, sexual misconduct, etc.). Liability issues are intertwined with *malpractice*. See also *malpractice*.

liability insurance Insurance designed to protect a person from the financial risks of a lawsuit.

libel Injury to a person's character through written means.

libido A *personality* component, according to *psychoanalysis,* that includes the basic sexual *instincts,* desires, and impulses with which all people are born.

licensed professional counselor (LPC) The title often given (in states that license professional counselors) to a counselor who successfully passes all criteria for *licensure*.

licensing board An official agency that is given jurisdiction over the regulation of licenses for a particular profession (e.g., counseling).

licensure Permission granted by a government, usually on the state level, allowing practice of an *occupation,* such as counseling, by an individual meeting professional criteria. Once licensure requirements are established, individuals cannot practice a profession legally without obtaining a license.

life expectancy The expected duration of human life.

life instinct A *psychoanalysis* term for an *unconscious* drive toward preserving and enhancing life. The life instinct is the balancing force to the *death instinct.*

life review The review of one's life in old age to find themes, meaning, understanding, and acceptance of what one has done.

life script A concept created by Eric Berne; a plan based on the interpretation of one's life experiences, which helps determine how a person interacts.

life script analyses A component of *transactional analysis* that examines people's basic plans involving *transactions* and *games.*

life skills Learned *behaviors* (e.g., problem solving, communication, planning), on both the interpersonal and *intrapersonal* level, necessary for effective living.

life skills training A type of *guidance* or *psychoeducational* activity (often carried out in groups), especially designed to help those who have a deficit of behaviors. Emphasis is on a "how-to" approach to learning new behaviors and may include the use of films, plays, demonstrations, role plays, and guest speakers.

life span   **1.** The average number of years men and women normally live.   **2.** The particular number of years a specific person lived.

life span development   The way a person matures from conception to death on a number of dimensions (e.g., physical, mental, behavioral, emotional, and moral).

life tasks   According to Adlerian theory, the basic challenges and obligations people face in life.

lifestyle   An *Adlerian counseling* concept for a person's unique, directional pattern of behavior based on a judging of both oneself and the outside world.

Likert scale   A technique developed by Rensis Likert that measures (on a multipoint scale) a person's degree of agreement or disagreement with a statement.

Most days I wake up happy.

5	4	3	2	1
strongly agree	mildly agree	don't know	mildly disagree	strongly disagree

Likert scale

limited license   A term that is used in connection with the protection of a title only. For instance, persons cannot call themselves *National Certified Counselors (NCCs)* unless they have successfully completed the requirements for and been granted this title by the *National Board for Certified Counselors (NBCC)*.

linear causality   Also known as linear thinking; the concept of cause and effect (i.e., forces are seen as moving in one direction with each causing the other). It is the opposite of *circular causality*.

A ———————→ B

linear causality

linear thinking   See *linear causality*.

linking   The process of connecting persons with one another by pointing out what they share in common. Linking strengthens the bonds between individuals and the group as a whole.

listening   A skill that is one of the primary means of conducting counseling. Listening involves hearing not only the *content* of a client's words but also the tone and inflection of what is being said (i.e., the *nonverbal*). Furthermore, listening in counseling involves hearing what is not being said as well as deciphering patterns.

locus of control   The idea espoused by Julian Rotter that individuals live their lives according to their view of controlling forces as either internal or external. When the locus of control is internal, people view themselves as being in charge of their own destinies. When the locus of control is external, people believe they are controlled by outside forces.

log   See *journal*.

logical consequences   An *Adlerian counseling* concept that stresses the negative social consequence for a client when actions are ill timed (e.g., not being invited to participate in a class function because of not paying attention in a class).

logico scientific reasoning   Reasoning that is characterized by empiricism and logic.

logotherapy   An *existential* psychotherapy, developed by Victor Frankl, that helps the client restore meaning to life by placing his or her problems in a larger spiritual and philosophical context. Logotherapy is uniquely existential in that it attempts to offer solutions to human concerns as they exist in the moment, rather than attempting to locate their roots in the past.

long brief therapy   Therapy so named because of the length of spacing between sessions (usually a month) and the duration of *treatment* (up to a year). Long brief therapy is also known as *systemic family therapy*.

longitudinal research   An investigation that collects information on the same individuals repeatedly over time in an effort to determine how phenomena change as people develop. Longitudinal research is considered more *valid* in most cases than *cross-sectional research,* but it also takes considerably longer.

long-term therapy   Treatment for *disorders* or problems that is extensive and extends over a number of sessions and at least a 6-month period of time.

loss   The process of ending, terminating, or losing a relationship, person, or experience. Loss is usually associated with *grief* and requires people to work through their feelings and come to resolution if they are to proceed developmentally.

low facilitative responses   Responses that are minimally helpful. Three such responses are (1) *advice/evaluation* (telling people how to behave or judging them), (2) *analyzing/interpreting* (explaining the reasons behind *behavior* without giving the client an opportunity for self-discovery), and (3) *reassuring/supportive* (trying to encourage someone, yet dismissing the person's real feelings).

LPC   See *licensed professional counselor.*

LSD   See *lysergic acid diethylamide.*

ludes   See *depressants.*

lysergic acid diethylamide   A *hallucinogen,* sometimes called acid.

m

magic shop   A warm-up technique in *psychodrama* that is especially useful for protagonists who are undecided or ambivalent about their *values* and *goals.* It involves a storekeeper (the *director* or an *auxiliary ego*) who runs a magic shop filled with special qualities. The qualities are not for sale but may be bartered for.

magnification   An exaggeration of something significant.

main effects   The individual effects of the *independent variable* on the *dependent variable.*

mainstreaming   **1.** The injection of a narcotic *drug* directly into the bloodstream through a vein.   **2.** The placing of developmentally delayed children into a regular classroom setting.

maintenance   A *behavior therapy* process in which a client consistently performs desired actions without relying on external help.

maintenance role   A *role* that contributes to the social-emotional bonding of members and the overall well-being of the *group.* When *interpersonal communication* in the group is strained, there is a need to focus on relationships. Persons who take on such roles are socially and emotionally oriented. They express themselves by being encouragers, harmonizers, compromisers, commentators, and followers.

majority   The primary group of people that sets the standards and tone for life within the culture in which it dominates. See also *minority.*

making the rounds   A warm-up exercise in *gestalt therapy groups* in which *confrontation* is heightened and group members are asked to say something they usually do not verbalize. A milder form of making the rounds, in which there is less confrontation but yet participation by all group members, is called *rounds* or go-rounds.

making wishes into demands   Using "should," "ought," and "must" in regard to an action. According to Albert Ellis, individuals who do this make themselves miserable.

maladaptive   Behaviors, thoughts, feelings, or characteristics that do not help a person obtain personal or societal goals and that are ill suited for the demands of life.

malpractice The failure to fulfill the requisite standard of care either because of *negligence* or ignorance that may occur through *omission* or *commission.*

malpractice suit A claim against a professional made by a "plaintiff" who seeks a monetary award based on a specific amount of physical, financial, and/or emotional damages.

maltreatment Actions that are abusive, neglectful, or otherwise threatening to another person's welfare. Maltreatment is often used as a general term for *abuse* or *neglect.*

managed care A wide range of techniques and structures that are connected with obtaining and paying for medical care, including in some cases counseling. Managed care involves the participation of a third party other than a *caregiver* and a *client.* The two most common third-party participants are a *preferred provider organization (PPO)* and a *health maintenance organization (HMO).*

mandala A *symbol* found in most cultures that represents, according to Carl Jung, the striving for the total unity of *self.*

mania A *mood disorder* in which there is elation and euphoria as well as a preoccupation with an activity or object.

manic-depressive illness See *bipolar disorder.*

manifest content The obvious meaning of dreams in dream *analysis.*

manipulators Individuals, often in groups, who use feelings and behaviors to get their way regardless of what others want or need. Often they are angry.

mapping **1.** In *brief therapy,* the sketching out of a course of successful *intervention.* **2.** In *structural family therapy,* the mental process of envisioning how the *family* is organized.

marathon group A type of *encounter group,* originated by George Bach and Fred Stoller in 1964, that seeks to help people become more authentic with themselves. Marathon groups usually are held for extended periods of time (e.g., 24 or 48 hours), during which group members are required to stay together. As time goes by, members become tired and experience a breakdown in their defenses and an increase in their truthfulness.

marijuana Often referred to as *pot;* a commonly used and controversial *drug* employed for recreational and, sometimes, medical purposes. Recreationally, marijuana produces a euphoric state, but prolonged use of marijuana impairs short-term memory, inhibits alertness, and causes lung infections. As a medical drug, marijuana is used primarily with cancer patients as a hypnotic, an analgesic, an anticonvulsant, and an antinausea drug.

marital schism Overt marital conflict that is *pathological.*

marital skewness A *dysfunctional* marriage in which one partner dominates the other.

marriage counseling Working with a married couple in *remedial* and *preventive* ways. Marriage counseling is usually *conjoint,* but sometimes it is *concurrent.*

marriage enrichment The concept and practice that couples and families stay healthy or get healthier by actively participating in activities that include other couples.

masculine mystique The belief that men are superior to women and therefore have the right to devalue and restrict women's *values, roles,* and *lifestyles.*

masochism **1.** A tendency for a person to seek out ways of being physically or psychologically hurt. **2.** A sexual *disorder* in which a person gets sexually excited by being threatened or harmed.

MAST See *Michigan Alcoholism Screening Test.*

Master Addiction Counselor A specialized certification in *substance abuse* counseling that is obtained after a professional becomes a *National Certified Counselor (NCC).*

masturbation The stimulation of one's own genitalia.

MAT See *Miller Analogies Test.*

maturation Growth and *development* common to members of a species.

MBTI   See *Myers-Briggs Type Indicator.*

MCMI-III   See *Millon Clinical Multiaxial Inventory-III.*

mean   A statistical *measure of the central tendency* that is the arithmetic *average* of the scores in a set of data. See also *average.*

meaning attribution   1. Assigning meaning or significance to an event or experience (e.g., a client's belief that his or her times of *depression* are valuable in helping the client understand the meaning of happiness).   **2.** A group leader's ability to explain to members in a cognitive way what is occurring in their group.

measurement   A procedure used to assign numbers to objects (e.g., test answers) in such a way that the numbers have quantitative meaning.

measure of the central tendency   A statistical term for describing the typical, middle, or central score in a distribution of scores. The *median,* the *mean,* and the *mode* are all used as measures of the central tendency. All these measures encompass different meanings of the term *average.*

median   A *measure of the central tendency* that is the halfway point or the midpoint of a distribution. In a set of *data,* the median is the point at which an equal number of scores are above and below it. The median corresponds to the 50th *percentile.*

mediation   The practice of having a third party hear arguments about a situation and then render a decision.

medical model   An approach to *helping* that is patterned after the orientation used by physicians in which the client is seen as having a disease or *disorder.*

meditation   A purposeful self-regulatory process that produces relaxation. Meditation can lower heart rate and blood pressure. In order to meditate, a person needs a quiet environment, an object to dwell on, a positive attitude, and a comfortable position.

mental age   A score on an *intelligence test* that is representative of one's mental ability regardless of one's *chronological age.* Mental age was first used by Alfred Binet as a term for the age at which a given number of test items were passed by the average child.

mental disorder   A clinically significant behavioral or psychological syndrome or pattern that occurs in an individual (per the American Psychiatric Association). At least one of three features must be present for a mental disorder to be diagnosed: *distress,* impairment, and/or significant risk. See also *disorder.*

mental health   A state of *positive wellness* and emotional well-being free from excessive *stress.*

mental health counseling   An interdisciplinary counseling specialty that is community based and comprehensive. Mental health counseling includes an emphasis on *development, environment, prevention,* and *treatment* issues. This specialty is recognized by the *Council for Accreditation of Counseling and Related Educational Programs (CACREP)* and the *National Board for Certified Counselors (NBCC).*

mental health counselor   An individual who provides professional counseling services to individuals, couples, families, and groups for the purpose of treating *psychopathology* and promoting optimal mental *health.* Mental health counselors work in a variety of settings, such as community agencies and hospitals, as well as in private practice. Some states, such as Florida, license counseling professionals as mental health counselors.

Mental Measurement Yearbook   One of the most comprehensive and definitive reference books published. It describes and reviews commercially published *tests.* Information on the *Mental Measurement Yearbook* can be found on the Internet at http://www.unl.edu/buros/catalog.html. See also *Buros Institute of Mental Measurements.*

Mental Research Institute (MRI)   Since 1959, a leading source of ideas in the area of *systems* studies, *psychotherapy,* and *family therapy.* MRI is located in Palo Alto, California; its Internet address is www.mri.org/index.html.

mental retardation   See *retardation.*

Mesmerism   Named for F. A. Mesmer, the original term for *hypnosis.*

meta-analysis   The analysis of a number of *research* studies on the same subject in order to decipher patterns and determine across-study findings or results.

metacommunication   The implied message within a message typically conveyed in a *nonverbal* manner. For example, a client who is not happy may cross his or her arms and frown.

metaphor   A *verbal* or *nonverbal* experience that occurs when two dissimilar objects are compared to one another for the sake of understanding one of the objects better. For example, on a verbal level, a client may describe himself or herself as "a dot who stays in one spot"; on a nonverbal level, a father who runs around in the morning waking up his family may be deemed "the family alarm clock." Counselors use metaphors to help clients gain *insight* into themselves and formulate their *goals.* For example, a counselor may say to a client who is trying to hold his or her family together, "You want to be the foundation on which your family is built."

method   **1.** The means by which counselors accomplish their purposes or *goals* in *treatment.* **2.** A procedural tool used in research that can be applied in various disciplines.

Metropolitan Achievement Tests (seventh edition)   A test used in school districts for *standardized testing* programs. The tests are used in kindergarten through the twelfth grade and focus on eight basic skills: vocabulary, reading, mathematics, spelling, language, science, social studies, and writing.

Michigan Alcoholism Screening Test (MAST)   A widely researched and used diagnostic instrument, composed of 25 items, that is self-administered. The MAST has been shown to correctly identify up to 95% of alcoholics.

microcounseling   An approach to teaching basic counseling skills (i.e., *microskills*), initi-

ated by Robert Carkhuff and Alan Ivey. The approach is based on the assumption that interviewing skills are complex and can be taught best if broken down into discrete behavioral units.

microskills   Human relations skills common to all theories of counseling, such as *active listening, empathy,* and so on.

middle adulthood   Ages 40 to 65; the period in which individuals realize that life is half over and death is a reality. These years are often full of family and work responsibilities.

middle childhood   Ages 6 up to puberty.

middle old   Ages 65 to 74.

middle school counseling   Counseling in school Grades 6 through 8 or sometimes Grades 7 through 9 by counselors educated to deal with the developmental and situational aspects of children and their parents at this time of life. Middle school counseling is both *preventative,* including the use of *psychoeducational* processes, as well as *treatment* oriented.

middlescence   A term used to describe the pluses and minuses of middle adulthood.

midlife   Ages 40 to 65. See also *middle adulthood.*

midlife transition   A time in *midlife* when individuals evaluate and make necessary adjustments to their lives to compensate for physical or psychological factors. This period—a time when people must give up their dreams and come to terms with reality and their own mortality—can be difficult for some individuals.

Milan family therapy   An Italian approach to working with families formulated by the clinical research team of Mara Selvini-Palazzoli, Luigi Boscolo, Gianfranco Cecchin, and Guiliana Prata, who in the 1970s became the most prominent leaders in *systemic family therapy,* their own approach to *strategic family therapy.*

milieu therapy   A form of *therapy* that focuses on changing the *environment* rather than the person.

Miller Analogies Test (MAT)   A *power test* consisting of 100 complex analogy items drawn from a number of academic disciplines. The MAT is a screening devise for predicting success in advanced graduate work.

Millon Clinical Multiaxial Inventory-III (MCMI-III)   A widely used instrument employed to assess *DSM-IV* categories of *personality disorders* and clinical syndromes. The MCMI-II yields 20 clinical scales divided into three categories: basic *personality* patterns (e.g., *antisocial, narcissistic*), pathological personality disorders (e.g., *borderline, paranoid*), and clinical *symptom* syndromes (e.g., *anxiety, alcohol abuse*).

mimesis   A way of *joining* with a family in which the counselor becomes like the family in the manner or content of their *communications* (e.g., joking with a jovial family).

minimal encouragers   Brief supportive statements that convey attention and understanding (e.g., "I see," "Right," "Okay," "Hmm," and "I hear you"). Minimal encouragers help clients reveal and explore information, especially in the beginning stages of counseling.

minimization   Making an event less important than it was or is.

Minnesota Model of Alcohol Treatment   Also known as the Minnesota Model; a *treatment* approach that integrates *self-help* with professional counseling and involves three levels of treatment: *detoxification, rehabilitation,* and *aftercare.* The model is nationally publicized by the Hazelden Foundation (800-257-7810; http://www.hazelden.org/index.cfm).

Minnesota Multiphasic Personality Inventory-2 (MMPI-2)   A revision of one of the oldest and most widely used *personality tests* in the world. The MMPI-2 is a pencil-and-paper objective personality test designed to be administered to clients ages 16 and above. Test results, which are translated into *T scores,* provide *data* on nine *abnormal* or potentially abnormal dimensions (e.g., *hypochondriasis,* *depression, hysteria, paranoia,* and *schizophrenia*).

Minnesota Point of View   A student personnel point of view, originated by E. G. Williamson, that was directive in nature. See also *clinical counseling.*

minority   A group of persons who because of cultural or physical distinctions are fewer in number and less powerful in a *culture* or society than a *majority.* Minorities are distinctive in regard to such dimensions as *ethnicity, religion, race,* and so forth. Often minorities are discriminated against.

minority model   A model, especially in *rehabilitation counseling,* in which people with *disabilities* are assumed to be a minority group.

miracle question   A *brief therapy technique* in which the counselor asks the client a question that is intended to help the client obtain a clearer picture of when he or she will be better. The question is, If a miracle happened tonight and you woke up tomorrow and the problem was solved, what would you do differently?

mirror technique   A *psychodrama* activity in which the *protagonist* watches from offstage while an *auxiliary* ego mirrors the protagonist's posture, gesture, and words. This technique is often used in the action phase of psychodrama to help the protagonist see himself or herself more accurately.

misdemeanor   A minor criminal offense.

mistrust   One of the *outcomes* in Erik Erikson's *psychosocial* theory of *development* that occurs when from birth to 1 year of age, a child is given inconsistent treatment or experiences. Mistrust is the opposite of *trust.*

mixed thoughts   One of four rational emotive behavioral therapy (REBT) types of thoughts. Mixed thoughts contain elements of each of the other three thought processes. See also *rational emotive behavioral therapy (REBT) types of thoughts.*

MMPI-2   See *Minnesota Multiphasic Personality Inventory-2.*

mode   The *score* or *value* that occurs most frequently in a distribution of scores; a *measure of the central tendency.*

model minority   A *stereotype* description of *Asian Americans/Pacific Islanders* that is the result of the significant educational and economic success of some members of this minority group in the United States. In fact, many members of this population live in poverty or suffer psychological distress. See also *Asian Americans/Pacific Islanders.*

modeler of appropriate behavior   A group leader who, through passive and active demonstrations, consciously models actions that he or she thinks group members need to learn. The ways of *modeling* can include deliberate use of *self-disclosure, role plays,* speech patterns, and acts of creativity.

modeling   Observational learning; a social behavioral method used to teach complex behaviors in a relatively short period of time by copying or *imitating.* Modeling is a part of Albert Bandura's *social learning theory.* See also *imitation.*

monodrama   Also known as autodrama; a *psychodrama* technique in which the *protagonist* plays all the parts of an *enactment,* with no *auxiliary* egos used. The person may switch chairs or talk to different parts of the *self.*

monopolizer   A group member who, because of his or her own *anxiety,* dominates conversations by not giving other persons a chance to verbally participate.

monopolizing   Taking up the group's time by talking and not giving others in the group a chance to participate.

mood   An *emotional* state of mind.

mood disorders   Disorders that have an *emotional* base. Mood disorders are classified by the *DSM-IV* as those that are primarily of a *bipolar* or *depressive* nature.

Mooney Problem Check List   A check list that is used to identify client *problems* in different content areas (e.g., health, economic security, self-improvement, personality, courtship, family life, sex, religion, and education). Different forms are available from middle school through *adulthood.* No scale scores are given; rather, counselors are helped to identify and discuss different types of problems that may be affecting clients.

moral development   The processes in which individuals, starting in childhood, learn about and come to adopt principles of right and wrong. Through these processes, they come to enact acceptable social behavior and to resist unacceptable conduct. Lawrence Kohlberg's *theory* of moral development, based on Jean Piaget's cognitive development theory, serves as an example of the processes and *stages* involved in this process.

moral principle   The principle that guides the *superego* so that it operates according to what is ideal (i.e., the moral teachings of a child's parents). Under this principle, there is a striving to be perfect.

moral therapy   An approach of the late 1800s to working with mental patients that included using the arts and occupational therapy.

morality   The judgment or evaluation of action. Morality is associated with such words as "good," "bad," "right," "wrong," "ought," and "should."

morita   A Japanese therapy for treating *anxiety.* In this approach, a client's attention is directed away from the *self.* Absolute rest and avoidance of distractions is emphasized.

morphogenesis   The ability of an organism, such as a family, to modify its functioning to meet the changing demands of internal and external factors. Morphogenesis usually requires a *second-order change* rather than a *first-order change.* For example, instead of talking, family members may need to try new ways of behaving. See also *first-order change; second-order change.*

morphostasis   The tendency of a person or system to resist *change* and remain the same way.

motivation   Behaviors initiated by *needs* and directed toward *goals*. Motivation is biologically based and acquired.

mourning   **1.** The expression of sorrow and *grief* that follows a *loss*. Mourning varies according to the person and the degree of loss. Prolonged mourning may lead to *pathological* behavior.   **2.** The final stage in a *group*'s *development* in which group members reflect on their past experiences, process memories, evaluate what was learned, acknowledge ambivalent feelings, and engage in cognitive decision making. Mourning is also known as *adjourning* or *termination*.

MRI   See *Mental Research Institute*.

multiaxial assessment   A way of organizing information about a client's *symptoms* along a continuum of five axes that is used in the *DSM-IV*. See also *Axes of the DSM-IV*.

multicultural counseling   According to Paul Pedersen, two or more persons with different ways of perceiving their environment (or two different *worldviews*) working together in a helping *relationship*. Differences may be the result of specific socialization, development, or environmental factors or a combination of such factors. The debate in multicultural counseling centers is on how broadly to define the term "multicultural." One side advocates that the term be confined to *ethnic* groups; another side proposes that the term be more inclusive and include, for example, people who are *disabled*, people who are *aged*, or people with a different *sexual orientation*.

Multicultural Counseling Competencies and Standards   A set of competencies and standards for working with clients who are from *minority* backgrounds. Published in 1992 in the *Journal of Counseling and Development* by Derald Wing Sue, Patricia Arredondo, and Roderick J. McDavis, the competencies have been widely discussed and adopted by a number of counseling groups.

multigenerational family   A household that includes members of more than one genera-tion (e.g., a child, a parent, and a grandparent). See also *extended family*.

multigenerational transmission process   Coping strategies and patterns of coping with *stress* passed on from generation to generation in families. In poorly *differentiated* persons, problems may result, including *schizophrenia*.

multimodal distribution   A distribution in which two or more *scores* have the same (also the greatest) *frequency*.

multimodal method   The use of *verbal* and *nonverbal* means for conveying information.

multimodal therapy   A cognitive behavioral therapy introduced by Arnold Lazarus. A basic assumption of this approach is that clients are usually troubled by a multitude of specific *problems* that should be addressed by a multitude of specific *treatments*. Thus, multimodal therapy utilizes methods from various approaches in an effort to help people make positive changes in their *BASIC ID*. See also *BASIC ID*.

multiple baseline design   A *research design* that permits greater generalization of the results. There are three types of multiple baseline research designs: across individuals, across situations, and across behaviors. Each emphasizes a different focus. The common trait of all three is that *intervention* is initially employed with a select individual, situation, or behavior while the researcher continues to gather *baseline* data on other persons, situations, or behaviors.

multiple intelligence   The idea that there are a number of kinds of *intelligence*. They include verbal/linguistic, logical/mathematics, visual/spatial, body/kinesthetic, musical/rhythmical, interpersonal, and intrapersonal.

multiple personality disorder   A term that describes the appearance of more than one *personality* within a person. This *disorder* is rare and dramatic and is known as a *dissociative identity disorder* in the *DSM-IV*. It has been popularized in such books and movies as *The Three Faces of Eve* and *Sybil*.

multiple transferences   A phenomenon in psychoanalytic groups in which group members can experience *transference* feelings with others in the group as well as with the group leader.

multiple-family group therapy   A procedure for the treatment of several families together at the same time. Created by John Bell in the 1960s, multiple-family group therapy requires the use of coleaders and has many advantages, including the fact that families can often serve as co-therapists for each other.

MUM effect   An effect that occurs when a counselor avoids *confronting* a client's *behavior*. As a result, the counselor is less effective than he or she would be otherwise.

music therapy   The systematic and primary or adjunct use of music as a way of bringing about therapeutic change. See also *American Music Therapy Association (AMTA)*.

musterbation   A word coined by Albert Ellis that refers humorously to the irrational thought process of demanding. When musterbation occurs, clients think they must have everything go their way. This "must" theme

leads to emotional difficulties when life does not go the way clients think it must or should.

mutual-help group   Groups in which members mutually assist one another; another term for a *self-help group*.

Myers-Briggs Type Indicator (MBTI)   A pencil-and-paper self-administered personality test based on the *theory* of Carl Jung. The MBTI is widely used in a variety of settings and yields scores on four dimensions of an individual's *personality:* extroversion-introversion, sensing-intuition, thinking-feeling, and judgment-perception.

mystification   **1.** A deliberate distortion and misrepresentation of another person's experience by misinterpreting it.   **2.** A term used to describe how some families mask what is going on between family members by giving conflicting and contradictory explanations of events.

mythopoetic   A *treatment* for men developed by Robert Bly. Mythopoetic treatment involves the use of ceremony, drumming, storytelling/ poetry reading, physical movement, and imagery exercises designed to create a "ritual process."

n

N   A *symbol* for the number of people, *scores,* or objects in a group.

N of 1 research   The study of a single qualitative entity, such as a person. N of 1 research is usually employed in a historical study or a *case study*.

NA   See *Narcotics Anonymous*.

NACCMHC   See *National Academy of Certified Clinical Mental Health Counselors*.

NADT   See *National Association for Drama Therapy*.

NAPT   See *National Association for Poetry Therapy*.

narcissism   An excessive preoccupation with,

concern for, and love of oneself to the exclusion of others.

narcissistic group   A group that develops *cohesiveness* by encouraging hatred of an out-group or by creating an enemy. As a result, group members are able to overlook their own deficiencies by focusing on the deficiencies of the out-group.

narcolepsy   A *sleep disorder* characterized by irresistible attacks of sleep.

narcotics   A group of *depressant drugs,* such as *heroin,* methadone, codeine, morphine, *cocaine,* and *opium,* that relieve pain and *anxiety* but are addictive and may have major side effects (e.g., drowsiness, nausea, and vomiting). An overdose can produce shallow breathing, clammy skin, convulsions, coma, and possible death.

Narcotics Anonymous (NA) A *mutual-help group* based on the *Alcoholics Anonymous (AA)* philosophy and using a variation of AA's 12-step program. Narcotics Anonymous is inclusive in its definition of *addiction* and includes anyone who has used a mood-changing, mind-altering substance. NA's address is P.O. Box 9999, Van Nuys, CA 91409 (818-773-9999; http://www.wsoinc.com/).

narrative therapy A postmodern and *social construction* approach to change based on narrative reasoning, which is characterized by stories, meaningfulness, and liveliness. Counselors are seen as collaborators and masters of asking questions. According to the narrative family viewpoint, people live their lives by stories. The approach emphasizes developing unique and alternative stories in the hope that families will come up with novel options and strategies for living. In changing their stories, families are encouraged to *externalize problems* in order to solve them; blame is alleviated, and *dialogue* is generated as everyone works to solve a common problem. See also *reauthoring.*

NASP See *National Association of School Psychologists.*

NASW See *National Association of Social Workers.*

National Academy of Certified Clinical Mental Health Counselors (NACCMHC) A *certification* group originally established, in 1978, as an independently incorporated unit of *the American Mental Health Counseling Association (AMHCA)*. In 1993, the NACCMHC merged with the *National Board for Certified Counselors (NBCC)*. A professional who wishes to obtain the CCMHC credential must first become a *National Certified Counselor (NCC)*.

National Association for Drama Therapy (NADT) A nonprofit association incorpo-

rated in 1979 to establish and uphold high standards of professional competence and ethics among drama therapists. Its members use drama and theater to bring about symptom relief, emotional and physical integration, and personal growth. NADT is located at 5505 Connecticut Avenue, NW, Suite 280, Washington, DC. 20015 (202-966-7409; http://www.ncata.com/drama.html).

National Association for Poetry Therapy (NAPT) A nonprofit organization incorporated in 1981 and affiliated with the *National Coalition of Arts Therapies Associations (NCATA)*. Members are interested in the power of the healing word and represent a wide range of professional experience, schools of *therapy,* educational affiliations, artistic disciplines, and other fields of training in both mental and physical *health.* NAPT is located at 5505 Connecticut Avenue, NW, Suite 280, Washington, DC 20015 (202-966-2536; http://www.poetrytherapy.org/).

National Association of School Psychologists (NASP) The largest association of *school psychologists* in the world. Its purpose is to promote research-based programs that prevent problems, enhance independence, and promote optimal learning. NASP is located at 4340 East West Highway, Suite 402, Bethesda, MD 20814 (301-657-0270; http://www.naspweb.org/services.html).

National Association of Social Workers (NASW) The largest organization of professional *social workers.* NASW promotes, develops, and protects the practice of *social work* and social workers in the United States. NASW's address is 750 First Street, NE, Suite 700, Washington DC 20002-4241 (202-408-8600; http://www.naswdc.org).

National Board for Certified Counselors (NBCC) An independent not-for-profit credentialing body, founded in 1982, that established and now administers and monitors national counselor *certification.* NBCC identifies those counselors who have voluntarily sought and obtained certification and also maintains a register of certified counselors. This process recognizes counselors who have met predetermined NBCC standards in their training, experience, and performance on the *National Counselor Examination (NCE).* NBCC certifies counselors in the counseling specialties of career counseling, school counseling, clinical mental health counseling, and addictions counseling. NBCC's address is 3-D Terrace Way, Greensboro, NC 27403 (336-547-0607; http://www.nbcc.org/index.htm).

National Career Development Association (NCDA)   A division of the *American Counseling Association (ACA).* NCDA's mission is to promote the *career development* of all people over the *life span.* Their Internet address is http://www.ncda.org/.

National Certified Counselor (NCC)   A counselor who is certified nationally by the *National Board for Certified Counselors (NBCC).* Complete information on becoming an NCC can be found on the Internet at http://www.nbcc.org/info.htm.

National Clearinghouse for Alcohol and Drug Information (NCADI)   An information service of the Substance Abuse and Mental Health Services Administration (SAMHSA), a component of the U.S. Department of Health and Human Services. NCADI is the world's largest resource for current information and materials concerning *substance abuse.* Their address is P.O. Box 2345, Rockville, MD 20847-2345 (800-487-4889; http://www.health.org/index.htm).

National Coalition of Arts Therapies Associations (NCATA)   An alliance of professional associations, founded in 1979 and dedicated to the advancement of the arts as therapeutic modalities. NCATA represents members of six *creative arts therapies* associations: *art therapy, dance/movement therapy, drama therapy, music therapy, psychodrama,* and *poetry therapy.* The association is located at 2117 L Street, NW, Suite 274, Washington, DC. 20037

(202-678-6787; http://www.ncata.com/ home. html).

National Counselor Examination (NCE)   The exam a counselor must pass in order to become a *National Certified Counselor (NCC).* The exam is comprised of 200 multiple choice questions (recorded on a separate answer sheet) and scheduled for a 4-hour period. For more information, visit the *National Board for Certified Counselors (NBCC)* Web site at http://www.nbcc.org/info.htm.

National Defense Education Act (NDEA)   An enactment by Congress in 1958 following the Soviet Union's launching of its first space satellite, "Sputnik I." The act's primary purpose was to identify scientifically and academically talented students and promote their *development.* It provided funds through Title V-A for upgrading *school counseling* programs and through Title V-B to train counselors and established counseling and *guidance* institutes. In 1964, NDEA was extended to include *elementary school counseling.*

National Defense Education Institutes   Specialized training programs set up by the U.S. government at select colleges and universities from 1959 to 1967 that supported the expansion and improvement of *guidance* and *counseling* services nationally. These programs varied in length from long term (a year) to short term (a few months). They were located outside of regular academic programs and did much to increase the number of counselors in secondary and primary schools and the professional image of counseling.

National Employment Counselor Association (NECA)   One of the divisions of the *American Counseling Association (ACA).* NECA was originally established in 1966. Their Internet address is http://www.geocities.com/Athens/Acropolis/6491/neca.html.

National Institutes of Health (NIH)   The principal biomedical and behavioral research agency of the U.S. government. NIH is a component of the U.S. Department of Health and Human Services. Their address is 6001 Executive Boulevard, Room 8184, MSC 9663, Bethesda, MD 20892-9663 (301-443-4513; http://www.nih.gov/).

National Institute of Mental Health (NIMH) An institute that is a part of the *National Institutes of Health (NIH)*. The mission of NIMH is to diminish the burden of mental illness through research. NIMH's address is 6001 Executive Boulevard, Room 8184, MSC 9663, Bethesda, MD 20892-9663 (301-443-4279; http://www.nimh.nih.gov/).

National Rehabilitation Counseling Association (NRCA) The oldest association dedicated to promoting the rights of persons with *disabilities*. NRCA's mission is to provide *advocacy, awareness,* and *career* advancement for professionals in the fields of *rehabilitation*. Their address is 633 South Washington Street, Alexandria, VA 22314 (703-836-0850; http://www.nationalrehab.org/).

National Training Laboratories (NTL) A group training facility in Bethel, Maine, established by Kurt Lewin and associates in the late 1940s.

National Vocational Guidance Association (NVGA) The forerunner of the *American Counseling Association (ACA)*. Founded in 1913, it offered *guidance* literature and united those with an interest in vocational counseling for the first time.

Native American An individual who belongs to one of the 478 tribes recognized by the U.S. Bureau of Indian Affairs or another 52 tribes without official status. There is tremendous diversity among Native Americans, including 149 languages. However, there are common *identity* values among many Native Americans, including a harmony with nature, cooperation, holism, a concern with the present, and a reliance on one's extended family.

natural child Also known as the *free child*. A *transactional analysis* term for a division of the *child ego state*. It includes the sponta-neous, feeling-oriented, impulsive, pleasure-loving, creative, intuitive, and expressive part of one's personality. The natural child is responsive to *nonverbal* messages and can be self-centered.

natural consequences An *Adlerian counseling* concept that emphasizes living with the results of a particular ill-timed behavior that brings a negative result to the client (e.g., damaging an item through carelessness).

natural observation The collection of data on clients by observing them in their natural *environment*.

NBCC See *National Board for Certified Counselors*.

NCADI See *National Clearinghouse for Alcohol and Drug Information*.

NCATA See *National Coalition of Arts Therapies Associations*.

NCC See *National Certified Counselor*.

NCDA See *National Career Development Association*.

NCE See *National Counselor Examination*.

NDEA See *National Defense Education Act*.

NECA See *National Employment Counselor Association*.

necessary and sufficient conditions for change The conditions Carl Rogers outlined in 1957 that must be present for change to occur. These core conditions of counseling are *empathy, unconditional positive regard (acceptance),* and *congruence (genuineness)*.

need A necessity (e.g., food) that is required for one's welfare and overall well-being. A need may be psychological as well as physiological (e.g., love). The deficit of something that is a need motivates people to behave in ways to satisfy it.

needs assessment A structured *survey* that focuses on the systematic appraisal of the types, depth, and scope of problems or concerns within a specific *population*. Counselors in school and community settings can obtain a great deal of information about the populations they serve through the regular use of needs assessments.

negative feedback The input of corrective information to a person or a *system* in order to help keep a person or a system functioning within prescribed limits. Negative feedback diminishes or stops output.

negative group variables Factors in groups that include but are not limited to avoiding *conflict,* abdicating group responsibilities, group members anesthetizing themselves to contradictions within the group, and the group becoming *narcissistic.*

negative reinforcement An aversive stimulus whose removal is contingent upon performance of a desired action. The removal of the aversive stimulus is reinforcing for the person involved. For example, a mother nags her daughter until the daughter washes the dishes. The nagging could be viewed as a negative reinforcer, especially if peace and quiet is valued by the daughter.

negative thoughts One of four rational emotive behavioral therapy (REBT) types of thoughts. Negative thoughts concentrate on painful or disappointing aspects of an event. See also *rational emotive behavioral therapy (REBT) types of thoughts.*

neglect Omission of responsibilities; not paying attention to or taking care of. Children in neglect situations are often left to take care of themselves in regard to basic needs, such as food, shelter, hygiene, medical attention, or supervision.

negligence Failure on the part of a helping professional (e.g., a counselor) to take due care within accepted standards of *treatment.*

neo-Freudian Followers of Sigmund Freud who put more emphasis than Freud did on *adulthood* and *defense mechanisms.* Leading neo-Freudians include Anna Freud, Harry Stack Sullivan, Karen Horney, and Eric Fromm.

neurolinguistics programming (NLP) A *theory* of *communications* originated by Richard Bandler and John Grinder. Human behavior is understood by NLP practitioners as the way people process information in their environment through using one or more dominant senses. For example, a person with a dominant auditory ability might be one who picks up information best through listening.

neurosis **1.** In *psychoanalysis,* a functional *disorder* of the nervous system that is psychological rather than organic in nature; a disruption of *ego* functions. **2.** In present day treatment, an antiquated but still widely used term to describe individuals who have some emotional disorders but who are not psychotic. The word "disorder" is now used in place of "neurotic" when a *diagnosis* is made using the *DSM-IV.*

neutral cognitions One of four rational emotive behavioral therapy (REBT) types of thoughts. Neutral cognitions are those that are neither positive nor negative. See also *rational emotive behavioral therapy (REBT) types of thoughts.*

new epistemology An idea from the general *systems* approach of Gregory Bateson; also referred to as *cybernetics.* New epistemology emphasizes that the impact of the family counselor's inclusion and participation in a family system must be incorporated into *family therapy.* This emphasis is known as *second-order cybernetics.*

nicotine A *stimulant drug* found in tobacco products that produces a physical dependence and a euphoria in the brain similar to that of *amphetamines* and morphine. Nicotine is dangerous to the health of those addicted to it and is a major cause of cardiovascular disease, cancer, obstructive lung disease, and complications during pregnancy.

NIMH See *National Institute of Mental Health.*

NLP See *neurolinguistic programming.*

nominal scale The assigning of numbers for categories that represent the way individuals differ (e.g., the number 1 is assigned to European Americans, 2 to African Americans, 3 to Asian Americans, 4 to Native Americans, and 5 to Hispanics). A nominal scale simply classifies without ordering.

nominal-group technique A six-step process involving the generation both verbally and in writing of a number of ideas/solutions connected with a *problem*. The process requires less open exposure of members than *brainstorming;* ends with a vote, discussion, and revote on priorities for resolving a situation; and takes between 45 minutes and 1.5 hours. Although this group procedure does not lend itself to statistical analysis and may not yield a representative sample of opinion, it is an enjoyable process and a fairly quick and efficient way for counselors to obtain a good idea of major issues.

nondevelopmental factors Events in the life of clients that are unpredictable but important in counseling (e.g., the nature of a *problem,* the suddenness of its appearance, the intensity of its severity, and the present *coping* skills).

nondirective counseling See *nondirective therapy.*

nondirective therapy See *client-centered counseling; person-centered counseling.*

nonevent The nonmaterialization of an expected occurrence in life, such as getting married, having children, or advancing in one's career.

nonlinear causality See *circular causality.*

nonlinear thinking See *circular causality.*

nonmaleficence An *ethical principle* of helping that focuses on not inflicting harm on the *helpee.* The phrase "first do no harm" is one that is often used in defining nonmaleficence.

nonparametric statistics Statistical tests that are used when there is an assumption of sharp dichotomies but not of a *normal curve* distribution. Nonparametric *tests* require larger sample sizes in order to yield a level of significance similar to *parametric* tests. Examples of nonparametric tests are the Spearman rank-order correlation and *chi-square.*

nonsummativity The idea that a *family* is greater than the sum of its parts, making it necessary to examine the patterns within a family rather than the actions of any specific family member alone.

nontraditional career A *career* in which people of one gender are not usually employed.

nonverbal cues *Body language,* such as gestures, and physical appearance that make up more than 50% of the messages communicated in social relationships. Nonverbal behaviors are usually perceived as more honest and less subject to manipulation than verbal behaviors.

non-zero-sum game A game based on the assumption that there can be two winners and on the principle of *equitability.* At its best, marriage is a non-zero-sum-game in which disagreements and differences occur without one spouse being right (a winner) and the other being wrong (a loser). It is the opposite of *zero-sum games.*

noogenic neurosis A *disorder* characterized by Victor Frankl as the feeling that one has nothing to live for. This disorder is found in self-indulgent people who experience an *existential vacuum* (a sense that life has lost all meaning) and, in the extreme, feel a sense of normlessness and valuelessness.

norm Formal and informal *rules* or standards of behavior held to by a group or society; the expected behavior within a society.

norm group The group on which a *test* is *standardized.*

normal curve See *bell-shaped curve.*

normal distribution A smooth *bell-shaped curve frequency distribution;* the underlying basis for *inferential statistics.* Large group *test* results are frequently distributed in this way with the greatest number of cases near the *mean* and the frequency of cases trailing off on either side of the mean.

norming The third stage of *group development* (following *forming* and *storming*) in which members form an *identity* as a *group* and a sense of "we-ness" (i.e., *cohesion*). Norming, like storming, lasts only for a few sessions; it sets the pattern for *performing* (i.e., working), which is the fourth stage.

norm-referenced test A test in which the *score* is compared to that of other members of a *group. Standardized tests* are norm-referenced.

norms **1.** *Rules* and standards of behavior. Two types of norms important in counseling are *prescriptive norms* and *proscriptive norms.* **2.** The *average* performance and varying degrees of deviation of a set of test scores standardized on a representative *sample* that provide a basis for interpreting the scores of other individuals or groups.

no-shows Clients who do not keep their appointments and do not notify the counselor beforehand that they will miss their appointments.

now An important concept in *gestalt therapy* and other humanistic counseling approaches. Now can be expressed in the following formula: Now = experience = awareness = reality. The past is no more and the future not yet. Only the now exists.

NRCA See *National Rehabilitation Counseling Association.*

NTL See *National Training Laboratories.*

nuclear family A core family unit of husband, wife, and their children.

null hypothesis A hypothesis used in *experimental research* that predicts there will be no *significant difference* between *experimental* and *control group* outcomes.

nurturing parent A *transactional analysis* term that describes the positive aspect of the *parent ego state* in which nurturing behaviors toward others are displayed.

NVGA See *National Vocational Guidance Association.*

O

OA See *Overeaters Anonymous.*

object A term in *object relations* theory for a *significant other* (e.g., a mother) with whom a child forms an interactional, emotional bond.

object loss A *psychoanalysis* term for the loss of love from an external object.

object permanence Jean Piaget's idea of an understanding by infants that *objects,* such as people, do not disappear once they are out of sight. This ability is acquired in the *sensorimotor stage* of *development.*

object relations A *psychoanalytic* theory that explains *relationships* across generations. According to this theory, human beings have a fundamental *motivation* to seek *objects,* that is people, in relationships, starting at birth. An individual's relationships in later life are based on parent-child interactions and the *internalization* of images that accompany early object interaction.

objective A term that refers to *research, theory,* or experimental *methods* dealing with observable events that are not affected by the observer.

objective test A test that yields *scores* that are independent of any opinion or judgment of the scorer. An objective test is usually multiple choice in nature. Examples include the *Minnesota Multiphasic Personality Inventory-2 (MMPI-2),* the *Myers-Briggs Type Indicator (MBTI),* and the *Edwards Personal Preference Schedule (EPPS).*

observation method A research procedure in which the investigator directly observes a person or *environment* for periods of time and records *data* on what is seen.

observational learning See *imitation.*

obsession A persistent and uncontrollable thought or idea.

obsessive-compulsive personality disorder A disorder, listed under the broader category in the *DSM-IV* of *anxiety disorders,* characterized by perfectionist behavior, insistence on having others do things a certain way, preoccupation with trivial matters and rules, inability to make decisions or prioritize, and a limited ability to express warmth or tenderness.

occupation   A group of similar *positions* found in different industries or organizations (e.g., a programmer or a manager).

Occupational Outlook Handbook (OOH) A U.S. government reference book that contains information (e.g., job descriptions, job outlook, salaries) on select *occupations*.

occupational therapist   A *helping professional* who focuses on helping people with *disabilities* find useful and productive employment.

odd-even reliability   The *correlation* between the total *score* on the odd-numbered and even-numbered items on a *test*.

Oedipus complex   A conflict that occurs during the *phallic stage* (ages 3 to 5) of *psychosexual* development. According to the theory, during this stage, boys have a sexual desire for or *erotic* interest in their mothers together with hostile feelings for and fear of castration by their fathers. The complex is resolved when boys identify with their fathers and vicariously possess their mothers through such an identity. The Oedipus complex is the opposite of the *Electra complex,* a similar phenomenon in girls.

offender counseling   Counseling that is focused on working with persons who violate the *laws* of society and are in correctional or prison facilities or on probation. It is also referred to as *correctional counseling.*

OK positions   The four life positions in *transactional analysis* theory that influence a person's interactions with others. The positions are (1) "I'm OK; you're OK" (a "get-on-with" position); (2) "I'm OK; you're not OK" (a "get-away-from" position); (3) "I'm not OK; you're OK" (a "get-nowhere-with" position); and (4) "I'm not OK; you're not OK" (a "get-rid-of" position). Everyone operates from each of these four positions at various times, but well-functioning individuals learn to recognize

unhealthy positions and modify thoughts and behaviors accordingly. See also *scripts.*

old epistemology   Dated ideas that no longer fit a current situation.

oldest old   Ages 85 and older.

old-old   Ages 74 to 84.

old-timer   A more experienced member of a *self-help group.*

OLSAT   See *Otis-Lennon School Ability Test.*

omission   A term used in connection with malpractice for not doing something that should have been done.

omnibus test   A test (e.g., the *Otis-Lennon School Ability Test*) that measures a variety of mental operations.

ontology   Any matter related to the study or science of being or existence.

OOH   See *Occupational Outlook Handbook.*

open marriage   A marital arrangement in which marital *rules* and *relationships,* including sexual *fidelity,* are constantly being worked out as the couple focuses on their independence and *autonomy.*

open system   A *system* with relatively permeable boundaries that exchanges information with the world outside of it.

open-ended group   A group that admits new members at any time.

open-ended question   A question that leads to *self-exploration* into the "what" and "how" of behavior. Open-ended questions invite more than a one- or two-word response. See also *questioning.*

operant   B. F. Skinner's term for a *response.*

operant conditioning   A type of *learning,* originating out of research by B. F. Skinner, which emphasizes that behavior is a function of its *consequences.* The acquisition or elimination of a response is a function of *rewards* and *punishments.* The way people operate in regard to their *environments* is dependent on the consequences of their actions.

operation   Jean Piaget's term for a type of mental activity or thought process. An operation follows logical *rules,* whereas a preoperation is intuitive, *egocentric,* and less logical.

opium   A narcotic *drug* extracted from poppies and processed to make other drugs (e.g., morphine, codeine, and *heroin*).

oral personality   A term from *psychoanalytic* theory that describes a person whose satisfaction in life comes from orally oriented activities such as smoking, drinking, eating, and talking.

oral stage   The first stage in Sigmund Freud's *psychosexual* stages of development. This stage occurs during the first year of life. The infant derives pleasure from orally oriented activities such as sucking, biting, and swallowing.

ordeal   A *strategic family therapy* process, developed by Jay Haley, in which the counselor assigns a family or family member(s) the task of performing an activity (i.e., an ordeal) whenever the family or individuals involved display a *symptom* they are trying to eliminate. The ordeal is a constructive or neutral *behavior* (e.g., doing exercise) but not an activity that those involved want to engage in.

ordinal position   See *birth order.*

ordinal scale   A scale that orders or ranks scores or individuals according to some characteristic.

organism   A form of life composed of mutually dependent parts and processes standing in mutual interaction.

organismic   A descriptive term for a person as a whole entity with interrelated and interdependent parts.

orthopsychiatry   An interdisciplinary field that emphasizes the development of *mental health* in human life and the *prevention* of mental illness.

Otis-Lennon School Ability Test (OLSAT) One of the most widely used group-administered general *intelligence tests* with levels for primary through high school grades. The OLSAT is employed primarily for predicting success in cognitive and school-related areas.

outcome   The results of counseling. Outcome in counseling is usually linked to preplanned *goals* and *objectives* (i.e., a *treatment contract*) by counselors and clients.

outcome research   Research that emphasizes results rather than the factors producing them. It is typified by *measurement* before and after treatment on specified *dependent variables.* An example of outcome research is the effect of *person-centered counseling* on depressed persons.

outpatient   A client who receives counseling services in a nonresidential setting.

overcompensation   The continuous striving by a client to overcome or offset a perceived or actual weakness. *Motivation* for this striving comes from feelings of *inferiority.*

overcorrection   A *technique* in which a client first restores the *environment* to its natural state and then makes it "better than normal." For example, children who throw food in the lunchroom might be required to clean up their mess and wax the floor.

overculturalization   The mistaking of people's reactions to poverty and *discrimination* for their cultural patterns.

Overeaters Anonymous (OA)   A *mutual-help group* for individuals with compulsive eating disorders. The organization is based on the philosophy of *Alcoholics Anonymous (AA)* and a variation of AA's 12-step program. OA's address is 6075 Zenith Court, NE, Rio Rancho, NM 87124 (505-891-2664; http://www. overeatersanonymous.org/).

overgeneralization   Applying *learning* from a particular incident too broadly so that matters related to that incident are viewed as being the same in all circumstances or matters.

overidentification   A form of *countertransference* in which the counselor loses the ability to remain emotionally distant from the client.

overlearning   *Learning* material through repetition and practice to a point well beyond simple mastery.

overt behavior   An observable act.

PA   See *Parents Anonymous.*

Pacific Islander   See *Asian American/Pacific Islander.*

panic attack   See *panic disorder.*

panic disorder   Also known as a *panic attack;* the sudden onset of intense fear and anxiety that is completely unexpected and not linked to any environmental event. A panic disorder is accompanied by such symptoms as sweating, dizziness, chills, nausea, and fear of losing control. Panic disorders usually last only a few minutes.

paradox   1. A form of *treatment* in which counselors give clients permission to do what they were going to do anyway, thereby lowering client *resistance* to treatment and increasing the likelihood of *change.*   **2.** A form of treatment in which counselors ask resistant clients to do the opposite of what would be an ideal treatment in the hope that they will disobey and as a result get better.

parallel relationships   Relationships in which both complementary and symmetrical exchanges occur as appropriate.

parallel reliability   A type of *reliability* test in which two equivalent forms of the same test are administered to see how closely they *correlate.* See also *equivalence.*

parameter   The descriptive measure of a *population* (e.g., *mean, standard deviation*).

parametric statistics   Statistical tests used when it is thought that the *population* being described has evenly distributed characteristics that could be represented by a *bell-shaped curve.* An example of a parametric statistical test is a *t-test.*

paranoia   An unsubstantiated and unfounded suspicion of others and the fear that one is being watched, followed, talked about, and persecuted. In the extreme, paranoia can become a *personality disorder* in which the person becomes extremely distrustful and suspicious of others.

paraphilias   *Sexual and gender identity disorders* characterized by sexual urges and behaviors that interfere with social adjustment and relationships (e.g., *exhibitionism, fetishism, voyeurism, pedophilia,* and sexual *sadism*). Paraphilias are difficult to treat.

paraphrasing   A reflective statement by the counselor of what a client has said but restated in different words and in a nonjudgmental way. Paraphrasing helps a client know that the counselor is aware of the client's perspective.

paraprofessional   A category of mental health workers who do not have terminal degrees in counseling or other *helping professions* but who provide direct services to clients to supplement the services of professionals (e.g., a nurse's aide).

parent education group   A group that is *psychoeducational* in nature and that focuses on the raising of children. Rudolph Driekurs began setting up these groups in the 1950s using Alfred Adler's *theory* and ideas.

Parent Effectiveness Training (PET)   Thomas Gordon's parent education program that emphasizes *communication* skills. In PET, parents are encouraged to recognize their positive and negative feelings toward their children and come to terms with their own humanness. A major hypothesis of this approach is that *active listening* and *acceptance* will decrease family *conflicts* and promote individual growth.

parent ego state   A *transactional analysis* term for the controlling, limit setting, and rule making part of the *personality.* The parent ego state is dualistic: It is both nurturing and critical (or controlling). The function of the *critical parent* is to store and dispense the rules and protection for living. The function of the *nurturing parent* is to provide affectionate care and attention.

parentified child   A child who is forced to give up *childhood* and act like an adult parent even though he or she lacks the knowledge and skills to do so.

Parents Anonymous (PA)   A national mutual-help organization with local chapters patterned after *Alcoholics Anonymous (AA)* to help parents who are at risk for abusing their children. PA's address is 675 West Foothill Boulevard, Suite 220, Claremont, CA 91711-3475 (909-621-6184; http://www.ten97.com/pa/pa.htm).

Parents Without Partners (PWP)   A national mutual-help organization with local chapters that help single parents and their children deal with the realities of *single-parent family* life in educational and experiential ways. PWP's address is 401 North Michigan Avenue, Chicago, IL 60611-4267 (312-644-6610; http://www.parentswithoutpartners.org/).

parent-skills training   An educational model of teaching parent skills in which counselors serve as social learning educators whose prime responsibility is to change, through experiential activities as well as discussions, a parent's response to a child. Examples of parent-skills training programs are *Parent Effectiveness Training (PET)* and *Systematic Training for Effective Parenting (STEP)*.

parsimony   The idea that explanations of *behavior* should be as simple as possible and consistent with observations.

partial reinforcement   Also known as *intermittent reinforcement;* a *schedule of reinforcement* used to maintain a *behavior,* once it is established, through *continuous reinforcement.* In partial reinforcement, a *reward* is given at intervals that vary but are frequent enough to maintain the client's interest.

passive-aggressive behavior   Behavior that is covertly angry but overtly docile. A person with a passive-aggressive personality tends to pout and procrastinate as well as be obstruc-

tive, obstinate, and inefficient. Anger is often *unconscious* or hidden just below the surface.

pastimes   A *transactional analysis* term for superficial exchanges between people that allow them to spend time together without getting involved at a deeper level.

pastoral counseling   A specialized form of counseling rendered by clergy who have been trained in counseling and who also deal with spiritual matters. See also *American Association of Pastoral Counselors (AAPC)*.

pat on the back   A closing group exercise in which members draw the outline of their hands on a piece of paper that is then taped on their backs. Other group members then write positive and constructive closing comments about the person on the hand outline.

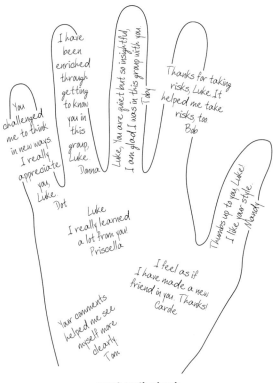

a pat on the back

pathological view of minorities   The view that some cultural *minorities* can never be helped sufficiently to fit in with the *majority* culture.

pathology   The study of disease, *disorders,* and *dysfunction.*

patient   The term used in the *medical model* for clients or counselees who receive help or treatment.

PCP   See *phencyclidine hydrochloride.*

Peabody Picture Vocabulary Test Revised (PPVT-R)   An individually administered *test* of vocabulary that is sometimes used as an abbreviated test of general *ability.* The PPVT-R consists of 175 plates with four pictures each. The examinee points to the picture that best illustrates a *stimulus* word given by the examiner.

peak experiences   Abraham Maslow's term for the both mystic and intense emotional feelings of joy experienced by *self-actualizing* persons. At such times, self-actualizing people feel at one with the world.

pedophilia   A disorder that can take a number of forms but, in all cases, involves gratification on the part of an adult through sexual contact with a child. Most pedophiles are males; most victims of pedophilia are female children.

peer   A person who is of equal status to another.

peer group   A group of equals along some notable dimension such as social status, intelligence, or age.

peer helpers   Students in educational settings who are specially trained to help their peers in dealing with developmental or situational concerns both by listening and referring them to appropriate sources for help.

peer supervision   Consulting between practitioners of equal status on a regular basis concerning issues and treatment of difficult clients or situations.

peer-counselor model   An aspect of *rehabilitation counseling* in which it is assumed that people with direct experience with a *disability* are the most capable of *helping* individuals with recently acquired disabilities.

penis envy   Sigmund Freud's idea that during the *phallic stage* girls initially envy boys for

their external sex organ and wish one for themselves.

people of color   A term used to describe individuals in the United States other than those who are white European-North Americans.

percentile   A value on a scale of 100 that indicates the percentage of cases at or below a given *score.* Percentile scores are often expressed as *deciles* and *quartiles.*

percentile ranks   A widely used *method* for showing the relative position of a person's score on a *norm-referenced* test. Percentile rankings range from 1 to 99, with a percentile rank of 50 being the *median.* Percentile ranks provide descriptive interpretation clearly and concisely by showing the percentage of persons in a reference group who score lower than a targeted person.

perception   The sensing of information through any of the five senses (i.e., sight, sound, touch, taste, and smell).

performance test   A test in which a person is required to make motor responses other than simple writing in order to show a certain skill or competence level. Performance tests are sometimes known as *work samples.*

performing   The fourth stage of *group development,* in which members become involved with each other and strive to achieve certain *goals.*

permission   **1.** Consent by a client to share information, usually records, with another professional.   **2.** A *transactional analysis* term for giving group members directives to behave against the *injunctions* of their parents.

permission form   A form used in clinical settings for clients to fill in and sign stating that they *consent* to the sharing of their *records* with another professional. *Legal* and *ethical* considerations mandate that permission forms be filled out and signed by the *client* any time a client's record is shared.

persecutor   A person in a *transactional analysis game* who appears to cause *problems.*

persona   Carl Jung's term for the *conscious,* outward, social appearances of people in everyday interactions. The persona is like a mask a person wears, especially in public.

personal growth A term that stresses *development* as a result of experiences such as travel or encounter and interaction with others.

personal growth group See *basic encounter group*.

personal growth issues Perceived deficits or needs within a person.

Personal Orientation Inventory (POI) A *personality test* created by Everett L. Shostrom. The POI is designed to measure *values* and *behavior* that seem to be of importance in the development of *self-actualizing* persons.

personal power A source of power employed more frequently in mature relationship situations. It is derived from the individual and his or her ability to persuade others to follow a select course of action. See also *power to resolve conflict*.

personal unconscious See *collective unconscious*.

personality A global concept that includes all the physical, mental, emotional, and social characteristics of someone that make that person unique.

personality disorders Long-standing, deeply ingrained, *maladaptive* behaviors that take many forms (e.g., *antisocial, narcissistic, obsessive-compulsive*). Personality disorders are highly *resistant* to *treatment*. They are listed on Axis II in the *DSM-IV multiaxial assessment* system.

personality inventory Any of a number of objective or projective methods that analyze one or more aspects of an individual's *personality* (e.g., *attitudes, temperament, values*). Examples of methods include the *California Psychological Inventory (CPI)* and the *Rorschach inkblot test*.

personality test Any of several methods (e.g., checklists, personality inventories, and projective techniques) of analyzing personality. A personality test may be either objective or projective.

person-centered counseling The name for the theory of counseling originated by Carl Rogers. It was previously known as *nondirective* and *client-centered therapy*.

person-environment interaction A *theory* that refers to the *congruence* between clients and their environments. Congruence is believed to lead to satisfaction, stability, and, perhaps, development.

Personnel and Guidance Journal The name of the flagship journal of the *American Counseling Association (ACA)* from 1952 to 1984.

persuasion The process of trying to positively influence a client to take needed action. Two direct persuasion techniques employed in counseling are the *foot in the door* and the *door in the face*.

PET See *Parent Effectiveness Training*.

phallic stage The third stage in Freud's stages of *psychosexual development*. In this stage, in which the chief zones of pleasure are the genitalia, children (between ages 3 to 5) attempt to resolve their sexual identities by working through conflicts (for boys, the *Oedipus complex;* for girls, the *Electra complex*). If this stage of psychosexual development is not resolved, individuals will experience future *intrapersonal* and *interpersonal* difficulties. Freud thought the basic ingredients of the adult *personality* had formed by the end of the phallic stage.

pharmacotherapy The *treatment* of *mental disorders* with prescribed medications.

phase of life A predictable and developmental transition in the *life cycle* such as entering school or retiring.

phases of sexual responsiveness Periods of sexual responsiveness including excitement, plateau, orgasm, and resolution.

phencyclidine hydrochloride An illegal *hallucinogenic drug* also known as PCP and angel dust. A water-soluble white powder substance, it can be ingested a number of ways (e.g., orally, smoked, snorted, or intravenously injected). It produces euphoria and numbness when taken in low dosages but may produce deliriums, convulsions, and violent behavior when taken in higher dosages.

phenomenological perspective   The idea that what is important is the person's perception of reality rather than an event itself.

phenomenology   The theory that individuals behave according to the way they perceive their worlds.

phenomenon   Anything that is perceived by an observer.

phobia   An irrational, exaggerated, and/or unrealistic fear of a specific object or situation.

phobic layer   A term in *gestalt therapy* for the client's attempt to avoid recognition of the aspects of the self that he or she would prefer to deny.

phony layer   A term in *gestalt therapy* for a client's pretense to be something that he or she is not.

photocounseling   The use of photography as the primary or adjunct means of working therapeutically with a client.

physiological characteristics   Characteristics such as skin and eye color, shape of head, and so forth.

pie chart   A type of *graph* used to display the percentage of *data* in a category. A pie chart is circular in form with a wedge of the circle identified with each category.

pilot study   A small experimental study that precedes a larger study in order to test proposed methodologies.

placater   One of Virginia Satir's four roles that a person takes when the person is not *leveling* (i.e., communicating clearly and directly). A placater is characterized as a person who avoids *conflict* at the cost of his or her integrity. Therefore, a placater may ingratiate, apologize, or eschew disagreement when just the opposite behavior is called for.

placebo   A sham treatment that has no known therapeutic value and is given in double blind research to test whether the targeted *treat-*

ment has an impact. Placebos are often given in medical research in the form of pills that look identical to the drug being tested.

placement   The locating and placing of people in *jobs*. A placement service is often performed by *rehabilitation counselors*.

play   Activities that have no goal other than the enjoyment that is derived from them.

play therapy   The use of *play* as a means of establishing rapport, uncovering what is troubling a child, and bringing about resolution. There are a number of theoretical approaches to play therapy. Play therapy takes place in a playroom that is specially designed, decorated, and furnished with the toys and equipment children need to use as tools for the dramatic scenes they direct with their counselors.

pleasure principle   The principle by which the *id* operates in Freud's schema of the *personality*. The id is dominated by the pleasure principle, seeking immediate gratification of its needs and avoiding unpleasantness or pain. It is the opposite of the *reality principle*.

pluralism   See *cultural diversity*.

POCA   See *Public Offender Counselor Association*.

poetry therapy   The use of the language arts as a primary or adjunct means of working with clients in treatment. The goals of poetry therapy are to promote understanding of the *self* and the individual in society, to accept and *change* feelings and behavior, and to enhance mental and social *wellness*. See also *National Association for Poetry Therapy (NAPT)*.

POI   See *Personal Orientation Inventory*.

polarization   The division of a group into different and opposing *subgroups* or camps. Such a division can lead to a stalemate, *conflict,* or the forming of *coalitions*.

polysubstance abuse   The abuse of two or more *substances* simultaneously.

population   A statistical term for all members of some defined group.

position   A group of tasks performed by one person.

position power A source of power most often used when there are immature relationships between individuals. Position power is derived from the status of people's titles. See also *power to resolve conflict.*

positioning *Acceptance* and exaggeration by counselors of what clients are saying. If conducted properly, positioning helps clients see the *absurdity* in what they are doing. Positioning is often used in *family counseling.*

positive addiction William Glasser's idea that some activities, such as meditation and jogging, may be therapeutically beneficial.

positive connotation A type of *reframing* in which a client's behavior is labeled as benevolent and motivated by good intentions.

positive correlation A pattern of points in a *scattergram* that tend to run from lower left to upper right and to occur when high scores on one *variable* are associated with high scores on the other variable.

positive feedback Any *stimulus* that when added to a situation increases the likelihood that a *response* will occur.

positive regard Love, *warmth, acceptance,* and respect given to a client by the counselor.

positive reinforcer A material (e.g., food, money, medals) or a social action (e.g., smile, praise) that individuals find significant and rewarding and are willing to work for.

positive risk A unilateral action not dependent on another for success. See also *caring days.*

positive thoughts One of four rational emotive behavioral therapy (REBT) types of thoughts. Positive thoughts focus on helpful aspects of an event. See also *rational emotive behavioral therapy (REBT) thoughts.*

positive wellness Health-related activities that are both *preventive* and *remedial* and have a therapeutic value to individuals who practice them consistently. Such activities include eating natural foods, taking vitamins, going to a health spa, *meditating,* participating in regular exercise, and exploring a variety of *humanistic* and *transpersonal* approaches to *helping.*

possibility therapy See *solution-focused family therapy.*

postconventional morality The last two stages of Lawrence Kohlberg's six stages of *moral development,* in which behavior is governed by a set of consciously held *ethical principles.* See also *moral development.*

posttest The administration of a *questionnaire* to a person after he or she has received *treatment.* Comparison is made between *pretest* and posttest results.

posttraumatic stress disorder (PTSD) A *disorder* following a *trauma* (e.g., an accident, rape). PTSD is characterized by a cluster of *symptoms* such as sleep disturbance, nightmares, *flashbacks,* and *anxiety.*

pot A slang term for *marijuana.*

potency The use of appropriate counseling *techniques* in certain situations in order to bring about *change.*

power **1.** The ability to get something done. In families, power is related to both *authority and* responsibility. **2.** A term in research for the ability of a statistical test to find a difference in *data* when there is one.

power test A test in which ample time is provided so that those taking it can complete all the items. The items are usually arranged in order from easiest to most difficult (though most are difficult). Examples include *intelligence, achievement,* and *aptitude* tests.

power to resolve conflict A strategy that involves the imposition of someone's will on someone else. The source of power may either be derived from one's position *(position power)* or one's person *(personal power).* By using power, a leader is able to quickly resolve a crisis, but the use of power creates a *win-lose atmosphere.*

PPO See *preferred provider organization.*

PPVT-R See *Peabody Picture Vocabulary Test-Revised.*

practicum A supervised short-term experience in which counselors in training learn to do counseling through *supervision*. A practicum experience is a prerequisite to an *internship*.

preadolescents   Ages 8 to 12 years.

preauthorization   The authorization by an insurance company or *managed care* provider to treat a client before the client is given treatment. In many cases, preauthorization is necessary for reimbursement.

preconscious   A term in *psychoanalytic* theory for the area of the mind in which materials not immediately available can be recalled to *awareness* if given enough prompting.

preconventional morality   The first two stages in Lawrence Kohlberg's six-stage theory of *moral development*. See also *moral development*.

predictive validity   A type of *validity* that exists when the *criterion* for what a *test* is measuring is not available until after the test is administered.

predisposition   The tendency to develop in a certain way under the right conditions. For example, the child of schizophrenics may be predisposed to develop schizophrenia especially if placed in a stressful and nonsupportive environment.

preferred provider organization (PPO)   A health care organization in which the PPO contracts with select mental health practitioners, physicians, and hospitals in a community for services. Clients can go outside the PPO network (unlike in an HMO), although they pay more for a non-network provider's services. See also *managed care*.

pregenital stages   The first three stages (*oral, anal,* and *phallic*) of Sigmund Freud's stages of *psychosexual* development.

prejudice   Preconceived opinions or judgment about someone or something formed without just grounds or sufficient knowledge. Prejudice thinking is often adversarial, demeaning, and degrading.

Premack principle   David Premack's behavioral intervention. The principle states that *behavior* that occurs at a naturally high rate of *frequency* may be used to *reinforce* behavior that occurs at a naturally low rate. Thus, a client may be assigned *homework* in which he or she must first do less pleasant tasks, such as study, before being allowed to engage in *leisure* activities, such as *play*.

premature termination   Termination that occurs when individual clients, couples, or families abruptly quit counseling without having achieved preset *goals* or when counselors must end the experience because of unexpected situations (e.g., illness, extended and unexpected family emergencies). Premature termination makes it difficult for clients and counselors to reach *closure* in regard to clinical concerns or *relationships*.

preoperational stage   The second stage of development in Jean Piaget's four stage theory of *cognitive development*. The preoperational stage (lasting from age 2 to age 7 or 8) is marked by a huge increase in a child's vocabulary and creative imagination and consists of two substages: *intuitive thinking* and *preconceptual thinking*.

preschool- and early school-aged children   Children between the ages of 5 and 9.

prescribing the symptom   A type of *paradox* in which clients are asked to continue doing as they have done. This technique often leads to clients either admitting they have control over a *symptom* or giving it up.

prescriptive norms   *Norms* that describe the kinds of behaviors that should be performed. See also *norms*.

presenting problem   The initial concern a client presents as a reason for coming to counseling.

pretend technique   A technique originated by Cloe Madanes in which the counselor asks clients to pretend to enact a troublesome behavior (e.g., a fight with one's spouse). By acting as if they were so engaged, clients learn to control a once involuntary action.

pretest   A *test* administered to a client before *treatment* to establish a *baseline*. Pretest results are compared to *posttest* results.

prevention   The use by counselors of educational or behavioral means (e.g., instruction or rehearsal) to help clients avoid or minimize potential *problems.*

primacy effect   The idea that all things being equal, those things that are learned first in a sequence are remembered best. It is the opposite of, but complementary to, the *recency effect.*

primal horde   Sigmund Freud's conceptualization of a *group.* Freud thought leaders within the group function as parental figures.

primal therapy   Arthur Janov's therapeutic approach that focuses on the recognition and expression of *affect.* Janov first makes clients miserable and then encourages them to relive miserable feelings of their *childhoods.* The culmination of the approach is a primal scream that supposedly rids the client of negative emotions and sets the stage for his or her healthy *development.*

primary affiliation group   A group that people most identify as belonging to (e.g., a *family* or *peer* group).

primary empathy   A *process* in which the counselor listens for basic client messages and responds to them through *paraphrasing* and *reflection* of feelings so that the client begins to feel understood. See also *empathy.*

primary prevention   The attempt to stop problems before they develop through various actions.

primary process   A term in *psychoanalysis* for the *id*'s means of reducing tension by imagining what it desires.

primary reinforcer   A *reinforcer* that people will naturally work for (e.g., food).

principle of awareness   A *gestalt therapy* assumption that people are free to choose only when they are *self-aware,* that is, in touch with their existence and what it means to be alive. Awareness includes all sensations, thoughts, and behaviors of the individual.

principle of holism   A *gestalt therapy* term for *integration.*

principle of polarities   A *gestalt therapy* belief that if people are to meet their *needs,* they must first differentiate their perceptual field into opposite poles (e.g., active/passive, good/bad). According to the polarity principle, people fail to resolve *conflicts* because they are not in contact with the opposite of the situation.

private logic   An *Adlerian counseling* term for an individual's unique pattern of *thoughts, feelings,* and *attitudes.* Private logic guides a person's ability to understand, predict, and manage life experiences.

private practice   A practice in which a clinician assumes total responsibility for the nature and quality of the *treatment* provided and collects fees directly or indirectly in turn for such services.

private self   One of the four quadrants in the *Johari Awareness model.* The private self is known to self but not to others.

privileged communication   A client's *legal* right that guarantees confidences originating in a therapeutic relationship will be safeguarded and not disclosed to others.

proactive   A type of *intervention* by counselors acting as *change agents,* who attempt to improve conditions for clients through actions that foster changes in society.

probability   A statistical term for how often something is likely to happen outside of chance.

probe   A question that usually begins with "who," "what," "where," or "how" and that usually requires more than a one- or two-word answer (e.g., the question, How do you plan on getting a job?). A probe is used in counseling to gather information from a client.

problem   A matter over which the client thinks or feels he or she does not have the ability to solve. A problem may result from a deficit of behavioral skills or a novel and sometimes overwhelming event.

problem-centered group   A small group set up to focus on one particular concern (e.g., coping with *stress*).

p

process   The way in which information is handled (e.g., the *techniques* and *methods* used) in *interpersonal* relationships.

process observer   A professional human services person who is neutral in regard to a group's agenda and personalities and who can observe the group and offer *feedback* with regard to what and how they are doing.

process research   Research that focuses on the dynamics of *counseling*. Attention is directed to the mechanisms by which counselors help bring about improvements in clients. Process research is intense and demands a concentrated amount of time and energy.

profession   A discipline that has its own unique body of literature, prescribed course of study, membership organization, standards of conduct, and *ethics*.

professional association   A membership organization of qualified individuals who voluntarily join together to educate the public about issues, advocate for clients and agendas, maintain ethical standards, and promote the generation of a body of literature on subjects pertinent to their discipline.

professional liability insurance   Insurance designed specifically to protect a counselor or other helping specialist from financial loss in case of a civil suit.

professional self-disclosure statement   A statement given to the client by the counselor that outlines the counselor's professional qualifications, the conditions that will be adhered to in *treatment,* the fee, if any, that will be charged, and the rights and recourses open to the *client.*

profile   A *graph* that depicts a person's scores on a test or a series of tests.

prognosis   A prediction about the *outcome* of a *disorder* or the outcome of a counseling *intervention.*

programmed workbooks for parents   Instrumental *behavioral* books parents may employ to help their children and, ultimately, their families modify behaviors.

projection   A *defense mechanism* in which an unwanted emotion or characteristic is attributed to someone else in an effort to deny that the emotion or characteristic is part of oneself. For example, people may say that their bosses are angry at them instead of saying that they are angry at their bosses.

projective tests   *Personality tests* that are usually unstructured and require clients to respond to figural or pictorial stimuli. These tests yield measures that, in varying degrees, depend on the judgments and interpretations of administrators/scorers. They are meant to tap into the unconscious. Projective tests include the *Rorschach,* the *Thematic Apperception Test (TAT),* and the *House-Tree-Person (HTP) Test.*

promoting hope   One of the basic *curative factors* described by Irvin Yalom. If clients believe that their situations can be different and better, they are likely to work harder.

pro   A self-help group leader who gains his or her position from experience and longevity.

proscriptive norms   *Norms* that describe the kinds of behaviors that are to be avoided. See also *norms.*

prosocial behavior   Behavior that is *altruistic* in nature and that is undertaken to benefit society at large.

protagonist   The person who is the subject of a *psychodrama* enactment. He or she may play many parts.

protection   Care, on the part of a group leader, that keeps members of a group safe from psychological or physical harm.

provider   The term used by third-party payment organizations to describe a clinician who is offering services.

pseudo-individuation   A pretend *self.* This concept involves the attempt by young people who lack an *identity* and basic *coping* skills to act as if they had both.

pseudomutuality   The facade of family harmony that many *dysfunctional* families display that is a masquerade for serious internal conflicts.

psyche   1. Carl Jung's term for the totality of one's *personality*.   **2.** A synonym for the mind.

psychiatric nurse   A nurse who has advanced training and specializes in working with the mentally disturbed.

psychiatric social worker   A *social worker* who has advanced training and specializes in working with the mentally disturbed.

psychiatrist   A physician who has had specialized postdoctoral training in the *diagnosis, treatment,* and *prevention* of mental and emotional *disorders*. A psychiatrist is permitted by *law* to prescribe and use *drugs* as well as other physical means for the treatment of *mental disorders*.

psychiatry   A medical specialty that focuses on the diagnosis, *treatment,* and prevention of *mental disorders*.

psychic energy   Energy that emanates from the *id*. According to *psychoanalytic* theory, this energy is converted by the *ego* and *super-ego* into actions.

psychoactive drugs   A group of *drugs* that induce changes in a person's *mood, cognitions,* or *perception*.

psychoanalysis   A *theory* of *psychotherapy* that originated from the writings and work of Sigmund Freud. One's *personality* consists of three dynamically interrelated parts: *id, superego,* and *ego*. Children go through and must resolve tasks associated with *psychosexual stages* of development. Much of the emphasis in this theory is on the importance of the *unconscious* and sexuality in human behavior. Treatment focuses on the release of *anxiety* and *repressed* memories through such techniques as *free association, dream analysis, transference,* and *interpretation*.

psychoanalyst   A professional who has been educated in and uses the *theory* of Sigmund Freud (i.e., *psychoanalysis*) as the basis for his or her *treatment* of clients. Professionals who are psychoanalysts are primarily those holding degrees in *psychiatry* and *clinical psychology*.

psychodrama   Jacob L. Moreno's interpersonal group approach to exploring the human *psyche*. In psychodrama, participants act out their emotions and attempt to clarify *conflicts*. See also *American Society of Group Psychotherapy and Psychodrama (ASGPP)*.

psychodrama process   The three phases of psychodrama: warm-up (preaction), action, and integration.

psychodynamic theories   Theories of *treatment* that include Sigmund Freud's *psychoanalytic* theory and other closely related theories that are neo-psychoanalytic (e.g., the theories of Anna Freud, Karen Horney, and Otto Rank).

psychoeducation   Helpful strategies regarding areas of emotional and relationship functioning that are taught to clients so that they can prevent *dysfunction* from occurring and cope with life events.

psychoeducational group   A group whose primary purpose is to educate or instruct clients in regard to certain subjects or areas pertinent to their lives (e.g., a parent education group).

psychohistory   The study of historical events and people in light of modern psychologically based theories. Psychobiographies are often an outcome of this process (e.g., Erik Erikson's *Young Man Luther*). Prominent practitioners of psychohistory include Erik Erikson, Kenneth Keniston, and Robert Coles.

Psychological Abstracts   A reference to the international literature in psychology and related disciplines (e.g., counseling) that has been published by the *American Psychological Association (APA)* since 1927. Monthly issues, organized by subject area, contain summaries of English-language journal articles, technical reports, book chapters, and books. Cumulative author and subject indexes are published annually. For more information, visit the Web site at http://www.apa.org/psycinfo/ pa.html.

psychological test   A standardized measure of an individual's behavior. See also *standardized test; test.*

psychologist   A helping professional who has earned an advanced degree in psychology and whose coursework and *internships* are concentrated in clinical, counseling, or school-related areas. All states license psychologists, but the requirements for licensure differ from state to state.

psychometrics   The discipline of testing.

psychometrist   A testing and appraisal specialist whose primary job is the administration and interpretation of psychological tests and instruments.

psychomotor test   A test that measures a person's fine or gross motor skills.

psychopath   A lay term for someone with a serious *mental disorder,* often a person with what is considered to be an *antisocial personality disorder.*

psychopathology   The study of *disorders* and *dysfunctional* behavior.

psychopharmacology   The study of the effects of *drugs* in the treatment of *disorders.*

psychosexual   A term used to describe psychological phenomena based on sexuality. From a psychosexual point of view, sexually based forces and motives drive *development.* In psychoanalytic theory, each stage of development is characterized by the body area providing maximal *erotic* gratification. The four stages of psychosexual development according to Sigmund Freud are *oral, anal, phallic,* and *genital.* There is a *latency* period between the phallic and genital stage (see chart below).

psychosis   A term used to describe serious *mental disorders* such as *schizophrenia.*

psychosocial   A term that underlies Erik Erikson's theory of human *development,* which deals with the resolution of social *crises* and the development of social competencies. The term refers to events or behaviors that relate to social aspects of life. Erikson's eight stages of psychosocial development are *trust* versus *mistrust* (0 to 1 year), autonomy versus *shame* and *doubt* (1 to 2 years), *initiative* versus *guilt* (3 to 5 years), *industry* versus *inferiority* (6 to

p

psychosexual stages of development

Stage	Age	Emphasis
Oral	Birth to 1 year	Gratification through sucking, biting; chief zone of pleasure is the mouth.
Anal	1st to 2nd year	Gratification through the withholding or eliminating of feces; chief zone of pleasure is the anus.
Phallic	3rd to 5th year	Gratification through stimulation of the genital area, sexual fantasy; resolution comes in giving up wish to possess opposite-sex parent and identifying with same-sex parent.
Latency	6th to 11th year	A period devoted to activity and achievement with peers; it is a quiet time sexually.
Genital	12th year on	This is the time of relating to persons of the opposite gender in an appropriate manner if previous stages have been resolved successfully.

11 years), *identity* versus *role confusion* (12 to 14 years), *intimacy* versus *isolation* (20s to 30s), *generativity* versus *stagnation* (40s to 50s), and *integrity* versus *despair* (60 years and over).

psychosomatic Psychological symptoms, such as *anxiety,* that are manifested in physical ways.

psychosurgery Surgery employed in the *treatment* of *disorders.* Usually such surgery involves an operation on the brain.

psychotherapist A general term used to describe a *helping professional* who provides mental health *treatment* to clients. Many professionals can be described as psychotherapists. The *legal* qualifications for such a title vary from state to state.

psychotherapy *Cognitive, affective,* and *behavioral* means of helping troubled individuals change their thoughts, feelings, and behaviors so that they reduce their *stress* and achieve greater life satisfaction. See also *therapy.*

PTSD See *posttraumatic stress disorder.*

Public Law 94-142 The *Education of All Handicapped Children Act,* which was passed by Congress in 1975. The law requires that schools make provisions for the free, appropriate public education of all children in the *least restrictive environment* possible. Part of this process is the development of an *individual education plan (IEP)* for each child as well as the provision for due-process procedures and for identifying and keeping records on every child with a disability.

Public Offender Counselor Association The former name of the *International Association of Addictions and Offender Counseling (IAAOC).*

public self One of the four quadrants in the *Johari Awareness Model.* The public self is known to self and others.

punishment **1.** The presentation of an aversive *stimulus* or the removal of a pleasant stimulus. Punishment decreases the frequency of the occurrence of some undesirable *behavior.* **2.** A penalty imposed for an *illegal* act.

Purpose in Life **1.** A *test* that attempts to measure meaningfulness and meaninglessness in a person's life. **2.** The meaning a person derives from participating in some activity or event such as *work, family,* accomplishment, or *spirituality.*

PWP See *Parents Without Partners.*

q

Q sort A three-step *evaluation* procedure based on Rogerian theory. First, the client is given one hundred cards, each of which contains a self-descriptive sentence, such as "I am intelligent" or "I despise myself." Next, the client is asked to place the cards in nine piles, from "most like me" to "least like me." After this self-sort, the client sorts the cards again by placing them according to how he or she would ideally like to be. Finally, the counselor *correlates* the degree of similarity between the two sorts, before, during, and after counseling.

qualitative research Research that is characterized by an emphasis on *open-ended questions* and the collection of narrative *data* on many *variables* over an extended period of time. This approach is often utilized in *theory* building.

quality circles See *quality groups.*

quality groups Also known as *quality circles; work groups* or *task groups* first set up and utilized by the Japanese after World War II under the direction of W. Edwards Deming to assure work was done correctly and efficiently the first time.

quantitative research Research that is characterized by an emphasis on *closed-ended ques-*

tions and the utilization of large *sample* sizes to gather information. *Data* is gathered in a precise form frequently using standardized instruments and reported in a statistical format. Analyzed and deductive conclusions are made that tend to "prove" or "disprove" *theories* and assertions.

quartile   A *score* distribution segment that has been divided into fourths or quarters.

quasi kin   A formerly married person's ex-spouse, the ex-spouse's new husband or wife, and his or her blood kin.

quasi-experimental design   A *research design* in which the conditions of *treatment* are controlled by the experimenter (e.g.,

assigning specific subjects to certain groups in a nonrandom way).

questioning   A query that is used to gather information, increase clarity, stimulate thinking, or elicit further discussion. See also *closed-ended questions; open-ended questions.*

questionnaire   A *survey* instrument, similar to a structured *interview,* used to gather information or opinions on specific topics.

quid pro quo   A something for something relationship. In social economic theory, married partners will stay in a relationship because it is quid pro quo (i.e., spouses are both giving and receiving). If the relationship ceases to be quid pro quo, it is likely to dissolve.

race   An anthropological concept that classifies people according to their *physiological characteristics.* Race contributes virtually nothing to cultural understanding.

racism   *Prejudice* displayed in blatant or subtle ways due to recognized or perceived differences in the physical and psychological backgrounds of people. It is a form of projection usually displayed out of fear or ignorance.

racket   A *transactional analysis* term for one's self-indulgence in negative or nongenuine feelings (e.g., *guilt,* inadequacy, hurt, fear, or resentment).

radical behaviorists   Behaviorists who avoid any mentalistic concepts and concentrate exclusively on observable actions.

rainbows   See *barbiturates.*

random sample   A *sample* drawn from a *population* in such a way that each member of the population has an equal chance of being selected.

range   A statistical measure of *variability* that encompasses the width or spread of scores in a *distribution.* The range is calculated by sub-

tracting the lowest from the highest score in the distribution.

rape   Forced sexual intercourse without *consent,* usually with a girl or woman by a man.

rape myth   *Stereotypes* and myths that are prejudicial ways of thinking about *rape* and that lead to the victimization of women (e.g., "Only bad girls or women get raped"; "Anyone can resist rape").

rapport   The establishment of a warm, personal, and trusting relationship with a client by a counselor. Rapport is the foundation on which counseling is built.

ratio IQ score   An *intelligence quotient* derived by dividing a person's *mental age* score on an *intelligence test* by the person's *chronological age* and multiplying by one hundred. See also *intelligence quotient (IQ).*

ratio scale   A scale with a true zero point and equal units of *measurement.* Height and weight are examples of measurements on a ratio scale, but most *test scores* are not on such a scale.

rational behavioral therapy (RBT)   An approach to counseling formulated by Maxie

Maultsby. RBT emphasizes cognitive change in a way more behavioral than Albert Ellis originally conceptualized. It involves checking activating events as if one had a camera in order to be sure of *objectivity*. Disputation of a person's *self-talk* takes the form of a debate based on five rules for rational behavior.

rational emotive behavioral therapy (REBT) The theory of counseling established by Albert Ellis in the late 1950s and originally called *rational emotive therapy*. The emphasis of the approach is that it is people's thoughts about events, rather than the events, that are the source of emotional and behavioral difficulties. REBT focuses on helping clients *change* or modify their *negative thoughts* to *neutral, positive,* or *mixed* thoughts and thus think more rationally and behave more responsibly and with less *interpersonal* and *intrapersonal* difficulty.

rational emotive behavioral therapy (REBT) types of thoughts The four types of *thoughts* in REBT theory: *negative, positive, neutral,* and *mixed*. The theory proposes that individuals can choose to think in one of these four ways. See also *thoughts*.

rational emotive imagery (REI) A *rational emotive behavioral therapy (REBT)* technique for disputing *irrational beliefs (IBs)*. REI may be used in one of two ways. First, the client is asked to imagine a situation in which he or she is likely to become upset. The client examines his or her *self-talk* during that imagined situation. Then the client is asked to envision the same situation but this time to be more moderate in his or her self-talk. In the second way, the client is asked to imagine a situation in which he or she feels or behaves differently from some real instance. Then the client is asked to examine the self-talk used in this imagined situation.

rational emotive therapy See *rational emotive behavioral therapy (REBT)*.

rational self-analysis (RSA) A *technique* devised by Maxie Maultsby in which clients are instructed to write down significant events in their lives and their thoughts and feelings associated with the events. The beliefs of the persons are then evaluated for their degree of rationality and changed in accordance with the rules of rational behavior. This method of assessing clients' thoughts is useful in maintaining a record of therapeutic progress. The standard RSA format consists of six steps.

rationalization A *defense mechanism* in which a person finds reasonable explanations for unreasonable or unacceptable behaviors to make them sound logical and acceptable (e.g., "I did it because everyone else was"; "I really didn't think it was going to be worth the time I'd have to spend, so I didn't do it").

raw score A *score* that has not been converted into a derived score such as a *standard score*.

RBT See *rational behavioral therapy*.

reaction formation A *defense mechanism* in which *anxiety*-producing thoughts, feelings, or impulses are *repressed* and their opposites expressed. For example, a host at a party may shower a disliked guest with attention. A reaction formation is often detected because of the intensity with which the opposite emotion is expressed.

real self The essence of a person (i.e., the person's true thoughts, feelings, etc.). In an *incongruent* person, the real self is in sharp contrast to the *ideal self*.

reality principle The principle by which the *ego* operates in Sigmund Freud's schema of the *personality*. Under this principle, reality is seen as that which exists in the outside environment. In order to deal with reality, the ego must sometimes delay immediate gratification. It is the opposite of the *pleasure principle*.

reality therapy A counseling theory originated by William Glasser in the 1960s that focuses on the present and seeks to help clients *change* by evaluating what they are doing, making new plans, and then implementing them. Reality therapy is pragmatic and has behavioral overtones.

reality-oriented groups   Groups that are set up for older individuals who have become disoriented with regard to their surroundings. These groups, while educationally focused, are therapeutically based in that their emphasis is on helping group members become more attuned to where they are with respect to time, place, and people.

reassuring/supportive response   A *low facilitative response* in which the counselor's intent is to encourage someone, yet the response itself dismisses the person's real feelings.

reauthoring   An aspect of *narrative therapy* that encourages individuals and families to change the emphases in their stories and focus on aspects of their lives that have not been previously emphasized.

REBT   See *rational emotive behavioral therapy.*

recall   A *psychoanalysis* term for reviving or reinstating a past experience from memory.

recency effect   The idea that all things being equal, those things that are learned last in a sequence are remembered best. It is the opposite of, but complementary to, the *primacy effect.*

recidivism   The relapse of treated clients into *behaviors* they were displaying before *counseling.*

reciprocal inhibition   A *behavior therapy* approach created by Joseph Wolpe based on the idea that an individual cannot feel anxious and relaxed at the same time. Thus, clients are taught to relax before they deal with *anxiety* producing situations. The most classic example of reciprocal inhibition is *systematic desensitization.* See also *systematic desensitization.*

reciprocity   The likelihood that two people will reinforce each other at approximately equitable rates over time. Many marital behavior counselors view marriage as based on this principle.

records   Written summaries of client/counselor sessions. Records of clients are legally protected except under special circumstances. Records allow counselors an opportunity to document their work with clients and afford counselors *legal* protection against suits if they show counselors followed a *treatment plan* based on an appropriate *diagnosis.*

recycling   A process in which individuals who have not benefited from a counseling experience go through a similar experience again and learn lessons missed the first time.

red birds   See *barbiturates.*

redecision school of transactional analysis   An approach to *transactional analysis* in which the emphasis is on intrapsychic processes. Individuals are encouraged to change their *life scripts.* Redecision is based on the premise that early life decisions are reversible if clients reexperience their decisions both intellectually and emotionally.

redefining   Attributing positive connotations to symptomatic or troublesome actions. The idea is that symptoms have meaning for those who display them whether such meaning is logical or not. Redefining is one way of lowering *resistance* to counseling.

redundancy principle   The fact that a family interacts within a limited range of repetitive behavioral sequences.

referral   The transfer of a *client* to another counselor. The referral process itself involves four steps: (1) identifying the need to refer; (2) evaluating potential referral sources; (3) preparing the client for the referral; and (4) coordinating the transfer.

reflection   A counseling technique similar to a *restatement* but dealing with *verbal* and *nonverbal* expression. Reflections may be on several levels; some convey more *empathy* than others. Some are based on rephrasing a client's feeling; others are based on rephrasing the client's *content.* An example of a feeling-based reflection would be a counselor responding to a client's silently sobbing over the loss of a parent by saying, "You're still really feeling the pain."

reframing   A process in which a *perception* is changed by explaining a situation from a different and more positive context. For instance, a misbehaving child may be said to be "behaving younger than his years" rather than being "incorrigible." Reframing allows people to make new responses because the situation is now seen in a new way.

registration   The lowest level of credentialing. It requires a practitioner to submit information to the state concerning the nature of his or her practice. Usually a professional organization, such as a state counseling association, assumes the responsibility for setting standards necessary to qualify as a registrant and maintains a list of names of those who voluntarily meet those standards.

registry   A voluntary listing of persons who use a title and/or provide a service. Registry is the simplest and least restrictive form of credentialing.

regression   **1.** A *defense mechanism* in which a person returns to an earlier stage of *development.* For example, a child under *stress* may begin to wet the bed during early adolescence after suffering a *trauma.* Virtually all people regress if placed under enough pressure or stress.   **2.** A statistical technique used to predict scores when a person knows the *value* of one set of *scores* that *correlate* highly with another.

regression toward the mean   The tendency of an extreme value when it is remeasured to be closer to the *mean.*

rehabilitation   The reeducation or restoring to healthy conditions of individuals who have *handicaps* and who have previously lived independent lives.

Rehabilitation Act of 1973   Federal legislation that broadened the interpretation of those eligible for *rehabilitation* services.

rehabilitation counseling   A counseling specialty that focuses on serving individuals with *disabilities* and *handicaps.* The practice of rehabilitation counseling requires knowledge in areas of medical terminology, *diagnosis,* prognosis, vocational evaluation of disability-related limitations, and job placement in the context of a socioeconomic system.

rehearsal   A processing *technique* in which individuals practice behaviors or repeat materials so that the action or information becomes permanently encoded and stored in their memories.

REI   See *rational emotive imagery.*

reinforcement   Any *stimulus* that increases the probability of a *response.*

reinforcer   A *stimulus* event that increases the probability that the response that immediately preceded it will occur again.

relabeling   A *technique* utilized in counseling, especially with families, to bring about change by giving a different perspective to a *behavior.*

relapse   The reoccurrence of *dysfunctional* behaviors once they have been treated.

relationship   The degree of psychological and emotional closeness between a counselor and client. The nature of a relationship often determines the *outcome* of therapeutic situations.

reliability   The consistency, dependability, or repeatability of a *test, measurement,* or classification system.

religion   The institutionalized and codified expression of one's beliefs in the transcendent in an integrated *system* that is oriented toward helping people find meaning, purpose, and spiritual connectedness in life. Major world religions include Judaism, Christianity, Islam, Hinduism, Buddhism, Confucianism, and Taoism. See also *spirituality.*

reluctant client   A client who has been referred by a third party and is frequently unmotivated to seek help (e.g., many school children and court-referred clients). Such individuals do not wish to be in *counseling,* let alone talk about themselves. Many reluctant clients terminate counseling *prematurely* and report dissatisfaction with the process.

remarried families   Also referred to as *stepfamilies,* reconstituted families, recoupled families, merged families, and *blended families.* Regardless of terminology, these families consist of two adults and stepchildren, adoptive children, or foster children.

remediation   The process by which counseling procedures are implemented with the *goal* of correcting a situation.

reminiscing therapy   A therapy, originating in the 1960s, that is based on the importance of *life review.* Reminiscing therapy helps individuals who have not yet fully realized their own older life stage to comprehend and appreciate more fully who they are and where they have been. In this approach, persons share memories, increase personal *integration,* and become more aware of their lives and the lives of those their age. *Insight* gained from this process helps these persons to realize more deeply their finiteness and to prepare for death.

remotivation therapy groups   Groups aimed at helping older clients become more invested in the present and future. Group membership is composed of individuals who have "lost interest" in any time frame of life except the past.

reorientation   An *Adlerian counseling* technique in which clients are encouraged to act differently and take more control of their lives. Such a procedure means taking risks, *acting "as if"* they were the persons they wished to be, and *"catching oneself"* in old, ineffective patterns and correcting them.

REPLAN   An atheoretical model of helping developed by Mark Young. "R" stands for relationship, "E" for efficacy and self-esteem, "P" for practicing new behaviors, "L" for lowering or raising emotional arousal, "A" for activating experiences and changing perceptions, and "N" for providing new learning and experiences in changing perceptions.

replication study   The repeating of an *experimental* study in the exact same way as a means of verifying the findings.

repression   The *defense mechanism* on which others are built. Using this most basic mechanism, the *ego* involuntarily excludes from *con-sciousness* any unwanted or painful thoughts, feelings, memories, or impulses. The ego must use energy to keep excluded areas from consciousness, but sometimes the repressed thoughts slip out in dreams or verbal expressions. Repression is considered the cornerstone or foundation stone of *psychoanalysis.*

rescuer   A person in a *transactional analysis game* who is seen as a problem solver or hero to the victim.

research   A systematic procedure for investigating facts and observations. Research in counseling is for the most part *applied research* that links basic science and theory to issues of counseling practice.

research design   The way a research study is set up. Five commonly used categories are exploratory, descriptive, developmental, *experimental,* and correlational.

resilience   The power to recover readily or spring back from *stress, trauma,* or other negative conditions in life.

resistance   Any *behavior* that moves a client away from areas of discomfort or *conflict* and prevents the client from developing (e.g., getting bogged down in details and becoming preoccupied with the unimportant).

resistant client   A client who is unwilling or opposed to *change.* Such an individual may actively seek *counseling* but does not wish to go through the pain that change demands. Instead, the client clings to the certainty of present behavior, even when such action is counterproductive and *dysfunctional.* Some resistant clients refuse to make decisions, are superficial in dealing with *problems,* and take any action to resolve a problem (i.e., do anything a counselor says). One of the most common forms of resistance is the simple statement "I don't know."

respondent conditioning   A behavioral view that human responses are learned through association. See also *classical conditioning.*

response   The reaction of the mind and/or body to a *stimulus.*

response set The tendency for a person to respond in a relatively fixed or *stereotyped* way in a situation in which there are at least two choices on a test. For example, a response set on a true/false test might be to answer all questions true.

responsive listening An *empathetic* verbal response by the counselor that communicates *acceptance* and concern.

restatement Saying in slightly different words what a client has said in order to clarify its meaning. Restating helps provide support and *clarification* within the counseling *process.*

restraining A *paradoxical* technique of telling a client that he or she is incapable of doing anything other than what he or she is presently doing. The intent is to get the client to show he or she can behave differently.

restructuring Changing the *structure* of the family. The rationale behind restructuring is to make the family more functional by altering the existing hierarchy and interaction patterns.

retardation **1.** A delay in *development.* **2.** A term used to describe significantly lower than average intellectual ability or significantly slower than average psychomotor reaction.

reward An object, event, *stimulus,* or *outcome* that is perceived as being pleasant and therefore may be reinforcing.

RIASEC An acronym for John Holland's *career counseling* theory. The letters stand for the six types of *personalities* and *environments* in the *theory:* realistic, investigative, artistic, social, enterprising, and conventional. See also *Self-Directed Search (SDS).*

rigid boundaries Inflexible *rules* and habits that keep family members separated from each other.

risk-taking New behaviors that generate some *anxiety* but are taken by a client in order to change *behaviors* and reach therapeutic *goals.*

rituals **1.** A *family counseling* term for specialized types of *directives* that are meant to dramatize significant and positive family relationships or aspects of problem situations. **2.**

A *transactional analysis* term for simple and stereotyped *complementary transactions* like hellos and good-byes.

role A dynamic structure within an individual (based on *needs, cognitions,* and *values*) that usually comes to life under the influence of social stimuli or defined positions (i.e., status). The manifestation of a role is based on the individual's expectation of self and others and the interactions he or she has in particular situations.

role collision A situation in which there is a *conflict* between the *role* an individual plays in the outside world (e.g., that of a passive observer) and the role expected within the group (e.g., that of an active participant).

role confusion **1.** The opposite of *identity* in Erik Erikson's fifth stage of *psychosocial* development. Role confusion is a lack of clarity about one's identity. **2.** A situation that occurs when a member of a group does not know what role to perform. This often happens in *leaderless groups;* members do not know whether to be *assertive* and help to establish an agenda or passive and allow the leadership to emerge.

role incompatibility A situation that occurs when a person in a *group* is given a *role* (such as that of group leader) that he or she neither wants nor is comfortable exercising.

role induction Explaining before the fact what one's *role* will be in a situation. Clients benefit from role induction in *counseling* because they find out what their roles are at the beginning of the process, before mistakes are made.

role model A person who is exemplary and a standard of emulation.

role overload A situation that occurs when a person tries to fulfill a greater variety of *roles* than he or she has energy or time for. Role overload is a common phenomenon of newly divorced single parents.

role playing A procedure in which clients are asked to *act "as if"* they are the persons they ideally want to be. Clients practice a number of *behaviors* to see which work best. *Feedback* is given and, ideally, *insight* and *empathy* emerge from the *process.*

role reversal   The taking on of a *role* opposite of what one normally assumes (e.g., becoming *assertive* if one is usually passive). Through role reversal, clients experience new *thoughts, feelings,* and *behaviors* and expand their abilities to switch roles as well as *empathize* more with individuals who tend to be different from themselves.

Rorschach inkblot test   A *projective personality test* developed in the 1920s by Hermann Rorschach. The test consists of 10 standardized inkblot cards.

rounds   Also known as go-rounds; the process of giving members of a *group* an equal chance to participate in the group by going around the circle in which they are sitting and asking each person to make a comment on a subject that is presently before the group. Sometimes rounds are used to ensure group member participation. They are less confrontational than the *gestalt therapy group* process of *making the rounds.*

rules   **1.** Prescribed guidelines for conduct with others.   **2.** The guidelines under which *counseling* is conducted and that are a part of the *structure* of counseling that counselors must establish early on in a therapeutic *relationship.*   **3.** A *structural family therapy* term for the explicit or implicit guidelines that govern a family's interaction.

S

SAD PERSONS scale   A scale used to assess the risk of *suicide.* The acronym describes persons at risk. The letter "S" stands for sex (male), "A" for age (older clients), "D" for depression, "P" for previous attempt, "E" for ethanol (alcohol) abuse, "R" for rational thinking loss, "S" for social support system lacking (lonely, isolated), "O" for organized plan, "N" for no spouse, and "S" for sickness (particularly chronic or terminal illness).

sadist   A person who derives pleasure from inflicting pain on someone else.

sadistic personality disorder   A *personality disorder* in which a person seeks to impose mental or physical cruelty on someone else.

sadomasochism   A simultaneous tendency toward *sadist* and *masochist* behaviors.

sample   **1.** The number of people involved in a *research* study.   **2.** A subset of a *population.*

sampling   The *process* of selecting subjects who are members of the *population* that the researcher wishes to study.

sand play   A nondirective, *projective treatment* procedure, based on Jungian theory, that offers clients an opportunity to *project* internal and external troubling and *traumatic* experiences *metaphorically* with figures in a container of sand.

sandwich generation   Couples who have adolescents and their aging parents to take care of and are squeezed psychologically and physically between these two responsibilities.

SAT   See *Scholastic Aptitude Test.*

SAWV   See *Scale to Assess World Views.*

Scale to Assess World Views (SAWV)   A scale that measures a client's *worldview* using the following categories: human nature, social relationships, nature, time orientation, and activity orientation.

scaled score   A *score* that has been converted from a *raw score* to a standardized number. Raw scores on many tests must be converted to scaled scores before test results can be tabulated and reported.

scapegoat   A person who is designated or blamed by a group or a family as the cause of its difficulties or problems. See also *identified patient (IP)*.

scattergram   A *graph* that plots pairs of *scores* for individuals on two *variables*.

schedule of reinforcement   A way of initiating or maintaining *behavior*. In order to initiate a behavior, a schedule of reinforcement should be *continuous* (i.e., every *response* to a *stimulus* should be rewarded). In order to maintain a behavior, schedules of reinforcement operate on either a ratio (number of responses) or interval (length of time between rewards) basis. Both ratio and interval schedules are either fixed (occurring after a definite number of responses or a set period of time) or variable (occurring randomly).

schema   See *schemata*.

schemata   Jean Piaget's *cognitive development* term for a way of thinking; a unit of cognitive structure. A schemata is comprised of core beliefs and basic assumptions about how things operate.

schism   The division of the family into two antagonistic and competing *groups*.

schizophrenia   A *mental disorder* characterized by a loss of contact with reality, *withdrawal* from others, and a loss of interest in external activities. In addition, there is a breakdown of personal habits and an inability to deal with daily events. *Delusions, hallucinations,* and thought abnormalities are also usually present. Subtypes of schizophrenia include *paranoid, catatonic,* disorganized, undifferentiated, and residual.

schizophrenia and other psychotic disorders   A diagnostic category found in the *DSM-IV* that include disorders characterized by *symptoms* that reveal a loss of contact with reality.

Scholastic Aptitude Test (SAT)   A standardized *aptitude test* published by the College Board that measures a student's ability to do college-level work. SATs have two sections, one in math and one in English; scores for the two sections are added to give an overall score. Most colleges and universities require students to submit either SAT or *ACT (American College Testing)* scores as a part of the admissions process. The College Board address is 11911 Freedom Drive, Suite 400, Reston, VA 20190 (800-626-9795; http://collegeboard.org/index.html).

school counseling   Services that are systematically provided by professional school counselors and that are specifically designed for elementary, middle, and secondary schools. These services include such activities as classroom *guidance, career* decision making, teacher and parental *consultation,* personal *counseling,* and *group work*. See also *American School Counselor Association (ASCA)*.

school counselor   A professional counselor who has had specialized training in working with children and adolescents and who is employed in a school setting. See also *American School Counselor Association (ASCA)*.

school phobia   A fear of going to school. School phobia is often attributable to unresolved dependency issues or *separation anxiety*.

school psychologist   A *psychologist* specifically educated to work in school settings with students experiencing academic, behavioral, and emotional problems. The services of most school psychologists are tied to state and federal mandates for the comprehensive evaluation of students who may qualify for programs, such as special education. Three of the primary duties of school psychologists are *assessment, consultation,* and *intervention*. See also *National Association of School Psychologists (NASP)*.

School-to-Work-Opportunities Act (STWOA)   An act passed by Congress in 1994 that offered community funding of comprehensive programs that provided a wide range of career and employability skills information for secondary school students entering the job market after graduation. STWOA was not refunded in 1998.

score   Also known as a *test score;* a number on a test that when compared to other numbers takes on a meaning as to where a person stands in relationship to others on a measurement instrument. See also *derived score; raw score; scaled score.*

screening   1. A process in which potential clients are interviewed prior to their entering counseling to see whether they are suitable for *treatment.*   **2.** A process for selecting members of a group.

script analysis   A procedure in *transactional analysis* for understanding the life plan that an individual is following.

scriptotherapy   The use of writing as a primary or adjunct therapeutic tool in counseling.

scripts   A *transactional analysis* term for the habitual patterns of behavior that influence how people spend their time. Most people initially script their lives as a child in the "I'm not OK"/"You're OK" stance (characterized by powerlessness), but change to an adult stance in later life as they affirm an "I'm OK"/"You're OK" position (characterized by trust and openness). Other options open are "I'm OK"/"You're not OK" (characterized by a projection of blame onto others) and "I'm not OK"/"You're not OK" (characterized by hopelessness and self-destructiveness). See also *OK positions.*

sculpting   An experiential *exercise,* usually found in family or *group counseling,* in which individuals use *nonverbal* methods to arrange others (e.g., office personnel, family members, or social peers) into a configuration like that of significant persons with whom they regularly deal. The positioning involves body posturing and assists clients in seeing and experiencing their perceptions of *significant others* in a more dynamic way.

SDS   See *Self-Directed Search.*

secondary affiliation groups   Those groups with which people least identify (e.g., as a member of a club that one never attends).

secondary gains   Extra attention or other benefits a person gets from having a *disorder.*

secondary prevention   Raising *awareness* to address *problems* already in existence.

secondary process   A *psychoanalysis* theory term for the reality-based decision-making and problem-solving activities of the *ego.*

secondary reinforcer   A *reinforcer* that acquires its value by being associated with a *primary reinforcer* (e.g., money and what it can buy).

secondary school counseling   Counseling in schools that occurs in Grades 9 through 12 or 10 through 12 by counselors specially educated to deal with developmental and situational concerns of *adolescence* in educational settings. See also *American School Counselor Association (ASCA).*

second-degree games   A term in *transactional analysis* for the more serious games, compared with those of the first degree. The interactive process in second-degree games leaves those involved feeling negative. See also *games.*

second-order change   A qualitatively different way of doing something; a basic change in function and/or structure.

second-order cybernetics   The *cybernetics* of cybernetics.

sedative   A *drug* that tends to calm, moderate, or tranquilize nervousness or excitement (e.g., *barbiturates*).

self   The concept a person has of himself or herself.

self theory   Another name for the theoretical ideas of Carl Rogers. For Rogers, the *self* is an outgrowth of what a person experiences; an *awareness* of the self helps a person *differentiate* himself or herself from others.

self-actualization   A constant striving and need on the part of human beings to grow and realize their full potential; to be *autonomous* and healthy, according to Abraham Maslow. Self-actualizing persons are *motivated* by enduring and universal *values* such as truth, beauty, *wisdom,* and peace.

self-awareness An ongoing *process* in life of recognizing thoughts, emotions, senses, and behaviors that influence a person on multiple levels.

self-concept The way one thinks of oneself based on information from *significant* others and experiences. Self-concept includes self-image.

Self-Directed Search (SDS) A popular career assessment instrument based on the *trait-and-factor (RIASEC) theory* of John Holland in regard to personality and environment fit. The SDS is self-administered, self-scored, and self-interpreted. Scores are linked with the *Dictionary of Occupational Titles (DOT)* codes through the Holland codes. The SDS is applicable for persons ages 15 to 70 who are in need of *career guidance.*

self-disclosure A *conscious,* intentional technique in which clinicians share information about their lives outside the counseling *relationship.* The original work in this area was done by Sidney Jourard. For him, self-disclosure referred to making oneself known to another person by revealing personal information. Jourard discovered that self-disclosure helped to establish *trust* and facilitated the counseling relationship. He labeled reciprocal self-disclosure the *dyadic effect.*

self-esteem The evaluative, attitudinal component of the *self;* the affective judgments placed on the *self-concept.* Self-esteem consists of feelings of worth and *acceptance* and develops as a consequence of a sense of *identity, awareness* of competence, and *feedback* from the external world.

self-exploration A client's exploration of his or her *thoughts, feelings,* and *behaviors* and their usefulness or *consequences.*

self-fulfilling prophecy A prediction by persons that something will happen to them. Often a self-fulfilling prophecy will come true because of the way people live their lives or shape their *environment.*

self-help group A *mutual-help group* that does not include professional leaders but is led instead by group members. An example of such a group is *Alcoholics Anonymous (AA).*

self-instructional training A technique originated by Donald Meichenbaum for teaching clients to become aware of their internally generated *maladaptive* thoughts and to replace such *self-talk* with self-enhancing cognitions.

self-monitoring The keeping by a client of detailed, daily records of particular events or psychological reactions in order to evaluate what he or she is doing.

self-report inventory A *test* in which persons check off statements that are characteristic or not characteristic of themselves.

self-report research format A *research* method in which participants write out or check off ways that they are different as a result of an experience such as *counseling.*

self-talk The internal messages people give themselves. Self-talk is sometimes known as *self-verbalization.*

self-verbalization See *self-talk.*

senility A term to denote the deterioration of mental and physical capacities in old age.

sensitivity group See *basic encounter group.*

sensorimotor stage The first stage in Jean Piaget's theory on the development of human intelligence. During this stage (which lasts from birth to about age 2), children understand their world primarily through their senses and activities. An important milestone in this stage is the development of *object permanence.*

sentence completion test A *personality test* that is composed of a number of incomplete sentences that a person is asked to finish as soon as possible.

separation anxiety *Anxiety* experienced by children when they are separated from *caregivers* (e.g., their mothers) to whom they are emotionally attached.

serial art therapy A *creative arts therapy* procedure based on Jungian theory in which young clients are requested to draw a picture at each *counseling* session. Pictures are not analyzed, but clients are encouraged to draw images that help them heal. Serial drawings may be structured or unstructured.

service delivery   The providing of particular *counseling* or supportive services to clients or agencies in a community.

sex differences   The naturally occurring differences in males and females. According to research by Eleanor Maccoby and Carol Jacklin and their associates, four basic differences appear to be present from birth on. Boys excel in visual-spatial and mathematical tasks and are more aggressive; girls have greater verbal ability.

sex discrimination   Treating individuals differently, often in a biased fashion, based on their sex. Women have most often been the victims of sex discrimination.

sex roles   Cultural roles assigned to males and females based on their gender.

sex therapy   A specialized type of *treatment* that is aimed at helping couples overcome sexual difficulties in their relationships.

sexism   The belief (and the behavior resulting from that belief) that persons should be treated on the basis of their sex without regard to other criteria, such as interests and abilities. Such treatment is arbitrary, illogical, biased, counterproductive, and self-serving.

sexual and gender identity disorders   A *DSM-IV* diagnostic category of three very different *disorders: paraphilias*, *sexual dysfunctions*, and *gender identity disorders*.

sexual dysfunctions   A category under *sexual and gender identity disorders* in the *DSM-IV* that involves *problems* in the expression of one's sexuality (e.g., arousal disorder, premature ejaculation). Sexual dysfunctions are usually straightforward problems that respond well to behavioral interventions.

sexual orientation   The orientation people have toward being *heterosexual, homosexual,* or *bisexual.*

shadow   A Jungian concept for the *uncon-*

scious, unaccepted, and unrecognized parts of one's *personality* that are often negative.

shadowing   See *career shadowing.*

shame   **1.** Dishonor, disgrace, or other painful emotions one feels for having failed.   **2.** The opposite of *autonomy* in Erik Erikson's *psychosocial* development theory.

shame attack   A *rational emotive behavioral therapy (REBT)* technique, often in the form of *homework,* in which a person actually does what he or she dreads and then finds the world does not fall apart regardless of the *outcome.* For example, a man might go into a restaurant and ask for a drink of water without ordering food. Whether he receives the water or not is irrelevant. He finds through the experience that he can actually do something he fears.

shaping   An *operant conditioning* procedure that involves *reinforcing* responses that come successfully closer to the desired *response;* the process of *learning* in small gradual steps. Shaping is often referred to as *successive approximation.*

shaping competence   The procedure in which *structural family therapy* counselors help families and family members become more functional by highlighting positive *behaviors.*

shifting the focus   The technique of turning a client's attention to a different topic. This procedure is employed when a client seems to be rambling or otherwise avoiding an important area that needs addressing.

Short Michigan Alcoholism Screening Test (SMAST)   A shortened version of the *Michigan Alcoholism Screening Test (MAST)*. It consists of 13 questions and can identify over 90% of alcoholics who take it.

short-term counseling   Counseling that is set up to last a specific number of sessions and whose emphasis is usually limited. See also *brief therapy.*

sibling rivalry   The competition between siblings within a family unit, usually for attention.

SIGI See *System of Interactive Guidance and Information.*

significant difference A statistical term for a difference that is unlikely due to chance.

significant other A term coined by George H. Mead that refers to a parent, teacher, relative, or other person in one's life who is important and meaningful to that individual. Significant others influence a person's thoughts, feelings, and behaviors.

SII See *Strong Interest Inventory.*

silence A passive form of a *lead* in which the counselor pauses and allows the client to speak or elaborate on a topic. Silence encourages clients to talk or reflect.

single parent A person of either sex who has complete responsibility for the raising of his or her children. Single-parent situations are usually created by *divorce* or death of a spouse but may occur through *choice,* such as in adoption.

single-parent family A family that includes one parent, either biological or adoptive, who is solely responsible for care of self and child/children. Single-parent families are created as a result of *divorce,* death, abandonment, unwed pregnancy, or adoption.

single-subject research design A procedure in which counselors follow one of two methods in *evaluation.* In the first method they follow an *ABAB research design* to evaluate the relationship of an *intervention* on changes that may have occurred. In the other method, counselors employ a *multiple baseline design* that more randomly measures change across subject, *variables,* or situations.

SIT See *stress inoculation training.*

situation A *psychodrama* concept in which the emphasis is on the present, and natural barriers of time, space, and states of existence are obliterated. Under these circumstances, clients are able to work on past problems, future fears, and current difficulties in a here-and-now atmosphere.

situational interpretation A level of *interpre-*

tation that is context centered and emphasizes the immediate interactions of the client.

situational therapy Activity groups for children ages 8 to 15 based on *psychoanalytic* principles first created by Samuel Slavson.

Sixteen Personality Factor (16 PF) Questionnaire A *personality inventory* based on the trait theory of Raymond B. Cattell. The questionnaire measures self-reported opposite characteristics of individuals (e.g., reserved versus outgoing) on 16 different dimensions.

skeleton keys A concept in Steve deShazer's *brief therapy* approach. Skeleton keys are *interventions* that have worked before and that have a universal application.

skewness The degree of asymmetry in a *frequency distribution.* Skewness is positive if more scores are to the left of the *mean* and negative if more scores are to the right of the mean.

slander Injury to a person's character or reputation through *verbal* means.

sleep disorders A *DSM-IV* category of *disorders* that can be either primary (not caused by other medical conditions) or secondary (related to other specific disorders) in nature. There are multiple factors involved in *sleep disorders,* for example, *emotions, environment,* and *lifestyle.* Sleep disorders include insomnia, *hypersomnia, narcolepsy,* nightmares, sleep terror, and sleepwalking.

sliding fee scale The practice of charging clients a fee based on their ability to pay (i.e., on their income).

Slosson Intelligence Test-Revised (SIT) A quick (10 to 30 minutes) individual screening test of crystallized verbal intelligence normed for ages 4 years through 65.

SMAST See *Short Michigan Alcoholism Screening Test.*

snorting The ingestion of powdered *drugs* through rapid inhalation through the nostril.

snow See *cocaine.*

social construction An idea about the way things are or should be that is built more on the shared *perceptions* of members of a society than on objective reality. According to the social construction point of view, there is no objective reality and no universal human nature.

social desirability   A *response set* in which a person tends to give answers that are more socially desirable than accurate.

social ecology   The social context of a group.

social exchange theory   An approach that stresses the *rewards* and costs of interpersonal relationships according to a *behavioral* economy. If individuals give more than they receive, they may well *withdraw* from a *relationship;* if the exchange is even or in their favor, they will continue in the relationship.

social interest   An *Adlerian counseling* term that describes not only a person's interest in others but also that person's interest in the interests of others. Individuals with social interest have a need to and are willing to contribute to the general social good of others.

social learning theory   A theory developed by Albert Bandura that stresses the importance of *modeling* and *learning* through observation as a primary way of acquiring new behaviors and developing.

social modeling   See *imitation.*

social reinforcement   Attention given to an individual either verbally or nonverbally by a significant other that *reinforces* a *behavior* and makes it more likely to reoccur.

social science   The study of people. Social science subjects include anthropology, history, psychology, and sociology.

Social Sciences Citation Index   An index published by the Institute for Scientific Information (ISI). The multidisciplinary database contains searchable author *abstracts* covering the journal literature of the social sciences. It indexes 1,700 journals spanning 50 disciplines and covers individually selected, relevant items from over 3,300 of the world's leading scientific and technical journals. Their Web site address is http://hplus.harvard.edu/alpha/isi_socsci.html.

social time   Time characterized by landmark social events in one's life such as marriage, parenthood, and retirement.

social work   A *helping profession* that focuses on individual well-being in a social context and the well-being of society. Fundamental to social work is attention to the *environmental* forces that create, contribute to, and address problems in living.

social workers   *Mental health* professionals who are trained in case work, *group work,* and community organization approaches. They provide social services and counseling to individuals and families with medical, *legal,* economic, or social problems.

social-cognitive theory   A form of *learning* in which people acquire new knowledge and behavior by observing other people and events without engaging in the behavior themselves and without any direct consequences to themselves. Social-cognitive theory is also referred to as *observational learning, imitation, social modeling,* and *vicarious learning.*

socialization   The processes through which a child learns the *rules* and *norms* of a society.

societal regression   The idea that if a society is under too much *stress* (e.g., population growth, economic decline), it will regress because of too many toxic forces countering the tendency to achieve *differentiation.*

sociodrama   A group technique devised by Jacob L. Moreno that uses *role playing* in order to help persons learn about and understand social factors that influence human interactions.

sociogram   A tool of *sociometry* that plots group members' interactions with lines. In a sociogram, circles represent members in a group, and lines indicate persons closest to each other (see diagram on page 113).

sociometry   A *phenomenological* method for investigating and describing *interpersonal* relationships within a *group.* In sociometry, members of a group provide *feedback* about their interpersonal preferences (i.e., what attracts or repulses them).

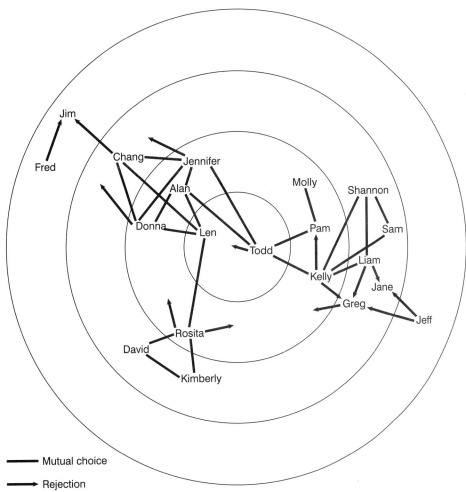

——— Mutual choice

———▶ Rejection

sociogram depicting choices and rejections of classmates

sociopath   A term used in relation to a *psychopath* that implies the *pathology* of the person is not an isolated, intrapsychic phenomenon but rather a complicated problem between the individual and society.

SOLER   An acronym devised by Gerald Egan (1998) that summarizes five *nonverbal* skills involved in initial attending. The "S" is a reminder to face the client squarely, which can be understood literally or *metaphorically* depending on the situation. The "O" is a reminder to adopt an open posture, free from crossed arms and legs and showing nondefensiveness. The "L" reminds the counselor to lean toward the client. Leaning too far forward and being too close may be frightening, but leaning too far away indicates disinterest. The "E" represents eye contact. Good eye contact with most clients is a sign that the counselor is attuned to the client. The "R" is a reminder to the counselor to relax. A counselor needs to be comfortable.

soliloquy technique   A *psychodrama* technique that involves the *protagonist* (i.e., the client) giving a monologue about his or her situation as he or she is acting it out. A variation on this activity is the *therapeutic soliloquy technique.*

solution-focused family therapy   An approach to working with families, originated by Steve deShazer and Bill O'Hanlon, that is systemic, brief, present oriented, focused on small changes, and geared to having client families examine exceptions to their typical ways of interacting. The approach emphasizes solutions (as opposed to problems) and family resources, including those that are both unique and universal.

somatoform disorders   *Mental disorders* that take the form of physical illnesses. The *DSM-IV* classifies *conversion reaction, hypochondriasis,* and *body dysmorphic disorder* under somatoform disorders.

specification   A *transactional analysis* term for the identification of the *ego state* that initiated a transaction. Specification takes place from the *adult ego state* of both client and counselor.

speed test   A test with a large number of items of the same or equal difficulty but having a short time for completion. Speed tests are often used in assessing clerical or mechanical skills.

spillover effect   The impact on others who are helping or watching a main character in *psychodrama* reach resolution on important issues. These "others" see themselves as interacting in a new and better way.

spirituality   A word that comes from the Latin "spiritus," meaning "breath of life." Spirituality refers to a unique, personally meaningful experience of a transcendent dimension that is associated with wholeness and *wellness.* It is an active process that involves a quest for meaningfulness in one's life. It is not the same as *religion.*

spitting in the client's soup   An *Adlerian counseling* technique in which the counselor points out certain behaviors to clients and thus ruins the payoff for the behavior. For example,

a mother who always acts superior to her daughter by showing her up may continue to do so after the behavior has been pointed out, but the reward for doing so is now gone.

split-half reliability   A method of computing test *reliability* in which one half of the test is correlated with the other half.

splitting   A *psychoanalytic* term for *object* representations being viewed dichotomously as either all good or all bad. The result is a *projection* of good and bad qualities onto persons within one's *environment.* Through splitting, people are able to control their *anxiety* and even the objects (i.e., persons) within their environment by making them predictable. However, those who engage in splitting pay a high price because of the misrepresentation of the person in question.

spontaneous recovery   The sudden reappearance of a *behavior* after it has been extinguished.

squeeze technique   An approach used in sexual therapy in which a woman learns to stimulate and stop the ejaculation urge in a man through physically stroking and firmly grasping his penis.

stability   See *test-retest reliability.*

stable coalition   A fixed and inflexible union (such as that of a mother and son) that becomes a dominant part of the family's everyday functioning. See also *coalition.*

stage   **1.** An identifiable period in a person's life. **2.** The area in *psychodrama* in which the action takes place.

stage theories   Theories of human *development* that propose human development goes through *stages,* psychological as well as physical, each building on the other. Examples of stage theories are those proposed by Sigmund Freud, Erik Erikson, Jean Piaget, and Lawrence Kohlberg.

stagnation   A part of Erik Erikson's seventh stage of *psychosocial* development where a person becomes self-centered and stagnant. It is the opposite of *generativity.*

stamps See *trading stamps.*

standard deviation The square root of the *variance* and the most widely used measure of *variability.* The wider the spread of scores from the *mean,* the larger the standard deviation.

standard error of the mean The *standard deviation* of the sampling *distribution.*

standard score A *score* that is used in a *norm-referenced* context and describes the location of a person's score within a set of scores.

standardization The administration of a *test* to a large number of people under standard conditions for the purpose of determining *norms.*

standardized test A *test* that is composed of empirically selected materials and administered under standard conditions with definite directions. In addition, a standardized test contains *data* on its *reliability* and *validity,* has information on scoring and appropriate use, and has adequately determined *norms.*

Standards for Educational and Psychological Testing A document recognized as the *criteria* against which *tests,* test procedures, test manuals, and other test information should be evaluated. The document was developed through the collaboration of the *American Psychological Association (APA),* American Educational Research Association, and National Council on Measurement in Education.

Stanford Achievement Tests (eighth edition) A major *achievement test* battery that is used in Grades 1.5 through 9.9.

Stanford-Binet Intelligence Scale (fourth edition) A popular individually administered *intelligence test.* Items on the Stanford-Binet are categorized according to age, with items at increased age levels being more difficult than items at early age levels. The Stanford-Binet is updated and revised periodically.

stanine A *standard score* scale consisting of the numbers 1 through 9 with a *mean* of 5 and a *standard deviation* of 2.

star Also known as explorer; Virginia Satir's term for the central character in the family reconstruction process.

statistical significant A difference in the *means* of *samples* that is not attributable to *chance.*

statistics The mathematical means researchers use in analyzing and interpreting *data.* Communication of these findings to others is done through numbers that describe a quality being measured.

statutory law Law passed by legislative bodies, such as state and national legislatures, and signed by an authorized source, such as a governor or the president.

STEP See *Systematic Training for Effective Parenting.*

stepfamily A *family* created when two people marry and at least one of them has been married previously and has a child. See also *blended family.*

stereotype A fixed image or thought of people, things, and places that is oversimplified, rigid, and often *prejudiced.* A stereotype allows no room for individual judgment (e.g., like Napoleon, all short men have a desire for power).

stimulant A *drug* of arousal including all forms of *cocaine, amphetamines,* and some prescription (as well as some over-the-counter weight-reducing) products.

stimulus Something that stirs people to action or effort and/or that excites them (e.g., a change in people's physical *environment* that introduces them to new individuals is a stimulus).

stimulus control Arranging the *environment* in such a way that a person can better control it in a desirable manner (e.g., if persons are tempted to overeat, they can make sure there is a limited quantity of snacks available to them).

storming The second stage of *group development,* in which there is *conflict* and turmoil as group members attempt to deal with issues.

The group moves from primary tension (awkwardness about being in a strange situation) to secondary tension (intragroup conflict). During storming, group members and leaders struggle with issues related to *structure,* direction, control, *catharsis,* and *interpersonal* relationships.

stranger anxiety   A fear of new and unfamiliar people usually found in young children. See also *separation anxiety.*

strategic family therapy   A systemic view of problem behaviors that focuses on the *process* rather than the *content* of *dysfunctional* interactions. Strategic family therapy strives to resolve presenting problems and pays little attention to instilling insight. This therapy is *brief* and limits the number of times a family can be seen.

strategic therapy   A term coined by Jay Haley to describe the therapeutic work of Milton Erickson in which extreme attention was paid to details of client *symptoms* and the focus was to change *behavior* by manipulating it and not instilling *insight.*

stress   A state of tension in a person accompanied by physiological arousal and strain. Stress interferes with *coping* and functioning; if it does not abate after a period of time, *distress* may set in, causing a person mental or physical incapacitation.

stress inoculation training (SIT)   A process in which clients break down potentially *stressful* events into manageable units that they can think about and handle through problem-solving techniques. Units are then linked together so that possible events can be envisioned and handled appropriately.

stress management   Specific strategies of a physical, mental, or *environmental* nature that a person uses to keep his or her *stress* low. For example, mental stress management might involve evoking relaxing images in one's mind before, during, or after a stressful situation; environmental stress management might take the form of avoiding whenever possible situations that produce high *stress.*

stressors   Particular stimuli that produce stress.

striving for perfection   **1.** An *Adlerian counseling* theory term for people's tendency to try to fulfill their own unique potential.   **2.** A term in *psychoanalysis* for the superego's attempt to live up to standards set by one's parents or society and to make life perfect as a result.

strokes   A *transactional analysis* concept for *verbal,* psychological, or *nonverbal* recognition of one person by another.

Strong Interest Inventory (SII)   An expansion of previous editions of the original Strong Vocational Interest Blank published in 1927. The SII is a pencil-and-paper self-administered career interest inventory that yields six general occupational themes and *personality* types (based on the acronym *RIASEC*—realistic, investigative, artistic, social, enterprising, and conventional). Results are displayed in basic interest scales, occupational scales, and professional scales.

structural analysis   An approach undertaken to understand what is happening within the individual through assessing how the three ego states (i.e., the *parent, adult,* and *child*), in *transactional analysis,* interact and express themselves.

structural family therapy   An approach, based on general *systems theory,* that advocates structural changes in the organization of the family unit. Particular attention is paid in this approach on changing interactional patterns in *subsystems* of the family, such as in the marital *dyad,* and establishing clear *boundaries* between family members.

structure   **1.** To set up *boundaries,* in counseling (e.g., the length of the sessions, when they will occur, and where).   **2.** A term in *structural family therapy* for an invisible set of functional demands by which family members relate to each other.

structured activities   See *exercises.*

structured life review   A procedure to help older people review their lives and become more integrated. Structured life reviews can take numerous forms, from individually telling one's story to someone else to a reminiscent group experience.

student personnel point of view   See *Minnesota Point of View.*

student personnel work   A variety of services (e.g., *counseling*, financial aid, placement, student center, admission) in higher education that are provided by professionals who interact with students in order to help them make the most of their college experience.

student services   A theoretical model for working with students in a college *environment* that emphasizes the student as consumer and mandates services that facilitate development. This approach stresses a cafeteria-style manner of program offerings that students select according to what they think they need.

study groups   A type of *task group*, typically involving three to four individuals who meet at least weekly to share information, knowledge, and expertise about a course in which they are all enrolled. The idea is that each group member will support and encourage the others and will obtain *insight* and knowledge through the group effort.

style of life   An *Adlerian counseling* concept for describing the way one prefers to live and relate to others. Adlerians stress that a faulty lifestyle is based on competitiveness and a striving to be superior to others.

style-shift counseling   A method of counseling in which as *needs* change, counselors depart from the *theory* they are using to another approach that is a better fit for the client.

subconscious   A *psychoanalytic* concept that includes aspects of the *conscious* and *unconscious*.

subgroups   Cliques of group members who band together, often to the detriment of the *group* as a whole.

subjective reasoning   A type of reasoning that places feelings on the same level as facts.

sublimation   A positive form of *displacement* in which a drive that cannot be expressed directly is channeled into constructive activities. For example, those who are unable to express themselves sexually may take care of children. Sigmund Freud thought sublimation was a major means of building civilization.

subpoena   A *legal* document ordering a person to appear in court at a certain time.

substance   A *drug* of abuse, a medication, or a toxin.

substance abuse   The habitual and often *addictive* use of *alcohol, drugs,* and tobacco. Drugs are any substance other than food that can affect the way a person's mind and body works. Drugs include *stimulants, depressants,* and *hallucinogens.*

substance dependence   People who use substances, such as *alcohol* or *drugs,* in a self-damaging way, usually with the knowledge that what they are doing is harmful.

substance-related disorders   A category in the *DSM-IV* that includes psychological and behavioral *disorders* associated with substance abuse (e.g., abuse of *alcohol, amphetamines, caffeine, cannabis, cocaine, hallucinogens, inhalants, nicotine,* opiates, *phencyclidine, sedatives,* or *polysubstances*) as well as induced disorders resulting from the abuse.

subsystems   Smaller units of the *system* as a whole, usually composed of members in a family who, because of age or function, are logically grouped together (e.g., such as parents). They exist to carry out various family tasks.

subtest   A subset of items on a *test* or a distinct portion of a test.

success identity   The development of a psychologically healthy sense of *self* by being accepted as a person by others. Especially important in this process is experiencing love and worth.

successive approximation The process of *learning* in small gradual steps; a procedure used in *shaping*.

suicide The intentional taking of one's life.

summarization Reflections by a counselor or client that recall significant events or learning experiences in a counseling session. Summarization prevents fragmentation and provides continuity and meaning. As a *technique,* summarization is best used at the beginning or end of a counseling session or after a lengthy *dialogue* in which several points were made.

superego A *psychoanalytic* concept for that part of the *psyche* that contains the *values* of parents and parental figures. The superego operates according to the *moral principle* by *punishing* the person through the *conscience* when he or she disobeys parental messages and by *rewarding* the person through the *ego ideal* when parental teachings are followed. The superego strives for perfection.

superiority complex A term in *Adlerian counseling* theory for the *overcompensation* by a person for feelings of *inferiority*.

supervision An intensive, interpersonally focused, individual or group relationship in which a more experienced *helping professional* is designated to facilitate the development of therapeutic competence in less experienced professionals.

support group A type of *self-help group* in which members share a common concern but in which there is a professional group leader.

supporting Providing encouragement and reinforcement for a client in order to create trust or encourage desired behaviors.

suppression The *conscious* mechanism of putting unwanted or unpleasant thoughts out of one's mind. Suppression is the opposite of *repression,* which is an *unconscious* process.

suppression of the conflict A strategy that consists of playing down *conflict.* It is often used when issues are minor. It keeps emotions under control and helps group leaders build a supportive climate.

surplus reality A *psychodrama* concept for psychological experiences that transcend the boundaries of physical reality. These experiences include relationships with those who have died, with those who have not been born, and with God and are often as important to people as their actual physical experiences.

survey A form of *research* that involves soliciting information from people using a series of questions. Survey *data* can be collected in four ways: through personal *interviews,* mailed questionnaires, telephone interviews, and nonreactive measures such as existing records or archives. Data are gathered in either a structured or nonstructured way with either a *cross-section* of people (many people at one point in time) or *longitudinally* (the same people at two or more points in time).

symbiosis An intertwined *relationship* between two people that is so *fused* that it is difficult if not impossible to distinguish a *boundary* between the two. This type of relationship is most often found in *dysfunctional* parent/child relationships.

symbol Something that stands for or represents something else by reason of association. Symbols play an important part in the theories of Sigmund Freud and Carl Jung. See also *mandala.*

symbolic drawing of family life space A projective technique in which the counselor draws a large circle and instructs family members to include within the circle drawings that represent the family and to place outside of the circle drawings of those people and institutions that are not a part of the family. Then the family is asked to symbolically arrange themselves, again through a drawing within a large circle, according to how they relate to one another.

SYMLOG An acronym for System for the Multiple Level Observation of Groups, a research instrument used in *group work* for examining *personality* and group relationships. The SYMLOG model yields a field diagram that pictures how members of a group are rated on three dimensions and how often members engage in any of 26 *roles* found in groups.

symmetrical relationship A couple *relationship* in which each partner tries to become competent in doing necessary or needed tasks. Members within these units are versatile. For example, a man or a woman can either work outside the home or care for children.

sympathy A *feeling* for someone (e.g., feeling sorry for a person who has experienced a significant loss). Sympathy is not the same as *empathy*.

symptom The manifestation of a *problem* by a client on either a physical or psychological level.

syncretism A sloppy, unsystematic process of putting unrelated clinical concepts together; a crude but first step in the process of learning *eclectic counseling.*

system A set of elements standing in interaction with each other. Each element in the system is affected by whatever happens to any other element. Thus, the system is only as strong as its weakest part. Likewise, the system is greater than the sum of its parts. Much of *family counseling* is based on *systems theory.*

System of Interactive Guidance and Information (SIGI) A *computer-assisted career guidance* system that contains five components: self-assessment (evaluate), identification of occupational alternatives (locate), review of occupational information (compare), review of information on preparation programs (plan), and the making of tentative occupational choices (strategize).

systematic desensitization A *counterconditioning* process in which a person's dysfunctional *anxiety* is reduced or eliminated through pairing it with incompatible behavior, such as muscular or mental relaxation. This is a step-by-step gradual procedure in which events that produce increasingly higher levels of anxiety are treated by pairing them with relaxation procedures and positive imagery one at a time.

Systematic Training for Effective Parenting (STEP) An *Adlerian counseling*-based parent education program.

systemic family therapy Also known as the *Milan family therapy;* an approach that stresses the interconnectedness of family members while emphasizing the importance of *second-order change* in families.

systems theory Also known as *general systems theory;* a *theory* that focuses on the interconnectedness of elements within all living organisms, including the family. Based on the work of Ludwig von Bertalanffy, systems theory proposes that any living organism, including a family, is composed of interacting components, that is, people who mutually affect one another. Three basic assumptions distinguish systems theory from other counseling approaches: (1) the idea that causality is *interpersonal,* (2) the basic assumption that *psychosocial* systems are best understood as repeated patterns of interpersonal interaction, and (3) the idea that symptomatic behaviors should be understood from an interactional viewpoint.

t

T score A *derived score* on a test with a fixed mean of 50 and a fixed *standard deviation* of 10.

TA See *transactional analysis.*

target population The *population* a consultant or counselor specifically wishes to help.

Tarasoff v. Board of Regents of the University of California A landmark *legal* case in counseling and psychotherapy in which the University of California was found *liable* for the murder of Tatiana Tarasoff by her boyfriend Prosenjit Poddar because the university had failed to warn Tarasoff and her family that Poddar had threatened to kill her. Although Poddar retracted his threat after he made it to a psychologist in the student health services, the California Supreme Court ruled that the failure of university officials to warn Tarasoff and her family was irresponsible. From this court decision came the principle of a *duty to warn* and the implication that *confidentiality* must be broken in counseling if a client is considered dangerous either to self or others.

task group   A group in which there is an emphasis on accomplishment and efficiency in completing identified work *goals*. Task groups are united in their emphasis on achieving a successful performance or a finished product through collaborative efforts and take the form of task forces, committees, planning groups, community organizations, discussion groups, and learning groups. Task groups are also known as *work groups*.

task setting   A procedure in *Adlerian counseling* in which clients initially set short-range, attainable *goals* and eventually work up to long-term, realistic objectives. Once clients make behavioral changes and realize some control over their lives, counseling ends.

TAT   See *Thematic Apperception Test.*

teachable moment   A time when people are ready and able to learn.

teaching to the test   See *coaching.*

team   A number of persons associated together in work or an activity, such as in athletic or artistic competition, who act and perform in a coordinated way to achieve a *goal*. Teams differ from basic *groups* in four main ways: They (1) have shared goals (as opposed to individual goals), (2) stress more interdependency, (3) require more of a commitment by members to a team effort, and (4) are by design accountable to a higher level within the organization.

team building   The effective development of a team through managing *conflict,* promoting *interpersonal* relationships, and achieving consensus.

teamwork   Work performed cooperatively by all members of a group.

teasing technique   A sexual therapy approach in which a woman learns to start and stop sexually stimulating a man.

technical eclecticism   An approach to integrating counseling *theories* that is best exemplified in the work of Arnold Lazarus. In this approach, procedures from different theories are selected and used in *treatment* without necessarily subscribing to the theories that spawned them. The idea is that techniques, not theories, are used in treating clients. Therefore, after properly assessing clients, counselors may use behavioral techniques (such as *assertiveness training*) with *existential* techniques (such as *confronting* persons about the meaning in their lives), if warranted by the situation.

technique   A discipline-specific procedure in *research;* a specific way, in counseling, of implementing part of a *theory*. For instance, *free association* is a technique in *psychoanalysis.*

teleological   Purposeful and *goal* directed behavior.

temperament   The overall *mood* or disposition of an individual.

Tennessee Self-Concept Scale:2 (TSCS:2)   A self-administered instrument consisting of one hundred questions on a *Likert scale,* ranging from "completely true" to "completely false," meant to measure different aspects of the *self* (e.g., self-satisfaction, personal self, family self).

terminal program outcomes   The most recognizable *goals* and performance objectives in *evaluation.*

termination   **1.** A transition event that ends one set of conditions so that other experiences can begin. Termination provides clients with an opportunity to *clarify* the meaning of their experiences, to consolidate the gains they have made, and to make decisions about the new behaviors they want. The decision to stop counseling should be made mutually whenever possible and should occur over a period of time rather than abruptly. Termination usually involves a four-step process: orientation, *summarization,* discussion of goals, *follow-up.* **2.** Another name for the final step in *group development.* See also *adjourning.*

tertiary prevention Efforts, equivalent to *therapy,* to reduce the long-term *consequences* of a *disorder.*

test Also known as a *psychological test.* A test is an objective or projective instrument that measures *behavior*(s) or reported behaviors and characteristics.

test anxiety Considerable concern over taking a test because of the fear that one might fail. High test *anxiety* is crippling; moderate test anxiety can be helpful and can increase a person's performance.

test battery A group of tests utilized in the *evaluation* of a person or group. See also *battery.*

test bias A test that *discriminates* against individuals or groups because of their backgrounds.

test interpretation The *interpretation* of a *test* as to the meaning of its *scores.*

test score Test results, usually reported in a quantifiable way.

test wiseness A person's capacity to receive a high score on a *test* by *learning* how to utilize the characteristics of the test or the testing situation (e.g., learning to avoid making errors, use time effectively, and devise strategies for effective guessing).

test-retest reliability The degree to which *scores* on a *test* are consistent, or stable, over time. Test-retest reliability is also known as *stability.*

Tests in Print (TIP) A comprehensive bibliography to all known commercially available *tests* that are currently in print. *TIP* is published by the *Buros Institute of Mental Measurements.*

Tetrahydrocannabinol (THC) The active ingredient in *marijuana* and similar *substances,* such as hashish.

T-group **1.** An approach to groups developed at the *National Training Laboratories (NTL)* in the 1940s in which primary attention is devoted to *theory, group dynamics,* and social material involving groups. **2.** A small group of people who spend a period of time together both for counseling and educational purposes. Participants are encouraged to examine their interpersonal functioning.

thanatos A *psychoanalysis* term for an *unconscious* drive toward ending life. It is one of the two basic *instincts* within the *id,* the other being Eros, the life instinct. See also *life instinct.*

Thematic Apperception Test (TAT) A *projective personality test* that is individually administrated. The TAT is made up of 20 cards with ambiguous pictures on them that the test taker is instructed to tell a story about.

thematical interpretation A level of *interpretation* that is broad based and covers the whole pattern of a person's existence, including behaviors that are self-defeating.

themes Specific topics or subjects related to the genuine interests of the participants, thereby holding their interest and inviting their participation. Many adolescent groups work best when they are structured around themes.

theoretical integrationism A form of *eclecticism* that requires counselors to master at least two theories before trying to combine them in an eclectic approach. The weakness of this approach is that it assumes some equality in counseling theories.

theory A formally stated and coherent set of propositions that purport to explain a range of phenomena, order them in a logical way, and suggest what additional information might be gleaned under certain conditions. A theory guides empirical inquiry and is useful in testing *hypotheses.*

therap-e-mail See *Internet counseling.*

therapeutic contracts Specific, measurable, concrete statements of what clients intend to accomplish. Therapeutic contracts place responsibility on clients for clearly defining what, how, and when they want to *change.*

therapeutic factors See *curative factors.*

therapeutic neutrality Accepting and non-judgmental behavior by counselors, especially when working with families. Neutrality keeps counselors from being drawn into *coalitions* and disputes and gives them time to assess the dynamics within the family. Neutrality also encourages family members to generate solutions to their own concerns. However, therapeutic neutrality may work against ethical decision making.

therapeutic soliloquy technique A psychodrama technique in which private reactions to events in the life of a protagonist (i.e., a client) are verbalized and acted out, usually by other actors (i.e., auxiliary egos). See also *soliloquy technique.*

therapist A synonym, in *mental health* circles, for the word *psychotherapist*. A therapist is a trained health provider. Since there are a number of different types of therapists (e.g., physical, occupational, etc.), professionals who work with the mentally distressed are wise to use a prefix such as psycho before the word therapist.

therapy A term sometimes used interchangeably with *psychotherapy* and *counseling*. Traditionally, therapy and psychotherapy have been used to describe psychological *interventions* with clients who have serious (as opposed to mild) disturbances and *disorders*. Therapy and psychotherapy are also traditionally associated with long-term treatment, although this distinction has become blurred in recent years with the onset of *brief therapy.*

third force A term used by Abraham Maslow to describe *humanistic approaches* to *counseling* and psychology. The first and second forces are *psychoanalysis* and *behaviorism.*

third-degree games The deadly games, often played for keeps, in *transactional analysis*. There is nothing socially redeemable about third-degree games. See also *games.*

thought The intellectual process of representing ideas, beliefs, and images in one's mind in an organized manner. The process of thought is developmental and individually manifested in reason and expression. Thought is an underlying base on which the theories of *cognitive counseling* and cognitive behavioral counseling have been built. See also *cognition.*

thought stopping A *cognitive behavioral theory* technique in which clients are taught how to stop unproductive *obsession* about an event or person through overt and mental procedures.

time out A *process* that involves the removal of persons (most often children) from an *environment* in which they have been reinforced for certain actions. Isolation, or "time out," from *reinforcement* for a limited amount of time (approximately 5 minutes) results in the cessation of the targeted behavior.

time sampling A *research* method in which *behavior* is observed during specific times with the aim of recording the frequency of a specific behavior.

TIP See *Tests in Print.*

title law Legislation requiring that counselors in private practice hold a state license or *certification* in order to use a professional title, such as "certified practicing counselor." A title law sometimes comes before more complete *licensure* legislation. In title law states, counselors may practice privately without the credential if they do not use the *legal* title.

token economy A system of *reinforcement* used in *behavior modification* in which students or clients contract to earn token points of varying amounts in exchange for fulfilling specific behavioral objectives. They may then "cash" their tokens in for a *reward.*

top-dog/underdog dialogue A technique in *gestalt therapy* in which clients are asked to examine the top-dog introjections they have learned from parents (usually represented by "shoulds" and "you" statements) and their own real feelings about situations (usually represented by "I" statements).

topic-specific groups Groups that are centered around a particular topic (e.g., widowhood, sexuality, health, or the arts). They are designed ultimately to improve the quality of daily living for older people. They also assist the aged to find more meaning in their lives and to establish a group of like-minded people.

tort   A wrongful act upon which *legal* action is designed to set right; the concept upon which *civil liability* rests. The legal wrong can be against a person, property, or even someone's reputation and may be unintentional or direct.

touching   A *nonverbal* counseling response usually meant to comfort or support. Touching can be controversial if not done judiciously and correctly.

tracking   A way of *joining* in which the counselor follows the *content* (i.e., the facts) of the client.

trading stamps   A *transactional analysis* term for particular feelings the *child ego state* collects.

traditional eclecticism   A form of *eclecticism* in which compatible features from diverse counseling sources are combined into a harmonious whole.

trait   An enduring characteristic of a person.

trait-and-factor theory   A *theory* that stresses that the *traits* of clients should first be assessed and then systematically matched with *factors* inherent in various occupations. Its most widespread influence occurred during the Great Depression, when E. G. Williamson championed its use. It has resurfaced in a more modern form, best reflected in the work of researchers such as John Holland. The trait-and-factor approach has always stressed the uniqueness of persons.

tranquilizer   A *drug* used to reduce mental disturbance, such as *anxiety* and tension. Examples of major tranquilizers are Thorazine, Stelazine, and Mellaril. Examples of minor tranquilizers are Valium and Librium.

transactional analysis   **1.** The name of the theory developed by Eric Berne.   **2.** The analysis of what people do and say to one another. Transactional analysis often involves diagramming *ego state* (i.e., *parent, adult, child*) transactions. The diagramming of trans-

actional analysis is *interpersonal*, in contrast to the *intrapersonal* diagramming of *structural analysis*. Transactions may occur on one of three levels: *complementary, crossed,* or *ulterior* levels.

transactions   Social action between two or more people, manifested on social (overt) and psychological (covert) levels.

transescents   Early *adolescents;* children in middle school.

transference   The *displacement* of *affect* from one person to another; the *projection* of inappropriate emotions onto someone else. Transference occurs when a person unconsciously reenacts a latter-day version of forgotten *childhood* memories and repressed *unconscious* fantasies in the counseling session. For example, a client might say to a counselor "You sound just like my mother" and start behaving as if the counselor were the client's mother.

transference pull   A client's reaction to the image of the counselor in terms of the client's personal background and current conditions. The way the counselor sits, speaks, gestures, or looks may trigger a client reaction.

transient children   Children who have moved to a new community and a new school.

transients   Individuals who move frequently and have no permanent home address.

transparent self   The self as revealed to another in an open and honest way. Such a process invites disclosure on the part of the listener and helps to build a *relationship*. This idea and *research* supporting it were the result of clinical work by Sidney Jourard.

transpersonal theories   Theories that propose humans possess the potential to ascend beyond their ordinary limits and attain higher levels of consciousness, including transcendence of self, cosmic awareness, ecstasy, wonder, and *altruism*.

transvestism   Sexual gratification through dressing in the clothes of the opposite sex.

trauma   An injury or nervous shock that is usually intense and unpleasant.

treatment Planned *interventions* to alleviate or modify a *disorder* or change a dysfunctional condition.

treatment contract A specific, concrete contract that emphasizes agreed-upon responsibilities for both counselors and clients. The contract lets each know when counseling *goals* have been reached. Behavioral approaches to counseling often make use of a treatment contract.

treatment plan A plan a counselor makes in regard to a client that includes information such as the theoretical approach to use, frequency of sessions, length of sessions, and so on.

triadic questioning The process of asking a third person how two other people in a family or group relate.

triangle The basic building block of any emotional system and the smallest stable relationship *system* in a *family*, according to Murray Bowen.

triangulate To focus on a third party. When people are stressed within their marriages, they tend to turn their attention to and project on a third party such as a child, a church, a school, or even a physical ailment.

triangulating The process in which interpersonal *dyadic* difficulties in a marriage or relationship are *projected* onto a third person or object (i.e., a *scapegoat*).

trust **1.** The first of Erik Erikson's virtues in his *psychosocial* model of development. Trust is developed in an infant when his or her *needs* are met consistently. It is the opposite of *mistrust*. **2.** The placing of confidence or faith in someone or something. If therapeutic progress is to be made, a client must develop trust in the counselor. Trust is gained through the counselor's display of his or her credentials and over a period of time as the client realizes the counselor understands him or her, wants to be genuinely helpful, and will not betray confidentiality matters.

trustworthiness The qualities of sincerity and consistency, in counseling. The counselor shows genuine concern about the client over time through patterns of *behavior* that demonstrate care. Many clients test the trustworthiness of the counselor by requesting information, telling a secret, asking a favor, inconveniencing the counselor, deprecating themselves, or questioning the motives and dedication of the counselor. Therefore, in order to facilitate the counseling *relationship,* it is essential that the counselor respond to the question of trust rather than the verbal *content* of the client.

t-test A commonly used statistical test that establishes whether a *significant difference* exists between two sample *means*. It is derived through a ratio: the difference between two sample means divided by an estimate of the *standard deviation* of the *distribution* of the differences.

Type A behavior Behavior that is characterized by time-urgent, competitive, and hostile behavior.

Type A stress Stress associated with a situation that is foreseeable and avoidable, such as not walking in a dangerous area at night.

Type B behavior Behavior that is characterized by patience, noncompetitiveness, and a relaxed attitude about time.

Type B stress Stress associated with a situation that is neither foreseeable nor avoidable, such as an unexpected death.

Type C stress Stress associated with a situation that is foreseeable but not avoidable, such as going to the dentist.

Type I error Rejecting the *null hypothesis* when it should be accepted; to claim there is a real difference in *data* when there is not.

Type II error Accepting the *null hypothesis* when it should be rejected; to claim there is not a real difference in *data* when there is.

u

ulterior transaction A *transaction* in *transactional analysis* in which two *ego states* operate simultaneously and one message disguises the other. Ulterior transactions appear to be *complementary* and socially acceptable even though they are not. For example, at the end of a date, one person may say to the other "Do you want to come in and see my etchings?" On the surface this question might seem to be coming from the *adult ego state.* In reality it is coming from the *child ego state:* "Want to come in and have some fun together?"

unbalancing When a counselor therapeutically allies with a *subsystem* in a family. In this procedure, the counselor supports an individual or subsystem against the rest of the family.

unconditional positive regard Total *acceptance* of the experiences of a client without conditions; a nonpossessive caring and acceptance. According to Carl Rogers, unconditional positive regard is a *necessary and sufficient condition for change* to occur.

unconditioned response A *response* elicited automatically by an *unconditioned stimulus.*

unconditioned stimulus A *stimulus* (e.g., food) that automatically elicits a *response* prior to *learning.*

unconscious The most powerful and least understood part of the *personality.* According to Freudian theory, the instinctual, *repressed,* and powerful forces of the personality exist in the unconscious.

undifferentiated family ego mass Murray Bowen's term for excessive emotional togetherness or *fusion* within a family.

undoing A *defense mechanism* in *psychoanalysis* theory in which a person engages in repetitive rituals to abolish the results of actions previously taken. For example, Lady Macbeth's action of repetitively washing her hands after urging her husband to commit murder is an attempt to "wash away" or undo what she has done.

unfinished business Emotional debris from one's past that interferes with present functioning. For example, if someone hurts another and fails to resolve the conflict with that person, he or she may avoid that person.

unimodal A *frequency distribution* in which there is a single *score* class that has the highest frequency (i.e., a single peak).

unintentional civil liability A lack of intent to cause injury.

universal approach to multicultural counseling An approach to *multiculturalism* that includes *ethnicity,* gender, *lifestyle,* age, *religion, disability,* and so forth. It is a more inclusive approach than the *focused approach to multicultural counseling.*

universalization A client's realization that he or she is not unique in regard to his or her concern.

unknown self One of the four quadrants in the *Johari Awareness Model.* The unknown self is not known to self or to others.

unprofessional Outside of or in violation of the conduct expected and required of a person in a profession.

unrealistic aspirations *Goals* beyond a person's capabilities.

uppers A lay term for *stimulants.*

utilization principle A foundation of *solution-focused family therapy* originated by Milton Erickson that states counselors should use whatever clients present in counseling as a basis and means for client solutions and *change.* Erickson believed that people have within themselves the resources and abilities to solve their own problems.

V codes   Conditions for which *mental health* services are sought, such as bereavement or an identity problem, that are listed in the back of the *DSM-IV.* V codes are not considered *disorders,* and most third-party payers do not reimburse mental health professionals if V codes are the only reason given for seeking *treatment.*

validity   The extent to which a *test* measures what it purports to measure, for example, certain *traits,* characteristics, *behaviors,* or constructs. Validity makes a test useful and meaningful.

values   Principles or qualities that are desirable. Basically, there are four domains of values: personal, family, political/social, and ultimate. Each has an impact on the other. *Ethics* are based on values.

variable   A property, *measurement,* or characteristic that varies and can be measured.

variance   A statistical *measurement* of how widely spread *scores* are from the *mean.*

venereal diseases   Sexually transmitted diseases such as syphilis, gonorrhea, and genital herpes that are infectious and spread through the exchange of bodily fluids.

verbal   Expression through the use of either oral or written language.

verbal test   A test that requires an oral or written response. It is the opposite of a *performance test.*

verbalizing presuppositions   An experiential *technique* in which the counselor helps families take the first step toward *change* by talking of *hopes* that the family has.

vertical stressors   Events dealing with family patterns, myths, secrets, and legacies. Vertical stressors are historical phenomena that families and their members inherit from previous generations.

vicarious learning   See *imitation.*

victim   **1.** A position in a *transactional analysis game* in which the person assumes a stance of appearing to be innocent.   **2.** A person who is *abused, neglected,* or *maltreated* by another.

visitors   A type of client, classified by Steve deShazer, characterized by no overt complaints and whose rationale for being in counseling comes from an exterior source, such as a court order. See also *complainers; customers.*

vocation   The *work* in which one is regularly employed. A vocation usually is composed of a number of *jobs.*

Vocational Preference Inventory (VPI)   A pencil-and-paper *personality test* composed of 160 items in which individuals are asked to circle *occupations* they like or might consider. The VPI is based on *RIASEC,* John Holland's theory of vocational adjustment.

vocational rehabilitation   A counseling specialty that focuses on serving individuals with physical, emotional, intellectual, and behavioral disabilities. *Rehabilitation counseling* practice requires knowledge in areas of medical terminology, *diagnosis, prognosis,* vocational evaluation of disability-related limitations, and *job* placement in the context of a socioeconomic system.

voice   Carol Gilligan's term for moral language. Accordingly, men's voice is based on individual justice and independence; women's voice is based on care, connectedness, and concern for others.

voyeurism   Sexual gratification through clandestine observations of other people's sexual activities or sexual anatomy.

VPI   See *Vocational Preference Inventory.*

v

W

WAIS *See Wechsler Adult Intelligence Scale.*

warmth A positive feeling as well as the ability to demonstrate genuine caring, concern, and *acceptance* of others.

warm-up An activity staged at the beginning of a *group* experience to help group members become better acquainted or to prepare them to become more relaxed or focus on areas they wish to explore.

washout period The period of time in *research* when there is no *treatment* given to a client.

WDEP system An acronym device created by Robert Wubbolding as a way of helping counselors and clients make progress in *reality therapy.* In this system the "W" stands for wants; at the beginning of the counseling process, counselors find out what clients want and in turn share their wants for and perceptions of clients' situations. The "D" stands for the direction of clients' lives and exploring that direction. The "E" stands for evaluation and is the cornerstone of reality therapy. Clients are helped to evaluate their behaviors to determine how responsible their personal behaviors are. The "P" stands for plan. A client focuses on making a plan for changing behaviors. The plan stresses actions that the client will take, not behaviors that he or she will eliminate. The best plans are simple, attainable, measurable, immediate, and consistent. Clients are requested to make a commitment to the plan of action. If the client fails to accomplish the plan, the client suffers the natural or reasonable *consequences* of that failure.

Web counseling See *Internet counseling.*

Wechsler Adult Intelligence Scale (WAIS) A popular individually administered intelligence test for individuals ages 16 and up. The WAIS is revised periodically and yields verbal, performance, and overall *intelligence quotient (IQ)* scores.

Wechsler Intelligence Scale for Children-III (WISC-III) A popular individually administered *intelligence test* for children ages 6 to 16 years. The WISC is revised periodically and yields verbal, performance, and overall IQ scores. The six verbal subtests on the WISC are general information, general comprehension, arithmetic, similarities, vocabulary, and digit span. The six performance subtests on the WISC-R are picture completion, picture arrangement, block design, object assembly, coding, and mazes.

Wechsler Preschool and Primary Scale of Intelligence (WPPSI) A popular individually administered *intelligence test* designed for children ages 4 years to 6 years 6 months. The WPPSI is revised periodically and yields verbal, performance, and overall *intelligence quotient (IQ)* scores.

Wechsler scale A *standard score* scale with a *mean* of 10 and a *standard deviation* of 3, used with the Wechsler *intelligence tests.*

Wechsler-Bellevue Scale The predecessor of the Wechsler series of intelligence tests developed by David Wechsler. The Wechsler-Bellevue Scale Form I, published in 1939 at Bellevue Hospital in New York, was strictly for adults; it was followed by the Wechsler-Bellevue Scale Form 2, published in 1947. The Form I version of the test was completely revised again in 1955 and became the *Wechsler Adult Intelligence Scale (WAIS).*

Weldon v. Virginia State Board of Psychologists Examiners A 1974 decision by the Virginia Supreme Court that stated that *counseling* was a profession distinct from psychology.

wellness A state of being that emphasizes good *health,* a positive *lifestyle,* and *prevention.* See also *positive wellness.*

w

wetanschauung   A German word for *world-view*. See also *worldview*.

we/they mentality   An overidentification with a particular *group* that tends to develop into an antagonism toward other groups. Other points of view are seen as "uninformed," "naive," or "heretical."

wheel   A group formation in which only the leader, or center spoke, has face-to-face interactions with others in the group.

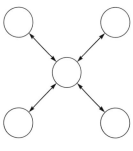

wheel

wheel or circle of influence   People who have been important to the star, or explorer, in Virginia Satir's *family reconstruction* model.

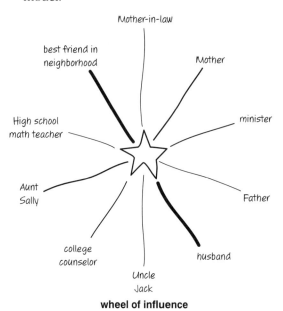

wheel of influence

white   A term used to describe individuals in the United States who are descendants of white European ancestry. See also *European American*.

Wide Range Achievement Test-3 (WRAT-3)   A frequently used and easily administered *achievement test* designed for a wide range of ages—kindergartners through adults. The WRAT-3 covers reading, spelling, and arithmetic.

will to power   An *Adlerian counseling* concept for a person's striving for *superiority* and dominance in order to overcome feelings of *inferiority*.

WISC-III   See *Wechsler Intelligence Scale for Children-III*.

wisdom   The ability to make effective choices among alternatives.

withdrawal   **1.** Removing oneself physically or psychologically from people or events that are disturbing.   **2.** The physical and psychological *symptoms* that occur in an addicted person when the use of *drugs* is discontinued. See also *detoxification*.

withdrawal from the conflict   A strategy that involves *group* leaders distancing themselves from *conflict* and postponing *interventions*.

word association test   A *personality test* in which a person responds with the first word that comes to mind after another word is read by the examiner (e.g., a response to the word "mother" might be the word "warm").

work   Activities that are engaged in for gain or *reward* rather than for pleasure that might be derived from them.

work group   See *task groups*.

work sample   See *performance test*.

workaholic   A person with *Type A behavior* who is a hard-driving perfectionist and in a hurry most of the time. Workaholics often prefer to act alone and have a hard time delegating authority. People with Type A behavior may be at higher risk than others of developing heart attacks and other stress-related conditions. Type A people can benefit from training in how to relax, how to manage their anger, and how to manage their time.

working out a compromise   A *process* in which each party involved gives up a little to obtain a part of what they want in order to avoid *conflict.* The result is a win-win situation in which cooperative behavior and collaborative efforts are encouraged. This approach is effective in groups in which there are limited resources.

working stage The most unified and productive *group* stage. It focuses on the achievement of individual and group goals and the movement of the group itself as a system.

working through A *psychoanalytic* technique that refers to the client's movement toward insight and understanding in the latter stages of a therapeutic relationship.

worldview An individual's perception of the world based on his or her experiences as well as the socialization processes of the person in interaction with members of his or her reference group (i.e., *culture,* country). Worldviews directly affect and mediate people's belief systems, assumptions, modes of problem solving,

decision making, and conflict resolution styles. The four most prevalent worldviews as proposed by Derald Sue are internal locus of control and responsibility, external locus of control and responsibility, external locus of control/internal locus of responsibility, and internal locus of control/external locus of responsibility.

wounded healers A term for fellow *helping professionals* and laypeople who have *insight* into their own suffering. It is assumed that these individuals are able to deal most effectively with the emotional pain of others because of their firsthand experience in having been psychologically hurt or "wounded." Such an experience helps them better understand clients' concerns.

WPPSI See *Wechsler Preschool and Primary Scale of Children.*

xenophobia An intense and persistent fear of strangers or foreigners.

Y A group formation that combines the structural elements of a *wheel* and *chain* group arrangement and has a perceived leader. The Y arrangement is similar to the chain in that group members may become frustrated in not

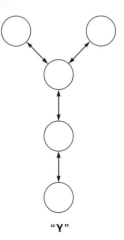

"Y"

having direct contact with each other and that information may not be equally shared.

YAVIS An acronym for young, *attractive, verbal, intelligent,* and *successful.* The acronym is used to describe the most successful candidates for traditional counseling.

yellow jackets See *barbiturates.*

yoga A form of *meditation* that involves a number of *techniques* such as breathing exercises, body postures, and focused concentration. Yoga is sometimes employed in counseling settings to help clients relax or gain *insight.*

young adulthood   The stage of maturation between 20 to 40 years old. The primary concerns of young adults, according to Erik Erikson, are establishing an *identity* and finding *intimacy*.

young-old   Individuals between ages 60 and 64.

z score   A number that results from the transformation of a *raw score* into units of *standard deviation*. A z score indicates how far above or below the *mean* a given score is.

zeitgeist   A German word that means "spirit of the times." Understanding the zeitgeist, or cultural climate, of an era gives one insight into the thoughts and actions of people of that period.

zero-sum games   Games in which there is a winner and loser. In marriages, some couples argue with the assumption that one must win and be correct and the other must lose and be incorrect. Zero-sum games produce feelings of resentment and revenge from losers and lead to more intensified arguments and behaviors. It is the opposite of *non-zero-sum games*.